DIESEL SPIRIT

THOUGHT PROVOKING INSIGHTS ON MINDSET, LIFE, AND SUCCESS.

ROGER MICHAEL MORELLO

LIFE IS A FIGHT.

We don't get to choose. We come into the world and inherit our circumstances, the people in our lives, and the conditions of our upbringing.

I was born in Bridgeport, CT and grew up in Stratford, CT. I grew up a fragile, scared kid in a home that quickly broke apart. As a small child I was often afraid of my father. Early memories of him throwing his weight around. Verbally and sometimes physically abusing my mother and sister, flipping over the dinner table as my sister and I peeked from the other room, slapping my sister's head into the wall verbally abusing her, belittling my mother telling her she's a loser and nothing without him, and a feeling of terror as he chased me to my bedroom when I tried to stand up for my mother.

My parents divorced when I was very young and time spent with my father right after was short lived and became nonexistent.

My mother tried her best as a single mom and had all the best intentions when I was younger. She was at a point in her life though, still young with a failed marriage and the burden of keeping a roof over our head, she wasn't around much. She dated a lot and worked three jobs. I was often alone as a young kid. There was a period of time as she was dating, different men would come in and out of my life.

I was bullied at school and by the kids on my street to the point I was afraid to walk out onto my own front porch for fear I would get beat up. I was always just smaller, weaker, and afraid.

When I was 12 years old, the childhood home I grew up in was sold and I've never gone back there since. My mother ultimately remarried a man I had no connection with. We moved to a new and very unfamiliar town, and I went to a new school. I became a burden on my mother's new marriage, would verbally argue with her new husband, and there were moments he got physical, slapping me in the face.

Coincidentally, unbeknownst to me, my father lived in the same town I was forced to move to with my mother when she remarried. With things worsening at my mother's I decided to go stay with my father. Not ideal, but sure beat living with my mother. She was happy about it, I was out of her hair and she could live in peace. I don't blame her. I was a problem, she didn't have to deal with me anymore. I didn't hear from my mother for years once I left and my relationship with her became nonexistent.

Up to this point at 12 years old I hadn't spoken to or seen my father since shortly after my parents divorced. Leaving my mother's new home to stay with my father at 13, I can still remember knocking on his door. He was a stranger to me. We sat in the kitchen and became somewhat acquainted with one another. No emotion, no genuine interest. For me it was just a place to stay. I was too young to go anywhere else and I had to leave my mother's.

My father was no kind of father. He really didn't care what I did. Zero guidance on how to be a man. I never had any sort of emotional connection with him. There were times we would argue and he would yell and try to throw his weight around with me like he did when I was a child. I was older though and he would get quiet when I gave it right back to him. He had a big mouth but was a coward deep down. Any man that treats the family he created like he did is a coward. I did learn many lessons from him though. I learned what type of man and father I don't want to be. Everyone in your life, good or bad, can teach you something.

Away from my mother and living with a father that was more of a stranger than a dad, I was a kid wandering in life, lost, and had no parental guidance. I became a very lost kid, got into trouble, suspended from school often and flunking every class, began using cocaine, marijuana, smoking cigarettes, and drinking alcohol at 13 years of age. I was definitely headed in the wrong direction in life from the start. I had no sense of normalcy, of home, of parental love and guidance.

At 15 years old I took a liking to weight lifting and competitive bodybuilding. It became an outlet for me. An outlet of positivity. It kept me out of trouble and made me value myself more. Made me more confident and enhanced my beliefs about what could be possible in my life. I entered my first bodybuilding competition at 16 years old. I lost the contest, placing third out of three competitors, but was determined to know what I needed to do to win.

After the contest I walked up to the head judge of the show, George Clark, and he told me he coached bodybuilders and that he saw a fire in my eyes. He took me under his wing and became my coach and mentor as well as a sort of father figure. He made me focus on my grades in school and I became extremely committed to bodybuilding. It was all I had. I felt like I was good at it. It gave me purpose. By the time I was 19, I would win Teen Mr. Connecticut, Teen Mr. America, and two Junior Olympic gold medals. My grades improved and I was straightening out. I was moving in a much better direction.

Unfortunately, by the time I was 19, the deterioration of the living conditions at my father's had reached a peak. He had a woman in his life, and her and her kids were his new family. I came out of nowhere at 13 years old, and I believe disrupted her plans. His girlfriend had it out for me, hated me actually. Did everything she could to make my life miserable there. She had children of her own my father was expected to care for and I didn't really fit into that equation. She wanted me gone. My father was extremely afraid to be alone and definitely had no intentions of choosing me over her.

I left my father's house. Packed the car and left. He came home to find me gone, didn't care, I haven't talked to him since. And so, my journey to who I am today began as a unique individual finding his own way.

Shortly after leaving my father's I had nowhere to go, so I went and stayed with my only sister in New Jersey for a short period of time. She had many struggles of her own, rooted from the same upbringing. She was independent also living a do or die, sink or swim kind of life. With that being said, understandably, she didn't have the capacity to worry about my mess of a life. My stay with my sister didn't last long. I was able to get my first apartment, which was a relief to become independent in my living situation. I lost the apartment after several months because I wasn't prepared to handle it. I became a fish out of water. I developed a victim mentality, blamed my parents, and my upbringing. I blamed everyone else but me. I was looking for someone to come save me and the realization that I would have to save myself frightened me to death. I didn't know how to deal with life.

The next three years would be three of the most hellish, destructive, and darkest years of my life. I became depressed. Life became extremely difficult and I wasn't prepared for it. I could lift weights but I didn't know how to handle life. Bodybuilding took a serious back burner to life. I fell off a cliff and my life began spiraling out of control. I became the complete opposite of the bodybuilding champion I was at 19 and I hated my life and myself.

Hard drugs, alcohol, hopelessness, severe depression, self-harm, stupid decisions, you name it. I had no control over my mind or my thoughts, and therefore no control over my life.

There were nights I was afraid to go to sleep because I was so high I was afraid I wouldn't wake up. Sleeping on any couch I could, wherever I could. Spending the night in a mental hospital because I cut my wrist, watching the sun rise for the first time in my life as I was up all night sitting, staring. Because I had nowhere else to go I lived with and became involved with people that were not good for me, bad influences, drug dealers, drug users, criminals, etc. Some of which are dead today. I was on a downward spiral, my life out of control, I was lost, hopeless, afraid, felt completely alone, and contemplated the point of living.

I needed help. I needed to get out of New Jersey. I didn't reach out to my past bodybuilding couch because I didn't want him to know what I had become. Desperate, I reached out to my mother and father and pleaded with them, even begged them to let me come live with them for a short time. I had an old weight lifting partner that was a General Manager at Bally Total Fitness and he assured me I had a job lined up whenever I could get back to Connecticut. I just needed a place to stay to get back on my feet.

My parents shut me down. I was on my own. No one came to help me. No one came to see if I was ok. No one felt sorry for me. If I was going to dig myself out of this life, this deep dark place my life had become it was going to be up to me. I was drowning and it was do or die, sink or swim.

I was going to need to become someone I was not to step into what I would become. I removed bad influences, changed my environment, and started making better decisions. I took any job I could to survive and was finally able to get another apartment with some roommates in New Jersey. I saved up $5000, ultimately made it out of New Jersey on my own, and moved back to Connecticut where I would embark on the next chapter of my life. One I thought was distancing me from the darkness I was so desperately trying to escape.

Life started making sense. I was healed, full of ambition, motivated, and in good spirits. I took the job at Bally Total Fitness that my old weight lifting partner still had waiting for me, worked my way up to General Manager, went on to manage several clubs in the State of Connecticut. I started competing in bodybuilding again, got a modeling contract in NYC, and met the woman I would eventually marry. She was it for me.

Life was good. I had a family in her family, a career that I liked, a stable home, and felt my dark days were well behind me.

I was wrong.

Bally Total Fitness went bankrupt, my bills and cost of living were through the roof, my income plummeted, and I was constantly stressed about money. I didn't know what I was going to do with my life. I had no college degree, was married and felt like a failure, and didn't really have any niche skill I could turn to. I switched careers to a totally new industry and absolutely hated it from day one. My back was against a wall and I was forced to take it. I had a tremendous amount of financial responsibility and was stuck. There were many days spent sitting, staring, stressing.

I would ultimately find out my problems didn't end there and were a lot worse than I could've ever imagined. My lovely bride was not what she seemed. I was being cheated on. In fact, I was being cheated on from before we even got married. She cheated, married me anyway, proceeded to live a double life for three years and got pregnant by the other guy while we were still married. One day I came home to a letter from Planned Parenthood following up on her abortion visit.

I was devastated. I thought my life had gotten better! My New Jersey days were long gone! How did I get here! I mean I was doing everything right. From the outward appearance of it, I was living a great life. How could this happen?

I was thrust back into a world of darkness. I was thrust into a world of aloneness, inner turmoil, and hopelessness all over again. I had worked so hard to distance myself from my past, to make the right decisions, and to live a normal, better life.

On my knees, in tears, I was alone and lost. Begging and pleading for someone to help me. I so desperately wanted to understand why I was such a failure in every aspect of my life, even though I tried so hard to do well. I just kept arriving back in this low, dark place. Not successful, not making progress. Life had beat me down to a pulp. I was completely, utterly, devastatingly, broken apart into pieces.

They say it's in these types of moments you come to yourself. It's in these types tragic, life altering moments true epiphanies occur. True awakenings.

And so it was for me.

Something happened in that period of time that I was by myself after my entire life had fallen apart.

Birth is traumatic. It's intense. You don't enjoy being born. In fact, you come out crying and screaming.

I was being reborn. A blessing was being bestowed on my life. I was in the infancy stage of a radical and transformative change of mind that would forever change me as a person, as well as the lens in which I viewed the world.

I became a student of life. I became determined to understand why my life was what it was, why the people in my life were who they were, did the things they did, and acted the way they acted.

Also, what was my contribution? How was I personally responsible? How did I ultimately arrive to the point I found myself in every aspect of my life?

I hated my corporate job, I had no emotional connection to the work and it was a highly political environment. I was always held back because I couldn't kiss up. But none the less, it was the only opportunity I had at the time and knew there was a possibility to make more money than I had ever made in my life. It was my only hope. My only chance. It was in the palm of my hand and there for the taking if I could muster up the mindset and drive to do it.

I wasn't handed anything or given the special treatment reserved for the biggest ass kisser. I made it happen anyway. I figured ways around the politics and created opportunities for myself within the company through newly built sales relationships with new clients. I wasn't given established clients so I went out and got my own. I worked tirelessly and became the top sales manager in my office as well as second best in the entire northeast. Hopeless, uncertain, afraid, doubtful, heart broken, and confused. I worked. I put my feelings and emotions aside, I sucked it up, became good at it, and took full advantage of that possibility. It wasn't until over a year later that I tripled my income.

As I started to see some success I started to believe in more and more possibility. I started to explore more possibility. I exposed myself to it. I was looking for it. I was determined to make something of this life.

I was determined to silence the whisper of my entire past that I should be a nobody. That I should be what everyone thought I was and said I was.

Belief compounds over time with success.

When life exposes you to something greater, lose something lesser. When life gives you an opportunity to break out and become something extraordinary…RUN.

I had more money in my hand than I ever had in my life from my job, I caught a glimpse, and I never looked back. Everyone else around me was buying new cars, expensive houses, other material items and I purchased a single two family home with the money. That single decision forever changed the course of my life.

I dove in and began to educate myself on rental real estate and become involved with it any way I could. Mornings and nights before and after work were spent studying and working towards my real estate business. While everyone else was wasting time I was working, studying, and dreaming.

I became a student of success. I studied highly successful, self-made, men and woman. I studied their actions, mindset, and philosophies. All of which were very different than my own. Very different than what I ever knew. A complete contradiction to everything I knew to be true.

I began to understand how the events of my life were a blessing. I thought I was drowning but life was preparing me. Life was taking me through steps and stages. I needed to go there, to get where I was going. I sensed and felt a spiritual guide had become present in my life. I began seeing signs on regular basis. My eyes were wide open. I was conscious. I was clear. The universe began working in my favor.

Today, I'm not scared anymore. Today, I know how to stand up to life. Today, I believe in miracles because I am a witness to one.

That miracle is me.

As I write this, I'm 38 years old and free. I never have to work for anyone else or any corporation again in my life and the future is brighter than I could have ever imagined it to be. I'm in control of my own life, in control of who I am and want to be, and have direction to get there. It didn't come easy. It took a lot of work on me.

Today, Morello Properties LLC consists of 27 properties. $4 million in income producing assets and growing. To me it's not just a legal business entity. It's not just about how many properties, asset value, money, or any other stats.

It's a living, breathing testimony.

It's a reflection of a spirit that just won't take no for an answer. A spirit that resolves to defy the odds, overcome all adversity, and will never back down.

It's a reflection of a diesel spirit.

The bigger and more profound it grows, the more diesel my spirit becomes.

If you take anything from this, know that circumstances don't matter. You can be greater than your circumstances as soon as you decide to be.

It doesn't matter what life throws at you when you become fully equipped.

Fully equipped with a diesel spirit.

The following pages are a collection of thoughts, insights, and beliefs, written based on and inspired by a story of struggle and adversity. They are the reflection of a mindset cultivated through challenge, self-discovery, and hardship.

They represent transformation.

These are the words of a diesel spirit.

Embrace the Struggle

Your current struggle is an opportunity. But only if you let it be.

I am who I am today because of what I've been through. Period. I'm grateful for my adversities, not ashamed by them. They're a gift.

I wouldn't change a thing. Not one single thing.

Every brick life threw was used to stand on.

And, here's the greatest gift of all your struggle gives, which is a gift that keeps on giving....

Down the road when you have future struggles, which you will, you can look back at where you are right now and remember what you went through, how you overcame, how it didn't kill you, how you handled it and made it through, and how you took one of life's best punches, spit out the blood, put your mouthpiece back in and raised your fists.

Then won the fight.

You can remember how you dominated your life and how you were a bonafide bad ass.

Don't be sad or upset about your struggle, celebrate it. You are becoming strong. You are becoming indestructible. Believe that!

Dominate your life today and forever remember who the hell you are.

Planted

Sometimes not getting what you want is a wonderful stroke of luck. We don't realize how something that is falling apart on us today is actually setting us up for something much better.

It's only in hindsight we realize why certain things in our lives were just not meant for us.

It might seem like all is going to hell. Like it's the end of your life as you know it.

I can tell you my friend, sometimes, when you're in a dark place it may seem like you've been buried, but actually you've been planted.

Don't quit. Don't ever surrender to the tragedies of life. Be patient, your harvest will be abundant.

Estimation

The amount of work it takes to be highly successful is highly underestimated. The early mornings when everyone else is sleeping. The sacrifice and suffering it takes to obtain something no one else can see but you. To step outside the box and have the strength of mind and character needed to withstand and endure the "chatter" of critics.

Doing what 99% of people on this earth won't do to have what 99% of people on this earth won't have. Whatever it takes, no matter how long it takes, no matter what. This is a mindset that is widely misunderstood, which is why there's a fraction of people that have it.

I know and will forever know what I've endured and continue to endure to reach my goals. I'm far from where I want to be but its cause and effect. If I do the work today I'll have success tomorrow.

There is no maybe.

When you respect the man looking back at you in the mirror, that's all you need.

Count the Cost

Many people want all the benefits of success but very few want to pay the price.

I've spent countless hours working and dreaming while others were fraternizing and enjoying recreation.

There's a certain satisfaction in knowing I'm getting ahead while others are wasting time. It lifts my spirit knowing I'm doing something most people won't.

If you do what most people won't you'll have what most people can't. It's really that simple.

To he who much is given, much is required. I have gratitude and excitement for the work. Every second spent gets me closer. I must make them count. My fulfillment is in the progress.

Not About Me

It's all good, I'm not mad at you.

See I understand what you see on the outside is a reflection of what's on the inside.

I understand your behavior and attitude demonstrate your inner conflicts to the world.

I understand your attitude problem, bitterness, and straight up intolerable personality is a reflection of your frustration with you.

I understand your failure to be open minded and see things differently is just a demonstration of your teeny tiny limited perspective.

I understand your denial about your life and the way you're living it is setting off bombs in your head.

I understand your verbal abuse towards me is just a reflection of your sick, twisted, wretched self-image you have of yourself.

I get it. No hard feelings.

I understand it's not about me.

Childish Things

When I was a child I spoke as a child, thought as a child, and understood as a child. When I became a man I put away childish things.

Who we are as adults is greatly influenced by our upbringing and early childhood development.

What childish things are you holding on to?

Unfortunately you don't get to choose how the story begins but you can sure as hell dictate how it's going to end.

Life is what you make it. Changing your story begins in your head. Change your perspective.

Become conscious, open your eyes wide, identify your childish tendencies and thought patterns, and change them.

Stop dwelling on yesterday and get busy living today because you're running out of tomorrows.

Break Free

You're not chained physically, you're chained mentally.

Many of us settle. We build routines around what we think we can't change. When you do this you get stuck.

I was stuck. Stuck in a life I didn't want because I was living up to the expectations of everyone else around me. Living up to the ideas of success that were influenced upon me, but weren't really my own.

I was forced to be someone I wasn't to fit into a culture that didn't resonate with who I was at my core. Forced to strive for something I had no emotional connection to.

Broke, frustrated, and completely fed up, I started studying powerful self-made businessmen that fit the vision in my head of what I wanted to be.

Early mornings, nights after work, and weekends became go time to strategically switch direction to move closer to the type of life I wanted. No vacations, no nights out, no nonsense, period.

Friday and Saturday nights were spent painting an apartment or reading a real estate investment book. Every free moment around my normal working hours and hours I slept, were spent doing productive activities that moved me closer.

Delay gratification. Suffer and sacrifice EVERYTHING in the short term to live content the rest of your life.

Lessons

People in your life can teach you some incredibly valuable lessons.

They show you how to be codependent on another person and completely lose your sense of self.

They show you how to be absent and unavailable to your children.

They show you how to brush problems under the rug and act like they don't exist.

They show you how to be a victim and blame everyone else but yourself.

They show you how to damage your health and well-being.

They show you how to be a puppet on a string for a pay check.

They show you how to quit and give up easily when things get hard.

They show you how to pretend to be happy to impress your friends and family.

They show you how to become whoever people want you to be to keep friends, intimate relationships, and marriages.

They show you how to spend money on things you can't afford to keep up on appearances.

They show you how to be bitter and angry because you're not living up to your potential.

They show you how an undisciplined life is an insane life.

They show you how to be fake.

They show you their true colors when they can no longer benefit from a relationship with you.

They show you how to deceive and manipulate everyone.

So, thanks for the life lessons. You're a great teacher. Thanks to you I know who I am and who I definitely don't want to be.

Not Too Close

You're a lot more conditioned than you realize. You are a common denominator of the 5 closest people to you on a daily basis. Notice similarities in who they are and who you are? In how they think and how you think? In how they act and how you act?

Miraculously their values and beliefs are your values and beliefs. Most people's thoughts aren't even their own thoughts.

Notice the same bullshit story they tell themselves as to why life is unfair and they can't succeed is the same story you're telling yourself?

You talk, act, and think very similar to the way they do. People rub off on you. Most people aren't even consciously aware it's happening.

Choose the people in your life wisely. Whether or not you want to be consciously aware of it, they are holding you back.

Develop your own thoughts. Develop your own standards. Even if it means standing alone.

Like attracts like. You'll attract who you become, lose the rest.

Advice

Sadly many people are misled and fail because they are listening to the advice of their parents, in-laws, siblings, friends, teachers, coaches, bosses, coworkers, etc.

Pay closer attention to the advice giver than the advice itself. Most people are full of it. It's not that they don't mean well, it's just that they have never actually done what you are wanting or trying to do and therefore can't advise you on how to proceed.

Knowing something isn't enough. What have they actually done? The proof is in the pudding.

We're afraid to go against the grain, upset someone, or be disrespectful to someone we love.

Advice always stems from the givers perspective. It's always a reflection of their perceived limitations based on what they've experienced, have done, or have failed to do. In some cases it's a pure manipulation that's in the advice givers best interest not yours. Just because they can't do something people want to convince you that you can't do something.

Never let anyone push their limitations on to you. Take a closer look at the advice givers in your life. Although they may mean well, they may be destroying your life and holding you back tremendously.

On Your Knees

Has life ever brought you to your knees?

It's brought me to mine more than once. Hopeless and afraid begging asking someone or something for help.

I was lucky though. No one came to help me. No one was there to tell me it was going to be alright.

I was forced to look for comfort within. I was forced to learn how to stand on my own two feet.

I was forced to pick myself up, figure it out, and get on with it.

I came to myself. Learned how to stand up again.

Complete metanoia. I was never the same again.

The battles you're facing are preparing you for some of the greatest achievements of your life.

Your lowest low will be the reason for your highest high.

I wear my battle scars proudly and solute the people that put them there.

The affliction you caused made me who I am today.

I am blessed to have been afflicted.

Who I am today is someone much better than you.

Revival

Revival. Defined as the improvement in the condition or strength of something.

If I said no more that single statement is enough to cause me to eat thunder and crap lightning.

There's no one as dangerous as someone who's making a comeback.

You haven't been in a fight until you've been in the ring a few rounds with someone that has affirmed a comeback.

The type that takes your best punch, gets up with a blood covered grin and motions you to come get some more.

Someone who's rising up.

Someone who is turning their dead ashes into pure fire.

Someone that is scratching and clawing to dig out of a hole, a dark place.

Somebody that has nothing to lose.

They've already gone as low as they can go.

They already lost everything. They already hit rock bottom.

Someone who's seen the light and is moving towards it.

They don't operate off of a cute fluffy affirmation, but a firm convicted decision.

A should becomes a must.

It's a come hell or high water, get out of my way kind of comeback.

They've already been distressed, through hell, lost everything, been through trouble, been embarrassed, and had their feelings hurt.

A person that has committed to unleash some fury that makes no sense. God bless you if you're in their way.

You will be met with an abrasive tenacity and grit that will leave you shocked and confused.

See, they have nowhere to go but up...and the person on the top of the mountain didn't fall there.

Sad or Unfortunate?

I've had many unfortunate circumstances and experiences in not only my life, but in my business. I don't look at any of them as sad or unfortunate. I'm certainly not bitter, I'm better.

That's not just a fluffy, cute little self-affirmation. It's a convicted belief that is fact.

My life is proof of it.

I've been able to rise above, dig my life out of the gutter, and build a successful real estate business because I don't have the interest, the time, or the mental and physical energy available to be bitter. Bitterness is unproductive. Bitterness is a waste of time.

Affliction hasn't just made me better, its made me unstoppable.

I can withstand things in life and business many cannot. Plain and simple.

I've withstood things and continue to withstand things due to the fact that I have a tremendous resolve and a relentless tenacity to overcome.

I have a resume of overcoming challenges and adversities. Therefore, in life and in business, I am not easily deterred. I am not easily discouraged.

I can rise to the occasion. I am just absolutely insufferably relentless. I will keep coming again, and again, and again, and again. I have a deep resolve and a dogged determination to never give in.

Frankly, I'm prepared to literally die before I would fail in bettering myself, my life, and my business.

I would have given up a long time ago if not for my afflictions.

Be thankful for the struggle. Be thankful for affliction. It's shaping, molding, and grooming you for what's to come.

Sad and unfortunate? No, no, no. More like hell yeah and thank you very much.

Admiration

I used to admire people that seemingly have it all.

I used to admire those that could buy all the finest luxuries.

I use to admire people that grew up in rich families and had inheritances.

I used to admire the pimped out ride I saw other people driving.

I used to admire titles and positions.

I used to admire people that grew up with close knit families.

I used to admire people that are famous or popular.

I used to admire those that have beautiful houses with white picket fences.

I used to admire beautiful, well thought out weddings.

I used to admire people that have such perfect relationships and significant others.

I used to admire those that have picture perfect marriages and children.

I used to admire people that are liked by everyone. People with lots of friends.

I used to admire people that were raised with love and perfect parents.

I used to admire people with perfect bodies.

I used to admire those that make more money than they know what to do with.

With all this admiration, there was always one thing I never gave the true admiration it deserves.

The one thing that can surely elude you regardless.

I now mostly admire people that have inner peace.

They're so bad ass.

Discovery Moments

Life gives you discovery moments.

Moments you realize not how tough life is...but moments you discover how strongly you've been created.

The tests and trials of life serve a purpose.

There are things about yourself that you don't know right now.

Strengths you don't know exist until you've been forced to use them.

Until you find yourself down on your knees or find your back against a wall.

Strengths that surface out of nowhere because being strong is the only choice you have.

Discovery moments happen in tight places.

Places that feel like everything is caving in.

Places that force you to fight back, to push hard, to survive.

It is in life's discovery moments we are being molded, shaped, and prepared for things that aren't immediately apparent or fully understood.

It is in the darkness we discover the light.

It is in tragedy we discover triumph.

It is in low places we discover great heights.

I know you feel broken. I know you feel betrayed. I know you feel lost, hopeless, and afraid.

Know that it's not what it seems. It's not what it looks like.

It's a defining moment.

It's a discovery moment.

You'll soon be able to discover and understand just how strongly you've been created.

Single

Ahhh, love is in the air.

The most beautiful and productive relationships are those where two people that are "whole" and "complete" alone, come together.

Becoming comfortable being alone is empowering and when two people who are comfortable being alone come together, it creates a powerful combination.

Sharing your life with someone becomes a valued option that enhances your life and adds to it, not a desperate necessity that forces you to settle for what's available.

Not a life of codependency, but a life of individuality together as one.

There's no issue in allowing your partner to blossom, be a unique individual, and be all they can be.

You don't take offense to it, become resentful, or feel like you have to compete.

You can be your partner's biggest fan and loudest cheerleader without feeling it somehow takes away from you.

You empower each other, not hold each other back for fear of losing them.

You don't need the other person to somehow complete you or turn a half into a whole. You don't need "another half".

You are not half a person.

Find completeness and wholeness alone, within yourself, then learn how to be whole while connected to your partner.

Stop the endless search for someone to make you happy.

It's important to learn how to create happiness and contentment within yourself, then find someone that adds to it.

It's OK to be alone. It's OK to be single.

Being with no one is better than being with the wrong one.

There's nothing odd or strange about you. There's nothing wrong with you.

In fact there's a lot right with you.

You are strong enough to wait for what you deserve, what you really want, and what adds to your life as opposed to subtracting from it.

Don't let loneliness steer you back to people and toxic relationships that aren't good for you.

Don't look for a relationship, then define who you are. Define who you are, then look for a relationship.

Second Chances

If you're lucky enough to get a second chance at something don't waste it.

Second chances are a gift.

An opportunity to grasp what you let slip through your hands the first time.

A chance to turn a wrong into a right.

A closed door that reopens.

Lost trust that gets restored.

A fleeting opportunity to do a great thing that resurfaces.

A broken heart that has the opportunity to love again.

A life that was almost lost but then found.

A tormented soul in darkness that catches a glimmer of light.

A help back up to your feet when you get knocked down.

A welcome back in when you've been kicked out.

A "let's start over".

A new chance to make a first impression.

Forgiven mistakes and forgotten lies.

A fresh start at a new life.

Don't take second chances lightly because you may be highly unlikely to see a third.

You'll be left always wishing, wondering, and praying for that second chance you took for granted...and already let pass you by.

Enemy Within

Everyone has an enemy within.

An enemy that rises up every now and again to spar with you in the ring of life.

Another version of yourself that fights you on the inside.

An invisible enemy declaring a war no one else can see but you.

A voice not heard by the outside world but oh you can hear it echoing in your head.

You can feel the pressure of the enemy breathing down your neck.

That tormenting whisper.

It's relentless criticisms and demands.

Telling you you're not good enough, you're nobody, you're exactly what they said you were, you're not capable, you're dumb, you're ugly, you're a failure, and you'll never make it.

The enemy within can drive you to a breaking point like no one else.

Drive you to a point where enough is enough. A tipping point.

Drive you to a point where shoulds become musts and indecisiveness becomes massive action.

A point that you submit and resolve to silence its voice once and for all.

The enemy within can drive you to do things you never knew you were capable of doing.

It can drive you to see in ways you never knew you were capable of seeing.

It can drive you to rise up to heights you never knew you could reach.

All along you've been fighting the good fight with an enemy no one else could see.

And suddenly you realize...

The enemy within is really no enemy at all.

The enemy within was your sparring partner...preparing you for the victory in the fight of life.

Behind Those Eyes

The appearance of a person's eyes is often the source of pure admiration.

It's not the outward physical beauty, or the forefront of what we see that's most important.

It's what's behind those eyes that matters most.

Behind those eyes there's a story being told no one really knows.

You're vision, how you see yourself and your potential, is a reflection of what's behind those eyes.

What's behind those eyes can blind you or give you sight.

You can be inspired by or disgusted by what's behind those eyes.

Your whole life, everything you see around you, is a forward projection of what's behind those eyes.

Your mouth speaks lies, but behind those eyes, you can't escape the truth.

You can have all the finest things money can buy.

You can have the most successful outward appearance.

You can put up a front to the world that you're happy and content.

You can be the best built man and the most beautiful woman.

You can be the most popular and most respected person on earth....

But, NO ONE can escape what's behind those eyes.

So, if you're secretly struggling and don't like what you see...

Remember it's the admiration you have for what's behind your own two eyes that will set you free.

Religion

Just because a person is religious, it doesn't make them closer to God than anyone else.

I'm not an extremely religious person.

I've never tried and still don't try to live "perfect" in a facade of neatness.

I didn't always believe in God.

I believed in me.

In fact, when asked if I believed in God, my answer would firmly and proudly be "no I believe in me."

I was and still am in some ways not what religiously fanatical people would consider to be a "godly" man...whatever that's supposed to be anyway.

It is through my ungodliness God looked down and said...

"I want that man."

Not because of my religiosity, my ability to "live right", righteousness, or ability to be perfect and never sin.

Not because I became a preacher, I'm not and don't intend to become a preacher.

Not because I never take my shirt off in a picture.

Not because I mask my problems, never say a curse word, never got divorced, never think an ungodly thought, or do an ungodly thing.

But because I was and still am in some ways anything but.

Because I didn't believe in him. I didn't love him. I didn't even consider him.

His power is made perfect in my weaknesses, my flaws, my broken places, my ignorance and lack of belief.

Not my ability to hide my sin.

I boast in my weaknesses not my religious perfection.

Religion is a man made invention.

I may not live up to what men say and I don't care, nor do I try.

But I forgive and dismiss them because they know not what they do.

No one is made holier than thou because they're religious.

It's what's underneath that counts not what's on the surface.

Pureness of heart and character, and an ability to submit to the fact that you're far from perfect is how God searches for man...

And, he chooses the least likely of suspects.

Excavation

Who were you before the world caused you to change your name?

Before the world got you in its grip?

Before the world stuck its dirty hands in the cookie jar of your mind?

Before the world dictated your beliefs about who you are and should be?

How brilliant and bright were you before the world tarnished you, creating that lackluster shine?

How far did you reach to grab great heights in life before the world slapped your hand and told you no?

How prominent was your voice before the world told you to keep quiet?

How creative and free were you before the world told you to get real and get back in line?

How big was that smile before affliction smacked it off your face?

How highly did you think of yourself before you heard someone tell you that you shouldn't?

You don't need to find yourself. You're not lost. You're not a quarter that fell between the couch cushions.

You're there, right where you always were.

You just need to perform an excavation in your head. An unlearning and reconditioning.

A defiance towards the opinions and inaccurate conclusions of other people.

Abundance in all aspects of life is all around us.

It's the mind that creates limitations.

Free your mind.

If you're willing to give it up...you can have it all.

Overly Thankful

You might laugh at what some people are overly thankful for.

Unless you know a person's personal testimony, you don't truly understand.

Things you take for granted, someone else is praying for.

Once you've been through hell and back you become thankful for crazy stuff.

Seemingly small and minor to many, but a straight up blessing to those that have been without it.

Little things that don't even make sense like being able to see in the morning, having a bed to sleep in, a blanket to cover yourself, a place to stay, a shirt and pants to wear, having money to put gas in your car, and being able to buy yourself something to eat or drink.

You don't notice or appreciate good health until you've been sick.

You don't notice or appreciate feeling happiness until you've been depressed.

You don't notice or appreciate peace until you've been disrupted and disturbed.

You don't notice or appreciate freedom until life locks you up.

You don't notice or appreciate a few bucks in your pocket until you've been broke.

You don't notice or appreciate good things people do for you until they stop doing them.

You don't notice or appreciate that job until you're sitting on the couch.

You don't notice or appreciate love and togetherness until you've been alone and unloved.

You don't notice or appreciate that beat up car until you've been thumbing it.

You don't notice or appreciate honesty until you've been manipulated and deceived.

You don't notice or appreciate a lot of the things you may take for granted right now.

You don't know what you got until it's gone and when you take things for granted, those things eventually get taken.

Appreciate what you have before it turns into what you had.

If you're a real big shot with all the finest things always remember the two real gifts you open every day of your life.

Your eyes.

Becoming

The greatest compliment is when a person who knew you when asks "when did you become?"

It's a question asked out of confusion and disbelief that a person they "knew so well" actually became something out of the character they were accustomed to.

It's a question that always comes from a person that doesn't understand the concept of change.

It's a question often asked by a timid soul that's too afraid to color outside of lines in their own life.

But, it's ok to answer silly people.

See, if they really must know...

You became when you made a commitment to become.

When you fell out with your old life and decided you wanted way more.

When you refused to submit to that type of limited thinking.

When you pushed forward in spite of fear.

When you decided to burn the book they were reading and write your own life story.

When you decided to stop pecking around with pigeons and fly with the eagles.

When you decided, unlike them, to cut your puppet strings and defy the puppet master.

When you decided to start dominating instead of tolerating.

When you decided to spray paint in the coloring book life they knew you from.

When you resolved to pay the price in advance and die before you would ever give up.

That's when you became.

Hopefully that might have answered the question.

Vibin High

The high vibe club.

High vibin gangstas in the high vibe mafia.

Only people that push you, challenge you, make you laugh, make you happy, and make you better are allowed.

Toxic and negative people? I'm sorry your application has been rejected and denied.

In this club we don't have time or energy for what you're talkin about....we're busy vibin.

We're busy thinking worthy thoughts, speaking inspiring words, and taking empowering actions.

When you're high vibe livin there's an unmistakable energy that radiates.

In this club we vibe so high we get on people's nerves.

Nothing can penetrate or affect us....cause we vibin.

We got a hop in our step....cause we vibin.

When you become a part of this club, magic starts happening.

Like a magic act, toxic and negative people disappear because they no longer know how to approach you.

Things start taking a turn for the better because the world around you is catchin your vibe.

Protect your energy, not everyone deserves it. You may be misunderstood by bitter, negative, unmotivated, uninspired people that aren't growing, reaching higher, or changing.

Keep your vibration high and your growth game on point...

The right people will catch your vibe and you'll become straight up gangsta.

Heart

A person that has heart is dangerous.

Talent and resources will only get you so far if you don't have any heart.

You never know a person's heart.

What they're willing to give up, sacrifice, and go through to see an expected end.

How hard they're willing to fight no matter the circumstances.

The man or woman that gets up again, and again, and again.

You can beat them to a pulp, they'll stand up, spit out the blood, put their mouth piece back in, and stay in the fight.

When you think they've had enough they motion you to come and get some more.

You can't discourage them easily.

STRUGGLE gives you heart. AFFLICTION gives you heart. ADVERSITY gives you heart. PAIN gives you heart.

Don't bet against a person with heart.

They just will not stop. They just will not throw in the towel. They won't tap out.

Put the worst set of circumstances on a person that has heart and it's game over.

Circumstances don't matter when you have heart. The odds don't matter when you have heart.

When you see a comeback, you're seeing a person's heart take flight.

Strip a man or woman of everything they have.

Take their money, their things, their resources, their relationships, and their security.

Pin their back against a wall.

Bring your best shot.

If they have heart....you're going to witness a strength and will you've never seen before.

It's called comeback power.

A power that is fueled by the heart.

I know you're down, depressed, uncertain, unstable, and unhappy.

Do you have heart?

How Bad?

Ever been short of breath?

It opens your eyes, creates panic, and is quite disturbing.

When you can't breathe all you want is your breath back.

All you can think about is that gasp of air you would literally die to take.

Your mind's focus and attention is completely immersed in the fact that you want that breath.

You NEED that breath. You MUST have that breath.

It's such an important need and want that you become frantic for it.

You scratch and claw for it. You would do anything for it.

You'd willingly give up and trade anything.

You'd walk to the end of the earth or climb the highest mountain.

Breath is a requirement of your life. It's non-negotiable. It's uncompromisable. It's not an if or a maybe.

When you approach that life change you want, the success you desire, like you approach that breath...

Then you'll get it.

Until then...

The fresh air of that life change or aspiration will forever elude you.

You'll always and forever be gasping and choking on the vile air of mediocrity and stagnation.

Do you REALLY WANT IT as bad as you want to breathe?

Seriously ask yourself that question.

True Strength

Those that disrespect and attempt to devalue other people disrespect and devalue themselves.

Arrogant, loud mouth people that talk negatively about others, prey on the weak, act out in anger or rage, throw tantrums, and push other people down to lift themselves up think these behaviors are a sign and a signal that they are strong. They falsely believe this is strength.

Silly people.

Say what you will as you say it from your average, misguided way of thinking and way of life.

Pump the brakes and turn that "strength" down a couple notches...

Here's a reality check for the uneducated, meager, and pathetic "big shots" of the world... these are signs of extreme weakness.

Deep down you have no control over who you are, the circumstances in your life, or the outcomes you desire.

Your soul is tormented, decrepit, and feeble.

Here's what you need to know boss.

When you're strong you don't need to act out and go overboard to display it or make it known.

When you've got "real" strength people will know it. People will tell you, you don't have to tell people.

It's displayed in your demeanor, your actions, and the overall outward reflection of the way you treat people and the life you live.

It's felt. It's understood without the need for your mouth.

To lift others up without feeling it takes away from you, is strength.

Humility, sensitivity, compassion, empathy, and kindness are what real strength is about.

Rawness and authenticity are strength, not your contrived existence.

See, your container doesn't have any content.

Strength is calmly smiling in the face of and walking away from "strong" people and their inadequate displays of "strength".

See, you're not fooling anyone.

Strength lies in how you make others feel about themselves, not in how you make other's feel about you.

True strength is the courage to admit weakness.

With all this being said, no hard feelings. I'm not mad at you.

I've got too much altitude in "real" strength to come down to your level.

Discouragement

Discouragement is a mysterious company keeper.

Discouragement can make one believe things about their circumstances that make them seemingly impossible to defeat.

Outwardly you appear determined, like you have it together, and are up for the challenge.

Inwardly, it's a secret fight in your heart, in your mind, and in your soul.

A subtle loss of confidence, enthusiasm, or a diminished spirit.

It can hide behind a smile, pretty makeup, and fancy clothing.

It'll catch a ride with you to work in the morning, or on the way back home.

Discouragement will take a seat at the dinner table and have a meal with you or tuck you in at night when you go to sleep.

Discouragement doesn't discriminate.

It often creeps in on the poor and homeless, but it won't stop there.

Discouragement is so bold it will pop in and visit the rich and privileged, as well as everyone in between.

If you listen to discouragement it can make you wonder...what is the point of trying?

What is the point of living?

Discouragement will prey on the most happy and cheerful, and it secretly weakens the biggest strongest people among us.

No one can escape discouragement.

A secret fight with discouragement can lead you down some dark alleys you're not sure you'll ever find your way out of.

Felt and believed strongly enough, discouragement will begin to trump any and all forms of encouragement, leaving you doubtful without any hope.

Don't give in to discouragement though.

Fight the good fight of faith in believing you are greater than your circumstances.

Rise up, fight back, and change your story.

Discouragement is no match for the believer.

It is hard, even for discouragement, to defeat the man or woman that never gives up.

Hope, faith, and belief are discouragements kryptonite.

Maintaining persistence in spite of discouragement is one of the most radical displays of courage that exists...

Disappointments are inevitable, discouragement is a choice.

Reignite that fire you allowed discouragement to extinguish...

Let it burn discouragement to a crisp.

Stay in the fight. Give it kryptonite.

Great Things

I've always had something inside of me that moved me to attempt great things.

It's just the way I'm wired.

I'd prefer an unknown heaven over a known hell any day of the week.

A lot of people don't live their dreams. They don't step out of the familiar, choosing misery over happiness and fulfillment.

Choosing known agony, torment, and discontent over unknown fulfillment, happiness, and bliss.

Moving in the direction of the unknown takes guts and courage, which is why so few do it.

Having limited visibility to what's in front of you and leaning into it anyway.

It's much easier to remain in a known hell where everything is familiar.

Where you know the outcome. Where you can kick your feet up and relax in knowing.

You don't have to be challenged. You have a better chance of avoiding what may be waiting around the corner.

The path is lit up. You can see every step.

And most importantly, after all, everyone will be pleased, satisfied, in agreeance, and at peace with the way you're living your life.

I'd rather try and fail then not try at all.

I'd rather stand and face the world boldly in triumph and say "THIS I have done!"

I'd rather throw my whole self at something and not get it, than live a life timid and afraid never knowing what would have happened had I not went for it.

I'd rather create than conform.

I'd rather be a hot mess of decisive action than a perfectly organized coward.

I'd rather chase the realization of a worthy ideal than stay put in a meager existence.

I'd rather try to reach for and grab something worthwhile no one can see but me.

Listen to that small voice calling you to step out.

Live every day like it is your last because someday it will be.

You can't grasp what you're not reaching for, see what you're not looking for, hear what you're not listening to, or taste what you're not taking a bite out of.

Bet the house on yourself. Even if you lose, you've won.

Tired

There are times you just get tired. Drained to the point you question your will to keep going.

To keep moving down the path of this journey you started and see it through to the end.

Inevitably along the way, self-doubt, disbelief, and discouragement creep in and start to get in your head.

The voices and opinions of other people convincing you that you can't do something begins to wear on you. You start to believe them.

How much longer can you stand up and stand firm?

Obstacles are put in your way to test whether or not you really want it bad enough.

It's OK to take a break. It's OK to rest. It's OK to stop, be still, clear your head, and re-calibrate.

It's OK to struggle...however quitting is not an option.

You have to remember why you started.

You have to remember what they said about you.

You have to remember where you come from...this wasn't meant for you.

You have to remember that person you aren't now, but are trying to become.

You have to remember, what if you can actually do this, oh how life would be.

You have to remember the self-respect you earn from taking life on and not giving up.

You have to remember that vision no one else can see but you.

You have to remember the outcome you desire.

Rise up inside yourself and remember the people you're proving wrong.

This is a fight. This is a test of your will, your strength, your endurance, your stamina, and your true desire.

If you give up easily then you never really wanted it in the first place.

You need to live for this. Bleed for this. Literally die for this...before you would ever give up.

Get up, stand up, slap yourself out of your stupor, put your big boy and big girl pants on...

Make it happen. Most won't but you will. Remember, something always seems impossible until it's done. DO IT.

Every champion was once a contender that simply refused to give up. Your future self will thank you for staying in the fight.

Don't give up on the person you are becoming.

Fight for Territory

Life is a fight for territory.

Anything you perceive to be yours you need to fight for it.

This has nothing to do with being a nice, kind hearted person.

Your family, your assets, your peace, your joy, your health, your life, your well-being.

Never let the enemy take your stuff.

You could be the nicest, most kind hearted, most beautiful soul on the planet.

But once a person crosses that fence...

You unleash a fury and a fight that rocks their world.

You reclaim by force. Not a tap dance. Not a beat around a bush. Not a cute gesture.

By force.

You didn't come this far to lay down and be walked on like a doormat.

You didn't go through all you went through to give up and let the enemy have their way.

A person can say whatever they want...

But once they attempt to threaten what you fought for, toiled for, and bled for...

They have a serious problem.

The problem is you.

You will not bow, you will not give in, you will not surrender, you will not settle.

The enemy better bring their best shot and be willing to give up their whole life for victory. Because you're willing to give up yours.

Encourage Yourself
When it boils down to it, encourage yourself.

It's not up to other people to encourage you. Encouragement needs to come from the inside.

When the going gets tough, self-encouragement is the deciding factor.

When there's no one there to pat you on the back and say "good job".

Encourage yourself.

With no crowd around you shouting "you can do it!"

Encourage yourself.

No pep rally, no family support, no one there to lift you up.

Encourage yourself.

When it's silent and you're alone with your thoughts, doubting yourself and your abilities.

Encourage yourself.

Everyone around can believe in you, but if you don't believe in you...

Encourage yourself.

At the conclusion of a trying day...

Encourage yourself.

I know you can't see the light at the end of the tunnel, but...

Encourage yourself.

When you can't rely on anyone else. When there's no one complimenting or celebrating you. When nobody cares.

Encourage yourself.

Life is a fight we often sometimes must fight alone. Personal battles on the inside. When you cry those secrets tears no one knows about but you.

Encourage yourself.

It's the sound of your own inner voice that will move you forward or hold you back.

Be your own biggest supporter, loudest cheerleader, and proudest encourager.

Tell yourself it's going to be OK. Tell yourself you got this. Tell yourself that you won't let you down.

You owe you and explanation.

You're counting on you to make it happen. Don't let yourself down. Encourage yourself.

Expectation

Expectation costs you something.

It's hard to want something and always be in a position of readiness expecting something to happen, because you might not get it. You might be disappointed.

It takes work to want something.

People fall into the abyss of not wanting anything at all because it's easier than wanting something and not getting it.

To stand in a position of expectation cost you more than it does someone that wants nothing at all.

So, most people just give up on all they want and expect and just accept what is.

But see, there are some radical people that never stop believing the best is yet to come.

Many get beaten in the battle, but some of us get better in the battle.

Some of us let the fire inside burn harder than the fire around us.

Some of us decide not to let the circumstances around us determine the conqueror within us.

To press on regardless of what it looks like right now, when there's no evidence around you....takes a stupid, ridiculous, irrational, radical belief and faith that you are greater than your circumstances.

The best is yet to come my friend.

But, it will only come to those that disregard the evidence, the way it looks right now, and press on.

Press on anyway no matter the circumstances, and get ready.

The universe will conspire to make it happen.

The best is yet to come.

Criticism

You'll never be criticized by people doing more than you. Only by people doing less.

You'll only be criticized by bitter people that do more complaining and excuse making than actually taking the necessary steps to better their life.

People that are not living up to their potential and have every reason in the world why not.

Those that have accepted defeatism and play the victim.

The woe is me mentality.

People that believe their own beautiful lies and fictitious stories as to why they can't do more.

People that feel the need to cut other people down so they can feel better and more accomplished in their average, meager existence.

The fact that some people even have the capacity, time, or interest in criticizing someone else who is trying to do something with their life says enough about them.

Truly successful people don't have time to worry about what other people are doing. They don't look them up on Facebook or other social media because they don't care.

They're busy.

It takes all their time and energy minding their own business. Working on progressing in their own life.

And, quite frankly, with a lot of people, there really is no need to look them up because you already know what you're going to find. People gossiping about other people, posting and sharing nonsense, or doing the same thing they've been doing the last ten years. Nothing ever changes, no surprise there.

If bitter, complaining people spent half as much time working on their own life as they do paying attention to someone else's they'd be shocked at how much they can accomplish.

There are some people that actually want to do something with their life.

Don't get mad when someone else is walking through doors when you just sit there your whole life and stare at them.

So, when you look that person up again and they're doing way more than you are, remember while you're crafting your next bitter critique, they're busy working and not giving a damn.

Codependency

Codependency...an excessive reliance on other people for approval and a sense of identity.

How about this idea...have an excessive reliance on yourself for approval and a sense of identity.

Be codependent on you. Be excessively desperate to be in a relationship with you. NEED you.

Realize that you are an actual person. There's a relationship going on every day you have with that person. You can try like hell to ignore it, run from it, escape it, or decide not to have it or participate in it.

You can run, but you can't hide. Eventually you will catch up with you.

So, how's that relationship going? Hopefully good because whether you realize it or not, it dictates the health of EVERY other relationship you have in your life.

In fact, look around, everything you see in your current life experience stems from the health of that relationship you have with you.

Love yourself, encourage yourself, keep yourself company, have meaningful conversations with yourself, take yourself out on dates, cook for yourself, clean for yourself, admire yourself, take yourself out for a walk, pamper yourself, believe in yourself, dominate yourself, and respect yourself.

Yourself, yourself, yourself, yourself.

Establish a firm sense of self and identity, find happiness within yourself, then invite other people in that add to it, contribute to it, and enhance it.

Don't feel bad for making decisions about your own life that upset other people. You're not responsible for their happiness. You're responsible for your own happiness.

Putting the keys to your own happiness in someone else's hands is never a good idea.

Handle your own keys, make several copies, label them real nice and put them on a nice, secure and shiny key ring.

Hang them up in plain sight so you can admire them daily. Have peace in knowing YOU hold the key to your own self-worth and happiness and you aren't codependent on anyone for anything.

When you hold the key within, you are empowered to stand alone, flat footed, which in my eyes is the equivalent of having superpowers like a comic book character.

Let whoever say whatever, just keep getting better. Be involved in your inner world more than the external one.

You're so busy looking high and low, everywhere else, and ignoring the scream from within to wake up and pay attention.

Until you shift your attention within, you will never be the best you can be for anyone or anything else.

You'll always just be endlessly searching for approval and a sense of identity that will forever elude you because you're not looking in the right place or depending on the right person.

The right place is within and the right person...

IS YOU.

Passing Through

It's a strange thing how many people come in and out of our lives.

Like a busy train station, one minute they're here, the next they're gone.

Some stay longer than others. Some overstay their welcome and need to be forced out.

Some only come for a period of time to serve a purpose and teach us lessons. Some of which are valuable and some we'd like to forget.

Some leave lasting impressions that stick with us forever. Some good, some bad.

Some only come when there's benefit, gone when it runs out.

Some we may see again, and some we may not. Some we miss, some we don't.

People you were like two peas in a pod with, and down the road became complete strangers.

One day they mean the world to you the next day they mean nothing at all.

See, people could be with you, but not really with you or for you.

They could be present, but not really connected.

I've learned to let people come as they come and go as they go.

I've learned if and when a person walks away, let them walk.

I've learned people are a dime a dozen.

I've learned out of all the people that come, and all the people that go...

There's only ever a few you can count on one hand that have a final destination in you.

Never lose yourself over people. Many are just temporary strangers passing by.

Passing by in a period of time waiting to catch a train to their next destination.

Face It

Face what you have to face.

When the weight of burden, chaos, or struggle gets increasingly heavy on you one of two things are going to happen.

You'll succumb to the weight and pressure and get crushed, or you'll dig deep, check your resolve, and rise to the challenge.

You'll either decide the weight is too much, or decide that you can and will muster up the strength to push against it.

When it seems like the weight of the world is bearing down on your shoulders it's no time to cry, no time to feel sorry for yourself, no time to be doubtful, pessimistic, or scared.

It's time to pick up the pace. It's time to press harder. It's time to push back.

It's time to face what you have to face and do what you have to do. It's no time to worry about hurting someone's feelings or being indecisive.

Make the decisions you have to make and approach the conflict in a strategic and non-emotional way.

You will never overcome any burden or struggle sent against you if you are overly emotional about it.

Believe you were given the incredible burdens and struggles you have because you are strong enough to bear them.

You are in control. You are resilient. This will not break you.

Don't decrease the goal. Increase the effort. To he or she much is given, much is required.

Come hell or high water, even if you have to toil 24/7, bleed, or literally die...

Handle it.

Leave Them Behind

An interesting phenomenon occurs when you start really being yourself.

When you start acting out in ways that are really who you genuinely are and talk truths about how you feel and how you see.

Those around you get so silent you can hear a pin drop. Some become distant and some literally just stop talking to you completely.

Once you give up the facade that "fit", you no longer resonate with or have similarities with who you used to.

Once you take off the mask and allow people to see who you really are and want to be, life can become a lonely place to be.

Only for a period of time, however, because you attract what you are.

You can't become who you want to be until you give up who you are.

When you become a butterfly you'll attract butterflies. Once changed, you never see a butterfly hanging around with caterpillars talking caterpillar language.

Butterflies leave the caterpillar world behind completely and unapologetically to be what they are...to float and flutter.

It's a very tough process no doubt, but a necessary one to level up.

Growth and change is painful.

But nothing is as painful as staying somewhere, stuck where you don't belong.

Don't be afraid to leave people that don't ever change or evolve behind.

Live your one life the way you want to live it now because the only thing that's going to matter when you're living out your final days is regret....

Not the people you pretended to be someone else to keep.

Nevertheless

Life doesn't always make sense. It's not always logical.

When hopelessness has you asking yourself "what am I going to do now?!"...you've just got to have a nevertheless attitude in life.

It's an extremely hard thing to do because it goes against your firmest beliefs. Beliefs that have been shaped by the lack of visual evidence.

When circumstances display no evidence of any light at the end of the tunnel, it takes a radical, silly, laughable, stupid, irrational, blind faith to adopt a nevertheless mentality and press on anyway.

I know your marriage isn't working out and you're getting a divorce, nevertheless.

I know you're broke, can't pay your bills right now, have no job, and losing your home or place to stay, nevertheless.

I know you lost a loved one, nevertheless.

I know you were lied on and cheated on by someone you loved, nevertheless.

I know you've been emotionally or physically abused, nevertheless.

I know that business failed or career took a nose dive, nevertheless.

I know you've been diagnosed with that health problem, nevertheless.

I know what they said about you, nevertheless.

I know how you grew up, how your parents weren't there for you, and where you came from, nevertheless.

I know your heart aches, you're tired, and don't know how in the world you're going to keep keeping on, nevertheless.

I know the cards you've been dealt in life, but...

Nevertheless, be that as it may, regardless, however, despite that, having said that, in any event, in spite of that, at any rate, anyhow, and anyway...

They say the people with the worst pasts, who have faced the worst odds, build the best futures.

You know why?

Nevertheless, they decided to make it anyway. That's why.

Not Your Fault

Sometimes people hurt you, and act like you hurt them.

To hurt someone deeply and treat the person you hurt as if they hurt you is a form of mental illness.

To them, their actions towards you are completely and utterly justified because you made them do it.

They did what they did to you because of something you said or something you did.

If you were different, perhaps they might have acted differently.

You're to blame. It's your fault they're mentally twisted.

Their actions were your responsibility not their own responsibility.

People who hurt you will pass the blame and responsibility of their pathetic behavior on you as a means to justify it to the world.

It's a means to deflect the spotlight off of them and their behavior.

They are trying to escape some truths about themselves.

Ugly truths, that forbid the world ever knew about, would tarnish their image.

The one thing to always remember, unfortunately for them...

God knows. You can't bamboozle God.

Enough said.

What Are You Thinking?

Everything you currently have and are experiencing in your life took shape in your mind before it showed up in your life.

You didn't even know it was happening. You're just busy living, blindly going through the motions of life, and...

BAM! You ask, "What the hell is going on with me and my life?"

Your mind can take you up or take you down. It can keep you in or get you out. It can make you rich or keep you broke. It can keep you stagnant or move you forward. It can keep you a prisoner or set you free.

Your situation, your set of circumstances, the way you live your life, the people you have around you, the way you spend your time, and what you make a priority, are all a manifestation of what's going on in your head.

Nothing ever changes in your life because nothing ever changes in your mind.

What needs to change in your mind?

You need a paradigm shift. A new way of thinking. A new perspective. A new way of looking at your life, yourself, and your situation.

If you're sitting their getting angry, rejecting this notion, and demanding you KNOW you KNOW, well then, there you go. Good luck staying stuck and miserable the rest of your life because that's exactly the fate you've decided. Don't be surprised when your outcome is the same no matter what you do, over, and over, and over, and over, and over, and over, and over.

And over.

If you're sitting there excited, curious, tearing up, feeling ready, feeling fed up, and ready to submit to the idea that you don't know what you may think you know and open your mind and your heart....

Congrats, there's a world of freedom and abundance that will be spilling over.

A freedom and abundance you are going to think into existence.

You attached some sort of meaning to everything in your life. Nothing has meaning until you give it a meaning.

If you give something a meaning you can take that meaning away. You can change that meaning. You can create new meanings.

Your life will head in the direction your mind tells it to.

Guard your thoughts. Own your thoughts. Don't allow anyone or anything to penetrate, manipulate, or dictate your thinking.

Whether you realize it or not, or want to admit it or not, that's exactly what you're doing every day of your life. You are not in control.

When you change the way you look at things the things you look at change.

It doesn't have to be this way or feel this way. Don't believe everything you think. Your altitude depends on it.

Your Whole Self

I'd hate to live and die and not know what would have happened had I not thrown my whole self at something.

Had I not committed, all in on that one desire. That one goal. That one dream.

To take the leap and go at it without an emergency brake on. Without limiting myself with disbelief.

Listening and trusting the sound of my own voice moving me forward, not the voice of others trying to hold me back.

To bet all my chips, the house, on me.

To know I left no stone unturned, I exhausted every possibility, and took each and every small advantage I could.

To know that when my life ends, I went for it. I didn't let anything stop me. I was courageous.

I was different.

I had the guts to do what many wouldn't do. I went where it was empty.

I took the unbeaten path. I didn't follow, I made my own way. I built my own vision, not someone else's.

I took every hit, every blow, and every punch life had to dish out and made it anyway.

I couldn't be administered, tied down, or controlled. I took my life and my destiny in my own hands and built something amazing.

Built something that would not have existed had I not come this way. Had I not imposed my will and the will of God.

And, when it's time to go, I will rest peacefully with a sly grin, content in knowing I lived a full life.

Standing boldly and proudly, looking back over my shoulder as I cross over into the light, full of satisfaction, whispering to myself...

"THIS I have done.

So and So

Many people have a so and so.

We spend our whole lives taking caution in our actions because we're afraid of what someone is going to say or think about it.

Well what is so and so going to think if I say this or that?

How is so and so going to feel if I don't want to do this anymore?

How is so and so going to react if I reveal the truth about how I feel?

We let so and so drown out our own inner voice, dictate what we do, and tell us how to live our lives.

All easy for so and so, however so and so doesn't have to live your life. You do.

So and so doesn't have to deal with the consequences of their "advice." You do.

So and so doesn't have to feel fake or like a fraud. You do.

So and so doesn't have to live with your feelings. You do.

So and so doesn't have to be tormented by the thoughts they want you think. You do.

So and so doesn't have to live miserably, unhappy, or unfulfilled as a result of you doing what they expect of you. You do.

It's time to stop putting so and so's opinion ahead of your own.

It's time to drown out the voice of so and so with the sound of your own inner voice.

It's time to stop living so and so's life and start living your own.

It's time to put so and so in check.

Life is just way too short.

So...who's your so and so?

Direction

I've learned that direction is the most important thing you need in life.

Peace, happiness, well-being, and fulfillment all stem from knowing you're on the right path, going the right way, doing the right thing.

I've learned a lack of a sense of direction can make you depressed, and want to give up on life.

A lack of direction fills your world with uncertainty, fear, and doubt.

You're easily manipulated when you have no direction. There are many that are naive, blindly following in a direction that leads them off the ledge of a cliff.

You're easily convinced to see the things people want you to see, hear things they want you to hear, and go places they want you to go.

When you have no direction it's easy to get off course. To travel down roads that aren't in your best interest. To move into areas that aren't good for you.

Lack of direction can put you in places you never wanted to be in. Places you have no emotional connection to. Places that cause you to hate yourself or your life.

Many spend their whole life going in the wrong direction, and don't realize it until it's too late.

Don't chase money, people, things, or status. Chase a sense of direction because with that, you'll obtain everything you've ever wanted and have the directed capacity and wisdom to keep it.

Right now you are moving in some sort of direction in your life.

Every day that goes by you are moving in that direction to where that path may lead.

Is it where you really want to go?

Get quiet, shut out the noise of every single person you have in your life around you.

Listen to yourself intently.

There you'll find the answer to that question.

There you'll discover direction.

Just on the Other Side

Your breakthrough is just on the other side.

I know you're tired. I know you're weak. I know your frustration is at its peak.

But it's just on the other side.

I know it seems like its not working.

But, it's just on the other side.

I know you've fought long and hard. You wonder how much more you can take.

There's a miracle waiting for you just on the other side.

If you can just get through this. If you can just stay in the fight a little bit longer. If you can keep toiling even though you're doubtful, uncertain, and afraid.

There's a multitude of blessings just on the other side.

Life is a fight. Your mind is the battle ground. The fight is in your mind.

Don't give up, don't give in. It doesn't matter how it looks or how it seems.

Keep reaching, keep stretching, keep pushing and shoving.

Because all though you have no evidence, and although it seemingly just makes no sense...

When life is trying to break you...but you don't break...

I promise you it's all going to come together. I promise you the doors will swing open, and something will be waiting for you...

And, it's going to be bigger than you think it is...

Just on the other side.

<u>Love Yourself</u>

As I began to love myself my relationship with everyone changed.

I developed a much lower threshold of tolerance for many things.

Things like...

My availability when they viewed me as an option.

My price tag when they didn't value me.

My acceptance of the mismatch between actions and the words coming out of their mouth.

My love only reciprocated with a like.

My explanation when they committed to misunderstand.

My respect when they lied to me like they lie to themselves.

My understanding when I didn't get an invite, text back, or phone call.

My assumption that they cared about me.

My passivity when I should have put my foot down.

My willingness to stand for a lack of follow through when I'm made a promise.

My trend of putting them first when they put me second...forth or fifth...or eighth.

My kindness when they took it for a weakness.

My desire to bend for them when they only appreciate when I break.

My presence when they deserved my absence.

My approval of an apology that didn't match the level of disrespect.

My satisfaction in what I was getting relative to what I deserved.

My ability to be fake so they will love, like, or accept me.

My attention when they took it for granted.

My agreement when they blatantly used me.

What can I say. Pain changed me.

It's really ok, you were just being you...

And, as you showed me who you really were...I started believing you.

Now I'm showing myself who I really am...and now I'm believing me.

I'm more than enough.

Don't take it personal...I'm just in love with me now.

See....

One of the things I finally realized that I don't have to do anymore is pretend things didn't hurt me that did.

I've finally learned that you can be a kind person with a good spirit...

And still tell people to go fuck themselves when needed.

Real Life

Growing up in a broken home, no father figure, doing drugs as an adolescent.

It was a fight.

Severe depression, life spiraling out of control, abusing drugs and alcohol to cope with life. The reality is my reckless behavior could have killed me a long time ago.

It was a fight.

Married, being manipulated, lied to, and used for years without even knowing it.

It was a fight.

Stuck in a job I hated, back against a wall, drowning financially, playing a part to fit in, absolutely hating my life.

It was a fight.

So beat down by life, I literally couldn't stand up, dropped down on my knees, literally begging and pleading for someone to help me.

It was a fight.

Made critical mistakes in business and damn near lost it all. Worked seven days a week, 16 hour days to save it.

Oh yes, it was a fight.

I'm not a self-proclaimed expert or professional on what people need to do to fix their lives or mentality.

I don't have magical, well-crafted answers, or fancy concepts with catchy labels to fix people's problems.

I'm a guy that has fought many fights in life and has come out the other side and won.

Through real, raw, and honest truth, I set out to give others permission to shine their own light and be set free.

I hope to give others strength to cast down demons, punch the devil in the face, and claim their victory.

I speak from experience and pain.

I had to straight up fight to become the person I am today. I had to fight for peace, self-esteem, self-respect, self-love, happiness, joy, and freedom.

I had to fight enemies no one could see but me. Secret fights. I had to fight to create the life I have today.

Life is no joke. It will beat the living hell out of you if you let it. No one is exempt from the fights of life.

As soon as you stop fighting for what you want in life, what you don't want will automatically take over.

My testimony, my words are intended to give others the strength of mind to take life on.

It's not cute, it's not magical, and it's not mystical. It's reality.

Underdog

Underdog stories are the ultimate motivation and inspiration.

There are many that are underdogs in life. People that weren't born into anything, no special advantages or resources.

Struggle and scarcity is a way of life. It's what they know.

When you see a person that is given an opportunity and works at it with an unusual, relentless, and obsessive tenacity and grit...

You are seeing an underdog in life.

You are seeing a person that is working harder and longer than everyone else because their motivation is different.

Their motivation is fueled by images. Images of their past, where they've been, the struggle they know.

These are the people that get told they're gripping the bat too hard, working too hard, and need to relax.

An underdog in life that is trying to escape struggle, hardship, and hopelessness has a work ethic that is not widely understood.

Give an underdog at life an opportunity to gain a shred of hope and see a ray of light that will lead to a better life, distancing themselves from the world they know, and they will gladly and enthusiastically work themselves to death to obtain it.

There's no such thing as working too hard.

They will suffer whatever they have to suffer, sacrifice whatever they have to sacrifice, and do whatever it takes for however long it takes to realize that opportunity. To take advantage of that one chance.

Give them that one chance and you will see the true strength of the human spirit blazing uncontrollably. Ruthless, like a wild fire.

I can spot an underdog in life from a mile away. I don't even have to talk to them or know them to spot them. I can watch their actions when given a chance and identify them immediately.

How they keep coming back for more, won't take no for an answer, and simply just won't quit no matter how much the odds are stacked up against them.

Oh, yes indeed, I know an underdog when I see one.

It takes one to know one.

Envy

Envy will suck the soul right out of your body, diminish your spirit, and give you the false illusion that you're not good enough.

Most people only put their best foot forward.

They display what they want you to see and nothing more. Only revealing the good stuff and concealing the rest.

They want you to see black and white, not true colors. They want you to see the welcome home mat, but not behind closed doors. The windows to their soul are hidden behind expensive curtains.

You never really know people like you think you do. In fact, you would be shocked by some of the things people hide.

It always looks great from a distance. Masked with a smile, pretty makeup, fancy clothes, and valuable items.

Get up close enough, you'll see every person has a chink in their armor somewhere. Somewhere, to some capacity, everyone has some sort of brokenness.

I've learned to see through to the real person. I look past and don't even acknowledge the presentation. I don't admire the wrapping paper and pretty bow.

I've learned not to believe everything I hear or admire everything I see.

Everybody's got something. Nobody is perfect. Everyone has issues.

That's why people that act like they've got it all together are laughable. No one has it all figured out. No one has it all together all the time.

Some people that seemingly have it all, the ones people admire most, suddenly blow their brains out.

People that display these picture perfect lives, families, kids, and careers...but are afraid to sit in silence to address the bombs going off in their head.

They're afraid of what people would think if they only knew. Their image is more important than their happiness. Their opinion of themselves is trumped by the opinion of everyone else.

Until you face the fact that you don't know everything...

Until you face the fact that there are chinks in your armor and things you need to address in your life...

Until you give up this facade...

And most importantly, until you stop caring about someone else's opinion about it...

You will always be quietly desperate, lacking inner peace. Desperate to be free from the agony you secretly battle within.

The secret agony that is your life.

Don't ever compare yourself to other people and be envious because through the facade...

They have issues just like you.

Create an envious life for yourself, not based on how it appears perfect and untethered.

Create an envious life for yourself based on perfect imperfections, authentic presentation, and admirable vulnerability.

These are the types of people I envy and want to be like.

Beautifully Broken

It's not always a person's strength that is most beautiful and inspiring.

Not their elegant, eloquent, or successful appearance.

Not even their riches, the car they drive, the expensive house they own, or their flashy appearance.

What's more deeply beautiful and inspiring is a person's struggle.

Their vulnerability.

I know you got success, show me your beautiful struggle.

I know you've got a fabulous after, show me your beautiful before.

I know you got a good clean up, show me your beautiful mess.

I know you've come up, show me your beautiful beat down.

I know you've got glory, show me your beautiful lowliness.

You're magnificent and beautiful, show me your beautiful obscurity and ugliness.

Triumphant you are, show me your beautiful failures.

Everybody is a bit broken somewhere, and that's ok.

Inspire the world not by how perfectly you've been put back together...

But by how beautifully you've been broken.

Profitability

Some relationships just aren't profitable.

Some people's love, concern, and reciprocity cost too much.

There comes a point you've done all you can do, given all you can give, said all you could say, tried all you could try.

You've got to know when you can't afford it. When it's costing you peace, mental health, and the ability to live productivity...it's too expensive.

You need to go on a budget.

You've just got to say, "look if we haven't gotten anywhere by now"...

If they don't love you by now, if they don't value you by now, if they don't reciprocate by now, if they don't care by now...

When people show you they don't care, believe them.

If they miss you, they'll call. If they want you, their actions will prove it. If they care, they'll show it.

If not, they're not worth your time.

You need to focus, life is too short. Be wise enough to know the things you just can't help anymore.

You're running out of time. You only have so much energy and only so much focus.

You've got to focus on areas and in people that you can make progress and be profitable in.

You've got to say "I did all I can do with that", and move on.

Set your face in a new direction.

There's a difference between giving up on someone and knowing that you've just had enough.

Your life will get better when you embrace a simple fact...

It's better to be alone than chase people that don't really care about you.

Humility

Just because you're flying high in life, everything is going exactly the way you want, and you're the bomb...don't be so quick to be critical of others.

Be careful about throwing rocks because you're not done living yet.

You never know what you're going to have to go through.

Life is crazy sometimes. Life will sometimes act like it has no sense. Like it's drunk off a fifth of gin. Life can flip on you in the blink of an eye.

Life will make you shut up.

It'll knock you right off your high horse, send you down to your knees, and humble your fine self.

Some of the most humble, kind, empathetic, and compassionate people are those that have been humbled by life.

Some have learned humility the hard way.

So, if you're a real big shot, reading this with a pompous and arrogant smirk...

I'm not mad at you, just stay far enough away from me so I don't get hit when life smacks it off your face.

Human Spirit

Bold, spectacular feats can only be accomplished by the human spirit.

It's quite a mysterious thing really.

This deep inner roar in a person that unleashes a persistent fury on anything in its way.

Images of struggle, adversity, affliction, and pain ignite and spur the awakening of this spirit that was lying dormant.

Your spirit is stronger than anything that can happen to it.

No one is exempt from the tests and trials of life, but some get beaten in the battle and some get better in the battle.

Don't shy away from what's trying to beat you down. Don't back away from what's wrong with you, your pain, or your problems.

Lean into them...

Because you see, it's what's wrong with you that's going to make what's right with you.

Lean into them...

Because it's the pain in you that will release the power in you.

Lean into them...

Understand that it is your problem that will provoke your power.

A unique power fueled by the human spirit. By your spirit.

Comeback power.

Connections

People rub off on you. Connections matter. Be careful who you're connected to.

Birds of a feather flock together. You can't surround yourself with blindness and expect to see.

Everyone wonders where to begin in making life changes and changing their mindset.

The answer is simple. Your environment.

People, situations you're in, some commitments you've made, and the life you created are holding you back more than you'd like to admit.

You can't let other people convince you that you should have the same perceived limitations that they do.

You could be trying to do great things, but if it's in a bad environment, it'll always end up dead going nowhere.

When a seed won't grow, you change the environment it grows in, not the seed.

You need an environment where you can flourish.

If you want to fly you've got to give up the things that are holding you down.

Don't be afraid to grow. End bad habits, leave dead end jobs, and cut off toxic, unhealthy, and limiting relationships.

Your mental health needs to take priority over any friendship or relationship. Be willing to lose anyone or anything before you lose your mind.

I know you're thinking it's easier said than done.

There's no doubt that changing your life is hard. That's why the majority don't do it, stay where they are, and make excuses. Excuses like it's easier said than done.

Anti-Social

Anti-social behavior doesn't mean there's something wrong with you.

Being somewhat anti-social is a sign of intelligence.

The more intelligent you become, the less you speak.

In fact, there are many that could probably benefit greatly from being a little less social.

It's not that anti-social people don't like people, they just may not be interested in you.

Anti-social people are just selective as to who they choose to be social with. They're selectively social.

I find that people that often have a lot to say, are the same people that would be better off shutting their mouth.

Idiots always have a lot to say. Out loud so you can hear them.

When a person seems anti-social, it simply may be due to the fact that they have zero interest in what many people are talking about.

People drain you. They're complicated and exhausting. It's better to hear silence than gossip stories about other people and other minor insignificant matters.

Many don't think before they speak. Anti-social people simply think more than they speak.

Silence is a source of strength in a loud mouth world.

When you decide to speak, add value to the world.

Otherwise, you're just devaluing yourself.

Every time you open your mouth, you tell the world who you are.

Inner Voice

Be so emotionally strong that you're able to shut down every voice but your own.

Your inner voice should be the loudest voice you hear at all times.

Too many people are listening to everyone else around them that their inner voice is silenced to the point of non-existence.

It's hard to listen to your inner voice in a world that is constantly trying to drown it out.

People have all this advice as to what's right for you and what's not. They can tell you about everything that's going on in your life.

How you should or shouldn't feel, how you should or shouldn't think, where you should or shouldn't go, who you should or shouldn't be, what you should or shouldn't do, how you should or shouldn't do it, who you should or shouldn't date, who you should or shouldn't marry, why you should or shouldn't work somewhere, what you should or shouldn't do with your money.

Should or shouldn't this. Should or shouldn't that.

STOP.

A lot of people that have all of this advice aren't even doing what they should or shouldn't be doing half the time. Many have a PhD in knowing what you need to do in your life and have no real direction for their own.

People can give all this advice on how to go fishing and catch fish but when you look in their boat they haven't even caught anything.

Keep your eyes in your own boat.

In their defense, many people do have good intentions when telling you how to think and live your life...so be nice, don't be rude.

Agree, nod your head yes like you understand and agree, then do what you were going to do anyway.

Offend People

I've really come to thoroughly enjoy "offending" some people as much as possible. In fact, the more I'm disliked the better.

Have you ever noticed how sometimes complete strangers support you more than the people you know?

As ridiculous as it sounds, there are people that will actually take offense to you becoming better and successful, thinking that you believe you're on some kind of pedestal or high horse.

Personal growth isn't met with a pat on the back I'm so happy for you, but a you think you're so great and better than everyone else.

You can't help but smile when asked or it's said...

"Who do you think you are?"

"When did you become so knowledgeable about life?"

"You think you're better than me?"

"You think you're smarter than me?"

"You've changed."

"You think you're so great!"

"I don't even know you anymore."

"What's your deal?"

Questions and statements like this, to a person that is improving their life, are so weak, pathetic, ignorant, and blind.

Pay close attention to who doesn't clap for you when you win.

Then "offend" the hell out of them as much as possible.

Let whoever say whatever just keep getting better.

All About Yourself

Here's your permission. Forget other people. Focus on yourself first.

They don't agree. Validate yourself.

They don't accept you. Self-acceptance is the best acceptance.

No respect. Its ok, self-respect trumps their respect.

Unloved, can't find a good date? Romance and fall in love with yourself.

I know they don't like you. Good thing you like you.

Don't explain it to them. You owe yourself an explanation.

So they walked out the door. Chase yourself.

They don't want to stay. Look in the mirror and beg.

You're always there for everyone else. Let you get taken advantage by you.

No family. Have a reunion with you.

They just won't forgive you. It's ok because you forgive you.

Betrayal and lies. Trust yourself.

Losing people left and right. Look around and find yourself.

You can't pour from an empty cup.

Everything in your life gets better when you get better. Your outer world is a projection of your inner world.

It's not selfish, it's necessary.

Think for Yourself

Many of the actions you take are not a result of your thinking.

Those with a PhD in life are not wise due to what they've learned, but because of what they've unlearned.

Growth is really just an unraveling and unlearning of all the garbage that's been fed to you your whole life.

Everything you believe you know to be true about yourself and how your life should be lived was programmed into your mind by somebody else.

Advice you get is always a reflection of the advice giver's perception and values. Their perceptions and values aren't always necessarily good for you.

Some of the most miserable periods of my life were a direct result of following someone else's advice and skewed perception for my own life.

Interestingly enough, after following their advice for a while, my life started to take shape and become a mirror image of theirs, which wasn't anywhere near what I really wanted for my own life.

Follow your parent's advice, your father or mother in-law's advice, your blind friend's advice, your teacher's or professor's advice, or even your spouse or significant other's advice, and miraculously your life begins to look eerily similar to theirs.

Don't allow yourself to be programmed. Question everything. Go against the grain.

It's YOUR life. Time is limited.

Follow that inner whisper, your heart and intuition. They know where you really want to go And most importantly...you don't owe

All Grown Up

Kid on the left 19 years old. Guy on the right 39.

What a difference 20 years makes.

Kid on the left, hopeful and naive. Guy on the right, accomplished and wise.

Kid on the left good at bodybuilding, sucked at life. Guy on the right, good at bodybuilding, expert at life.

Kid on the left, swallowed up by life. Guy on the right, makes life choke.

Kid on the left, thought he knew way more than he really did. Guy on the right, understands he doesn't know shit.

Kid on the left, didn't understand how his experiences were molding him like clay for his own good. Guy on the right, understands he's a clay pot piece of work.

Kid on the left, couldn't stand on his own two feet. Guy on the right, does back flips on stilts.

Kid on the left, went into an uncontrollable downward spiral. Guy on the right, consciously dictates whatever spiral he wants.

Kid on the left, afraid, a follower, impressionable. Guy on the right, look you straight in the eye and let you know how this is going to go.

Kid on the left, pushed out of his father's house because his stepmother hated him, had no real place to call home. Guy on the right, owns 26 of his own houses now, fuck her.

Kid on the left, ambitious but smacked in the face by life. Guy on the right, smacking is for little bitches, with clenched fists he's going to finish what that kid started.

Broken Pieces

Just because things are broken in your life doesn't mean you can't survive.

Like a boat that crumbles to pieces in the water, you can survive on broken pieces.

You think your life has lost shape to get you where you were going, but it just took another form, it didn't cease to exist.

You may never be able to piece it back together the way it was, but when life breaks into pieces and takes another form, grab a piece of what you have left and hold on until it gets you to where you want to go.

With faith and a radical belief, what's broken and scattered can be made whole again.

Stop focusing on what you lost and embrace what you've got left.

The most valiant and strongest among us are made through what they've survived and pieced back together.

With bits and broken pieces.

Bitter

Bitterness is heavy.

Your character and how you talk reveals what's going on in your heart.

Unmet expectations, anger, resentment, and unforgiveness.

When you let bitterness from past experiences bleed into your present, it closes the door on your future.

When you let the things on the outside contaminate the person on the inside you're only hurting yourself.

Don't let life make you change your name.

Like drinking poison and waiting for the other person to die.

It's over. They're long gone, done moved on with their life, the situation is over, and nobody cares. It's history. Let it go so you can move on with your life.

Clinging to negative experiences will keep you in the same place forever.

Some people remain bitter their whole life, watching life pass them by.

As long as you're refusing to let go of your past, you will never be able to reach for and grasp your future.

Put it away. Free yourself from the prison that is bitterness.

Become better instead of bitter.

Running Out of Time

We are visitors passing through in a period of time.

Someday your stay will end. Someday this "experience" you call life will be over.

Sorry to be so dreary and dramatic but it's the truth.

People get so caught up in things that don't matter in the grand scheme of things.

You have one opportunity, one life, and many choose to waste it focusing, obsessing, and holding onto insignificant matters.

Time is passing by.

People disrespect time. They take it for granted. Treat it like it's never going to run out. Like it's unlimited. Like it's this renewable resource and there will always be a constant supply.

It's only when you start to run out of something you begin to notice that it's scarce. The more you want and need something, and the less of it you have left, the more you value what you have left.

However you old you are, really stop and think about how many years you realistically have left.

YOU ARE RUNNING OUT OF TIME.

Your life may have been a disaster up until now, but really, what in the hell is worth sitting around, dwelling, complaining, and being sad over?

Stop overthinking and over analyzing it, and just do it already.

Does it REALLY matter what they said, what they think, what their opinion is?

People that left you, hurt you, betrayed you, didn't care about you. It just doesn't matter.

I live my life a very simple way. I look at my life and the use of my time through the eyes of the old man I will be at the end of my life.

That old man gives me a crystal clear picture and idea of what really matters and what doesn't.

I'm not fazed by much of what people are consumed by and dwell about because of one simple undeniable truth, fact, and reality.

I don't have time for it.

Don't Do It

We all admire successful and highly favored people and try to do what they do.

The real magic isn't in what they do, but in what they don't do.

They don't allow other people to run their life.

They don't become crippled by fear.

They don't stay stuck in comfort zones and comfortable situations.

They don't give up with the first sign of struggle.

They don't let the chatter of other people stop them.

They don't take no for an answer.

They don't entertain negativity, pessimism, or doubt.

They don't major in minor things.

They don't make excuses for their incapacities.

They don't put off and remain indecisive with the inevitable.

They don't dwell on the past.

They don't say, "it's easier said than done".

They don't gossip. They don't care.

They don't let anyone get comfortable disrespecting them.

They don't put off deleting people.

They don't go with the flow.

They don't try to please everyone or fit in.

They don't follow the crowd.

They don't drive a pimped out vehicle or live in a mansion with five dollars in their bank account.

They don't accept their circumstances.

They don't tolerate anything that is holding them down.

They don't shy away from confrontation.

They don't value anyone else's opinion of themselves over their own.

They don't complain about what they have the ability to change.

The secret is really simple.

You want to know what to do?

Don't do anything they wouldn't do.

What They Say

People will say all kinds of things about you.

I've had many say things about me, my character, who I am, what I'm about, what I'll do, what I won't do.

Funny thing is the people with the most repulsive, ignorant personalities and character traits are always the ones with the most to say.

People that possess a boat load of flaws in who they are, are always the ones that offer up the most profound critique.

Many have criticized me for faults they also possess.

They have a false appearance of virtue and goodness, however they're just as ugly as they perceive me to be.

The pot calling the kettle black. Hypocrisy at its finest.

But that's ok because the beauty I see doesn't come from them, it comes from within.

See, stop trying to change people's minds about you.

It doesn't matter what people think about you, because it's not what other people think about you that will control and shape your destiny.

Your destiny will be controlled and shaped by what you think about you.

Say whatever you want.

I can see through you.

Don't judge someone just because they sin differently than you.

Thank You

Thank you for the heartache.

It turned a tiny flickering flame into a blazing inferno.

Thank you for the affliction.

It saved my soul.

Thank you for the struggle.

It's building an empire.

Thank you for the suffering.

It unleashed my spirit.

Thank you for the adversity.

It's planting seeds of greatness.

Thank you for the agony.

It made a blind man see.

Thank you for the hurt.

It became a super power.

Thank you for the setback.

Addition became multiplication.

Thank you for the hardship.

It made a way out of no way.

Thank you for the trouble.

It woke a sleeping giant.

Thank you for the pain.

Wisdom is nothing more than healed pain.

For all of these reasons, sincerely, I thank you.

You introduced a man to himself.

You Did It

How you handle situations today will shape what your life is going to look like tomorrow.

Life responds to what you provoke it to do.

Wherever you find yourself in life, at some point, you made an appointment to be there.

Cutting off your nose despite your face, making a bad situation worse.

Making decisions that have permanent effects based on temporary feelings.

Compromising and giving up a blessing because you can't control your temporary and immediate urges.

Blame whoever you want, but the reality is you put yourself there.

Compounded like interest over time...

You're simply experiencing a culmination of small decisions you chose to make.

Eventually all the dots connect and the picture of your life takes shape.

Your life is a direct reflection of who you are. You don't get in life what you want. You get in life what you are.

If you don't take the time to work on who you are. You'll be spending a lot of time dealing with a life you don't want.

It's not anyone else's responsibility to assure you make good choices in your life.

Life is just fine. Life is amazing actually. The problem is you.

High Places

High places are seductive.

We all want to reach higher levels, rise above, and soar like eagles.

We often say the sky is the limit.

Everyone has an image of their high place.

But, there are secrets to high places. Things you must understand.

There are struggles on the way up. Things you must endure to begin to get your feet off the ground.

Elevation requires that you break the gravity of your environment.

The thing that keeps pulling you back. Holding you down.

Elevating to that high place may require you be separated and pulled apart.

Singled out. Elevation is lonely business.

You have to be willing to leave the pack. Elevation might require your isolation.

Elevation requires you check your baggage and limit your passengers.

It is the weight of the load that will determine your lift.

Elevation is frightening. You'll feel every kind of emotion on your way up.

Turbulence.

You'll be tempted to go back down, feet on the ground, where it's familiar, where it's comfortable.

But if you can resist, and have the courage to rise higher and higher into the unknown, someday you'll stand out...In the high place.

Interpretation

How you interpret things holds power. Many people live in the prison of their own perspective and perception.

Silly people have interpretations that are so far out in left field it's scary. So wrong, so stupid, and so misinformed.

Many interpret the intentions and actions of others in a skewed, distorted, and biased way because it's a reflection of their own insecurities and low self-esteem.

When you outwardly interpret things like this without even knowing the person, the truth, or all the facts you make yourself look ridiculous.

Often times a person's interpretation in regards to what they think something means is better off kept to themselves.

In private, to themselves, where nobody can read it or hear it.

When you understand people will always only see things from their level of perspective and perception, you just stop explaining yourself.

Let people interpret things however they want. Ultimately it's not their interpretation that defines an intention.

Their interpretation reveals the definition they have of themselves.

To all the great interpreters of the world, interpret this...

Don't mistake your opinion, perception, and interpretation with facts and truths.

<u>Confession</u>

I confess.

I'm not always poised. I'm human just like everyone else.

I'm not exempt.

I often feel many of the same emotions as others through this journey of life.

I don't always know if what I'm doing is totally the right thing.

I've made and continue to make mistakes, and suffer the consequences along the way.

At times I'm scared, uncertain, feel beat up and defeated.

I often fight with frustration and feel like I'm at my wits end.

I question myself, doubt myself, and sometimes struggle to keep going.

There are days I don't feel great or up to the challenge. I just don't feel like trying or fighting.

Given all this, there is one distinct quality that differentiates me from most people.

I simply have not and will not quit.

I simply stay in the fight longer than most people. I stay with problems longer than most people.

Many years of ongoing consistent sacrifice, dedication, and hard work. Spiritual stamina and endurance. Consistency.

This has made and continues to make all the difference.

The Little Things

You look at some people and wonder why they're so happy with things and accomplishments that are seemingly not that impressive to some.

It's a tiny little shack of a house or apartment but they put a real fancy wreath on the door.

The car is old and beat up but they take it to the car wash and vacuum out the interior.

It's a little mom and pop shop business but they put a nice sign above the door.

The job only pays minimum wage but they take pride and work harder than everyone else.

Their physical transformation hasn't made them a bikini model, but they work that thing and are glowing.

See, you have to have seen a person's before to have a true appreciation for the after.

Success stories come in many shapes and sizes. Victory is unique to the individual.

The before provides the true measure of the size of the blessing.

You're appreciation for where you are is directly related to where you had to dig yourself out of to get there.

What might not seem like much to many is a hard fought victory to someone else.

The value you place in anything is in direct proportion to the size of the fight you had to go through to get it.

You never know the depth of a person's struggle to get from point A to point B.

Be obsessively grateful for small things given to you in life, then big things will come.

That which is given to you can be taken away. If you will be faithful over a few, you'll be made ruler over many.

Be sure to count your blessings in life.

Paradise

I didn't always believe in God.

I always believed my way was the right way. I always thought that I knew. I had all the answers.

Until I became broken.

Brought to my knees, weak, begging, crying so hard it was painful, repeating myself over and over..."somebody please help me."

I willingly gave up all desire to save face. I had no more will to assert myself.

As I began to immediately become free from my infirmities, through blind faith and not by might, I became witness to things in my life, that weren't working before, begin to not only work...

But overflow.

Like someone had taken my hand, lifted me up, and carried me.

The more I looked for an explanation, the more it pointed me in the direction of the word of God.

I began listening to the word of God because I got tired of listening to the words of men.

I got tired of their thoughts and of their council.

I didn't begin listening to the word of God just to receive some sort of useful, nifty message.

I began listening to the word of God because I was drowning, and I desperately needed a lifeline to keep living.

My life started to make sense, by way of mercy, not my merit.

Greater is he that is in me.

There's a lot one can learn from Jesus Christ.

You are not afflicted. You are blessed.

No cross. No crown. "Today you will be with me in paradise."

Go Bigger

It's hard to go big when little has a grip on you.

There's power in being a misfit, a reject, being overlooked, not being counted, not being considered, and not being included.

There's a reason everyone has been stripped away, you've been left out, and you've been left alone.

If you're going to be highly favored, you're going to have to stand out, not fit in.

You can't stand out from or lead people that you're trying to fit in with.

You were meant to be an outcast with the world so you can be an incast with something bigger, something greater.

We all want more abundance in our lives, but you have to have courage to receive what you're asking for.

It takes courage to be an outcast. To be a marked man or a marked woman.

It takes courage to be who you want to be in a world that's constantly trying to make you what it wants you to be.

Forget however much success you think you have right now. I'm talking about an increase that is overflowing so much in your life, your head spins.

The more you try to be like others, belong, and blend in...

The further away you are from the truth. It's truth that sets you free.

Leave little behind. Gladly let society and the world as you know it go.

Step into something bigger.

Discomfort

It is good to be uncomfortable.

Embrace the discomfort that comes with moving from where you are now to where you are going next.

The moving from who you are now to who you are becoming next.

Discomfort is the key to happiness. You can't become happy with the life you're living until you are willing to accept the discomfort associated with changing it.

The more you are not willing to be uncomfortable the less your life will change, the longer you'll stay the same, and the less you will do with your life and with yourself.

You'll never meet anyone that is highly accomplished, or made dramatic shifts in their life that wasn't uncomfortable.

You can't go through life trying to avoid pain and struggle or you will never grow.

Discomfort gives birth to strengths you never knew you had, it's the only way you discover what's in you.

You're stronger than you give yourself credit for, but you'll never know until you test it out.

Your spirit and will are built through use. Tests and trials. Discomfort.

Strength isn't made clear in good times, it reveals itself in bad times, chaotic times. Uncomfortable times.

You either get uncomfortable and rise to the challenges of life or acquiesce to a dead comfort zone where nothing happens. Ever.

They say rough storms and seas create skilled sailors.

The greatest enemy to your potential is your comfort zone.

Construct

Sometimes your history determines the fierceness of how you fight what's in front of you.

Through your history, you develop a new construct to withstand the weight of what life is going to do to you.

Your history gives you an improved, grand design built to withstand, like a skyscraper.

Your history develops a blueprint of strength in character giving you more capacity to handle the loads you carry and the burdens you bear.

The reason there are some people that can bear more than others is in their construct.

How they're built. What they're made of.

What's hard for some is easy for others. What doesn't seem to phase one person, causes another to crumble.

It's in their construct.

All they've overcome, all they've been through, all they've survived, all they've endured.

These were all just the building material to an indestructible construct that will stand the test of time.

You're not afflicted, broken, torn apart, beaten down, or defeated.

You are marvelously made.

In times of need, don't ever forget your history.

Don't ever forget who you are and what you're made of.

The Gap

You're not who you once were.

That's clear. You know you know that.

But you're not who you're going to be either.

Many people live in the gap.

The gap of two different people. That who you once were and that who you're becoming.

The in between place.

It's in the gap you learn and become aware of who you really are and what direction your life needs to take.

It's in the gap you start the journey away from the safe place you've built, leave timidity, insecurity, fear, and small mindedness behind.

It's in the gap you start to strip away dead wood, cleanse your soul, and experience divine discovery.

It's in the gap your eyesight becomes clearer, your vision manifests, and what you're looking for reveals itself.

It's in the gap you feel an aloneness that is overwhelming at times.

But, you are not alone.

It's in the gap God does his best work in preparing you for a blessing you don't even realize is already ready.

Already waiting for you...

Waiting for you to become who you need to become.

Don't wait on God. God will call you out but he's not going to come in and get you. God is waiting on you.

Don't give up on the person you are becoming.

Close the gap.

Self-Reliance

When you depend on someone else to give you what you can't give yourself, you are always at the mercy of that person.

I'm not just referring to material things like a house, a car, money, or anything else that is material and tangible.

I'm talking about what you can't see.

There are things you consult with and depend on everyone else for...until you realize you are the only person you need to be good enough for.

There's a tremendous power in self-reliance and independence within yourself.

See, nobody can give you what's already yours.

You don't need to depend on someone else to have an identity.

They can't give you an identity that's already yours.

I know they don't accept you for who you are and you've been rejected.

They can't give you acceptance that's already yours.

They said they loved you, for better or for worse, until death do you part, but they were lying.

They can't give you love that's already yours.

They don't agree with you, they write you off, don't approve, and disagree.

They can't provide any validation that's already yours.

When you know yourself, accept yourself, love yourself, and validate yourself...

They can't give you what's already yours.

Checklist

I gave up on how life is supposed to be.

The infamous checklist.

You're supposed to go to college...check, you're supposed to get married...check, you're supposed to have children...check, you're supposed to get a house...check.

You're supposed to do or be this, you're supposed to do or be that.

Says who? I mean really.

Never let anyone else create a checklist for your life.

Everyone is different, don't get me wrong. You could live how you're supposed to, whatever that looks like. Check off each and every box and be totally fulfilled and happy. Congrats, you've won.

I've come to realize at least for myself, going against the grain and where it's empty gives me life.

It's where my happy place is.

Going up when others are going down, taking a left when the majority are going right, standing up when others are sitting down, running when others are walking.

On the exterior life may look very neat, well put together, prim and proper, and pieced together perfectly and eloquently.

But on the interior, there was a desperate need to break free.

It is torture living a life constantly putting on a fake smile, living in a tight place of quiet desperation.

Where you greet everyone you see as they come with a happy, uplifted facade, and they have no idea that behind that smile you're secretly in a tight place, desperate to get out.

The more I lived a supposed to life, the less happy I became.

It just felt stupid.

Create a life that feels good on the inside, not a life that just looks good on the outside.

After all you've only got one shot at it.

Sometimes things look better in your head than they do in real life.

The Man I Am

Pushed to the limit, I push back.

You can't phase what's already been phased.

You can't hurt me any more than I've once hurt myself.

The pain I once felt trumps any pain another can deliver.

I know pain. I've lived pain.

See...you don't understand what kind of man I am.

Pain is nothing more than power pellets to me.

The more I endure the stronger I get.

You don't understand what kind of man I am.

I've walked through the wilderness.

I've danced with the devil, so I can easily dance with you.

You're strong in flesh, I'll spiritually whip you to death.

You can't bend me far enough to break me.

You don't understand what kind of man I am.

You say I'm dreaming, I say I'm your worst nightmare.

You say I can't and I'll never, I say I CAN and I WILL.

You may be Goliath, I got God on my side and a rock.

You don't understand what kind of man I am.

You say enough is enough how much more, I say I'm just getting started.

You say this is who I am, I say no...

THIS is who I am.

Take your best shot, you're going to need a lot more bullets for that gun.

You don't understand what kind of man I am.

Inner Circle
You can't surround yourself with blindness and expect to see.

People that are stuck in a limited, defeated, bitter, and victimized mentality seek fraternity.

They seek shelter and sit on porches together. Pointing at and criticizing all those passing by, taking comfort in their incapacities.

Broke hangs out with broke, bitter hangs out with bitter, limited hangs out with limited, ghetto hangs out with ghetto, defeated hangs out with defeated.

Seeking comfort from other people that walk with the same exact limp as they do.

See, if everyone limps just like they do it's alright.

They take refuge in other people with similar perceived limitations so they don't need to feel challenged. It's considered normal.

A brotherhood and sisterhood of lameness and dysfunction.

Together, they live in a community creating routine around things they've convinced themselves they can't change.

If you want to walk a unique path you can never be common in your associations.

You are the common denominator...the median...of the five people that surround you every day of your life.

If you are not inspired by your circle, you don't have a circle...you have a cage. Choose wisely.

Unconditional Love

Love is passed around loosely.

You are disrespecting yourself if you are pouring your time, energy, and soul into someone who loves you conditionally.

If you lose someone's love they never really loved you. If the love was conditional it wasn't really love to begin with.

A parent's love for their children, intimate relationships, marriages, even friendships or any other personal relationships.

Real love has no conditions. Real love knows no limits. Real love isn't about convenience.

If you change, and are therefore not loved because you weren't the way you were before, you were never really loved.

Real love is when they see the bad in you and love you anyway. It's not based on certain unspoken rules and conditions.

Unconditional love is when you're hard to love but they love you hard anyway.

Unconditional love doesn't come through mixed signals. Do yourself a favor and take mixed signals as a no.

They cheated because their expected conditions weren't met, let them walk, it's not love.

The trick is to understand and be wise enough to know when you are being loved conditionally or unconditionally.

Conditional "love" is perfectly fine, just know and accept it for what it really is, don't be blinded by fake love. There's a difference between interest and love.

Love is profound. Don't get it twisted.

Spend your time and energy on those that love you unconditionally, no matter what, not on those that only love you when the conditions are right for them.

True, real, unconditional love bears and endures all things and is worth fighting for.

True, real, conditional love is not.

More Mind

You've got the skill and know how.

You've got more degrees than a thermometer.

You've got the perfect well thought out plan.

But do you have the mind?

A diesel spirit?

When life catches you off guard, when life moves on you, when life declares war, when life sucker punches you right in your mouth and you're spitting out blood....

And make no mistake...it will.

When life puts up a fight. Struggle, trauma, tragedy, loss, heartache, self-doubt, health, uncertainty, despair, inner turmoil, complacency, affliction.

What then? How will you withstand?

Skill and know how won't save you, degrees won't save you, the perfect plan and money sure as hell won't matter.

It's going to boil down to your ability to harness your will.

It's going to boil down to your relentless, insufferable, and indomitable will to win and refuse to take no for an answer.

It's going to boil down to how you persevere.

The resiliency and resolve you muster up to overcome no matter the circumstances.

How you keep taking another step no matter how it looks. No matter the odds.

When life pushes you....

YOU WILL BE DEFINED BY HOW YOU PUSH BACK.

Return life's pushes with an ass whipping shove.

Stand up to life and eventually life will yield to you.

Don't pray for more skill, know how, education, or perfect plans.

Pray for more mind.

It is with the mind. The rest is valuable and necessary...but secondary.

<u>Who I Am</u>

You're going to have people say stuff about you.

You're going to have people that will tell the world who you are based on their interpretation.

Some people get it twisted.

Don't get upset. Don't get angry or bitter. Don't even try to make an argument for yourself and explain.

Just get to work.

You're going to show them who you are.

Destroy misjudgments, misinterpretations, and false labels.

Develop yourself. Make something of yourself.

Remove any confusion and stand flat footed and unafraid.

Your actions and success will boldly and proudly tell the world....

"THIS is who I am".

You won't have to speak a single word to defend yourself.

The shine of your light will fade out any question as to who you are or what you're about.

<u>Destiny</u>

Destiny is defined as being a hidden power believed to control the events of what will happen as well as the events that will necessarily happen to a particular person or thing in the future.

Sometimes it seems like the wicked, wrong doers, those who possess low moral standards, and those that take advantage of and walk all over other people go forward while the righteous are held back.

People that don't work nearly as hard, weren't nearly as committed, or nearly as faithful.

Watching their prosperity becomes the source of your agony. The type of agony that's enough to make you question life as you know it and the point of continuing on.

Agony that causes you to wonder how and why bad things happen to good people while good things seemingly happen to bad people.

Agony that causes so much frustration you sabotage your own life and progress because you don't see a point in trying.

The agony of watching these people prosper can cause you to draw a premature conclusion about life.

Don't fret and make a permanent decision about the possibilities in your own life because you must realize that they will soon be cut off.

The doer of good deeds and the righteous will always prevail in the end.

We all create our own destiny.

It's not where you start, it's where you finish.

You reap what you sow.

Be careful what you sow.

You just might end up with a harvest full of weeds.

<u>You Know Not</u>

Many think they know more than they really do.

They overestimate their knowledge and don't know their own ignorance.

I used to be that way.

I used to think I was so smart. I used to think I had it all figured out.

You couldn't tell me anything. I had all the answers.

You know where that got me?

It got me sucker punched by life down on my knees begging for answers as to why what I knew so well wasn't working.

It wasn't until I humbled myself and submitted to the idea that I don't have all the answers.

Life forced me to tap out.

You can't learn what you think you already know.

Getting delusional that you already know all there is to know makes you stubborn in your beliefs and unwilling to accept new information.

This stagnates your growth potential.

Your life as it exists right now is a manifestation of what you think you know to be true.

Challenge those thoughts, beliefs, and assumptions. Know more about what you don't know than what you do know.

Smile and smirk with your arrogant self, the jokes on you.

Check Yourself

If you run from one thing you'll run from everything.

Constantly starting over. Constantly switching direction. Constantly taking the easy way out.

Until you buckle down and strap yourself in. Give yourself no way out. Venture out to the island and burn the boat...

You'll never realize your true potential in anything you do.

You'll always get so far...then when it gets hard or doesn't come easy...well it must be because it doesn't work.

There are people doing the things you've convinced yourself can't be done.

Facing the same circumstances, same obstacles, same difficulties, and breaking through to realize success.

They're doing them simply because they haven't accepted defeat as reality.

There's always a way if you're willing to find it. Where there's a will there's a way.

Where there's a burning desire and an indomitable will to make the thing happen, there's a way. You'll create a way.

The universe has a way of moving around and conspiring to work for the person that just will not give up.

When something isn't working the way you thought it should, try looking in the mirror, not at the thing itself.

Check yourself. Check your story. Check your real desire.

Don't fall back when it gets hard. Lean in, stand flat footed, and refuse to be denied.

Look inside and determine if this is really your true desire.

It works just fine. See, it's that you don't work. That's the problem.

Self-Leadership

Everyone in some way needs to be a leader in life.

Whether you're leading your peers, your family, your relationships, your business, or even just leading yourself.

You are promoted or demoted in life based on your threshold in your ability to handle and withstand pain.

Sometimes things will happen in life that will make you pick up the pace.

It's no time to cry, no time to panic, no time to get emotional or lose your head.

I am tested by tough situations regularly and I can tell you...how you remain level headed and handle them in your own life will make or break you.

If you're going to be a force and a leader in your own life, it's critical to learn to stay calm, cool, and collected in the midst of a storm.

Being optimistic and positive in the midst of a crisis or storm isn't ignorance or delusion, it's leadership.

To resist the urge to lose all your wits when all hell is breaking loose.

Approaching chaos in an unemotional, step by step, strategic way.

Only focusing on what you have the power to control and influence.

Staying calm and understanding what is the next right and logical move would be to move you out of the situation, then going all in with massive action in that direction.

Not spending one single second of thought or energy on what you can't control.

Rising to the challenge knowing you are capable, brave, and in control even when it feels like you're not.

Control your thoughts and emotions or they will use and abuse you. The higher you go, the more problems you'll have to deal with.

Handle tough situations like a boss, stay calm in crisis, and life will promote you accordingly.

Level head...level up...it's that simple.

Burning Desire

If you're perfectly happy with your current position in life, wouldn't ask for a single thing more, don't desire any further growth, progress, or leveling up...

Congrats, you've won, this isn't for you.

However, if you're wired different, you're not kidding yourself, accept no excuses, rationalizations, or lame stories and want more out of your life...

If you burn with desire to change, to grow, to become more, and to squeeze every ounce of blood out of this rock we call life...listen up.

Become uncomfortable every day of your life.

People become so domesticated and forget that inner fire. Their roaring fire dwindles down to a match stick flame.

Sabotaged by success or contentment, they lose that drive and that burning desire to grow beyond their current status or circumstances.

Force discomfort.

Create situations that force change. Force things to move.

Rattle your own cage. Become a wild beast. Challenge your normal.

Comfort zones are dead zones. Nothing worthwhile happens in a comfort zone.

Force unease. Force unbalance. Rock your own world. Flip it upside down.

See, this is where the magic happens. This is where growth occurs. This is where you become stronger. This is where you become unstoppable.

If you do not become uncomfortable you will not grow. Discomfort is your friend.

Become who you were before that thing watered you down and distinguished your fire.

Stop waiting for that light at the end of the tunnel and light that bitch up yourself.

Why Me?

"My life just never gets any better!"

"I mean why do these things keep happening to me?!"

"Things never go right for me!"

"What am I doing wrong?!"

"I just don't get it!"

"How did I get into this mess!?"

"It's just one thing after another!"

"Why is life so unfair!?"

Doing the same thing over and over and expecting a different result is ludicrous.

Every decision and choice you make has a compound effect on your life.

Good decisions and choices create positive compound effects.

Bad decisions and choices create negative compound effects.

Compound effects add up over time to create what you see all around you at this very moment.

If you would like different effects to compound, then you must make different decisions and choices to create them.

If you want to make different decisions and choices to create them, you must change the mentality and thinking process behind your actions and approach.

Better smarter thinking = creation of improved decisions and choices = creation of improved habits (approach) = a better life (compounded effect).

When you decide to touch fire you get burned.

Stop touching fire and you will not get burned.

When you decide to make dumb decisions and choices, life sucker punches you in your mouth.

Stop making dumb decisions and choices and life will pat you on the back instead of sucker punching you in the mouth.

Hope that's easy enough to understand.

Open Your Mind

The greatest wisdom there is lies in one's ability to acknowledge that they know very little.

Some people think they know everything.

So thick headed and hard headed, new thoughts, concepts and ideas are out of the question.

Stubborn to the point you can't tell them anything.

New doors can't open as long as your mind is closed.

Open mindedness is necessary to grow.

Many listen but don't hear. Through one ear and out the other, they reject things that can be life changing if they'd just humble themselves and be open to receiving.

Words are powerful and have the ability to mold and shape your thought process about yourself, your life, your possibilities, and your reality, and as a result, your behaviors.

You didn't think a certain way until you heard someone's words that influenced that thinking.

Be careful what words you let stick to you. The words you allow to ingraft themselves into your mind and into your soul will shape your life.

Look at your life. Look at your thoughts. They're tied together.

You're always one thought away from a completely different life. Think wisely.

Solitude

There's power in occasional and voluntary solitude and isolation.

Deep contemplation.

There are many things that influence and consequently hinder your authentic self from blossoming.

You'll understand yourself more when you take time and voluntarily remove yourself from your habitual environment, people, and social obligations.

It's a noisy world. We're constantly bombarded by it. The world is constantly competing for control over your mind.

People spend a lot of time evaluating other people and don't spend time evaluating themselves.

Self-reflection and introspection are vital to the process of bettering yourself. You need to understand how YOU really feel about your life and the thoughts YOU think.

Isolation allows you to hear yourself think, gather your thoughts, and become more creative.

Revelation, disillusionment, enlightenment, and strength of mind are fed in isolation.

You go through life gathering people and experiences that aren't good for you and not really what you want. You end up in places and around people you start to realize you don't even know how you got there.

You can be in a crowded room and feel extremely and completely alone. Everyone around you is partying and living it up, and you're sitting there feeling like you're about to cry.

Periods of isolation renews clarity and mindfulness around what and who you've gathered in your current life.

Around who and what you've become.

Isolation allows you to take stock of it, reevaluate it, reset it, refocus it, and redirect it slowly in a better direction that is more in line with who and where you want to be.

Wisdom is born in isolation. Great minds are built in isolation.

When you're not afraid to be completely, utterly alone, and not be defined by anyone or anything...

You've reached a dangerous and empowering level of freedom.

You've grown into a mentally strong person that can go and do whatever you want, regardless of what other people think, and regardless of how difficult it is to go there.

We spend a lot of time making friends and focusing on external relationships, but oddly still feel alone.

If you make friends with yourself, you'll never be alone.

Seize Opportunity

I've seized many opportunities in life that others who were given the same opportunity did not.

Life is an equal opportunity experience.

When opportunity knocks it's up to you to answer the door.

It's amazing how many people let opportunity pass them by unrealized.

Many could get clobbered right over the head with and an amazing opportunity and not even see it.

So many people love saying, "life is what you make it!"

But, they aren't making much. It's one thing to say it. It's a totally different thing to do it.

Many people aren't really doing as much as they think they are.

Success requires massive, obsessive action in a focused direction.

Not a million different directions, but one singular focused direction.

People allow others to dumb down their enthusiasm and work ethic because they don't want to stand out and be different. You'll be criticized when you out work everyone else.

Better to blend in, fit in, and be average like everyone else.

Don't let the chatter stop you. When you make excuses for your incapacitates you get to keep them.

When someone says you're gripping the bat too hard, grip it harder.

When someone says you're working too hard, work more.

When someone says you're going to burn yourself out, light that bitch up.

When you are working towards the realization of your worthy ideal it's impossible to work too much.

Those are THEIR limitations. THEIR perception of too much doesn't have to be yours.

Opportunity and success compounds like interest. One thing leads to another. Dominate everything you do and doors open in places you can't see in the beginning.

Bottom line is this...

When you do what other people are not willing to do, you will have a level of success other people will not have.

You don't judge a tree by the fruit it talks about or claims. You judge a tree by the fruit it actually bears.

Don't talk about it, be about it.

It doesn't matter what you say. What matters is what you actually produce. Don't think. Be. Don't talk. Do.

Confusion

Oh I'm sorry perhaps I just got confused.

You were there when I was struggling through the toughest most hopeless times of my life?

I looked I don't remember seeing you.

My shoes were on my feet when I checked, I don't remember letting you borrow them to walk a day in them.

Oh wait...you did see me suffering?

Was it from a distance? I don't remember you being up close.

I mean you must understand the pain I've felt I would imagine.

You know what I had to go through to get what I got? Really?

That's weird.

You don't seem as happy as I am about it.

Oh wow, you were there during the battle?

Well I fought a good fight!

I mean I don't have to tell you...you saw it right?

I'm sorry for the misunderstanding...I mean I must have a form of amnesia.

It's not that I don't believe you...I just don't remember.

I'm really trying to consider your opinion and take it to heart.

I'm just trying to justify what gives you the right to even speak on me or my life.

See...until then, you and your opinions just don't matter.

Sorry, not sorry.

Absolute Certainty

Life always has a level of uncertainty, but if you've lived long enough, there are some things you become absolutely certain about.

There are certain things you experience, and certain people you've associated with along the way that you just know for an absolute fact aren't for you.

Some of the best most useful lessons I've gotten were from those that I have absolutely no admiration for at all and from experiences that were a living hell.

Ways I don't want to act. Who I don't want to be. Thoughts I don't want to think. Things I don't want to do. Places I don't want to go. Parts and characters I don't want to play. Experiences I don't want to experience ever again.

I have quite a collection I must say.

So, salute all the people you dislike and don't admire, as well as give thanks for all the horrible experiences you've had.

You don't always get the people and experiences you want, you get the ones you need to move you in the right direction.

Even if they're more negative than positive.

Your Garden

Your current perceived reality is no more than an outward projection of the thoughts you think.

If you read something particular enough you will become that.

If you hear something particular enough you will become that.

You become what you think.

Somehow, someway, your thoughts were planted there, at some point.

Your current life experience is an expansion of something that snuck in and now you're seeing it play out.

Your ears are the gates to your world and your mind is like a garden.

What you let through those gates to be planted in that garden will make or break you.

It will empower you or weaken you.

Guard the gates of your mind. Plant good seed.

And most importantly, water it daily.

Or it will dwindle, weaken, and diminish. Like a garden that has not been tended to.

What you think you become.

When you begin to understand that the thoughts you think control your life, you begin to become real careful about what you think about.

You can't however find what you're not looking for. You won't look for what you think you already know.

Know you know not.

There are a million ways to learn how to cook.

Unfortunately you can't teach someone how to be hungry.

Confrontation

Sometimes, some things, turn in to dumb things...and you need to put your foot down.

Look the person right in the face and say what's got to be said.

Settling for situations and circumstances you don't desire, unfortunately, is all too common practice.

Fear, timidity, low self-esteem, and low self-worth cause people to play the victim to situations they have the power to change.

Stand up for yourself. Face whatever you have to face. Emotions aside.

You have to take control of your life and your outcomes. This has nothing to do with emotions or hurting someone's feelings.

Your mental health and well-being need to take priority over any friendship or relationship.

Be ready and willing to lose anyone or anything before you lose your mind, your dignity, your self-esteem, or self-worth.

Givers have to set limits because takers have none.

Some people will walk all over you and use you like a door mat if you allow them to.

You have the power to change a lot more than you think.

What you allow will continue.

If you won't confront it, then you are choosing it. Therefore don't complain about it.

<u>Receiving</u>

You can't make a person comprehend a message they aren't ready to receive.

Words stop going through one ear and out the other...

When struggle and hardship become disturbing and hopeless.

When you feel alone in a room full of people.

When treading water becomes drowning.

When a slight hiccup becomes utter devastation.

When minor discomfort becomes chronic debilitating pain.

When your life falls apart and you submit to the idea that you don't know how to pick up the pieces.

When you realize you're sleeping with the enemy.

When the doctor reveals the diagnosis.

When you shed tears from time to time for seemingly no reason and don't know why.

When your wants and needs become frantic desperation.

When you destroy your life and have nothing left except the last drop down to the bottom of every bottle.

When a small crack becomes shattered pieces.

When the truth comes out and it rocks your world.

When you're in prison but not behind bars.

When you discover their true colors.

When you were forced to say goodbye to them...forever.

When you're crawling in your own skin and your worst enemy is you.

When you swing around on that barstool and realize it's not fun anymore.

When a vibrant smile becomes a blank possessed stare.

When you're down to your last dollar in your checking account and the shut off notice is in the mailbox.

When your life doesn't look the way you'd thought it would look at that age.

When your back is pinned and the walls are closing in.

When silence is deafening.

These things make words strike a chord, it is then you will pay attention.

When the student is ready the teacher will appear.

Today is the Day

Today is the day.

It ends today.

No more sorrow. You've cried your last tear.

You're forgetting those things that are behind and reaching to those things that are before.

Give the sympathy card back, give the flowers back.

You'll no longer be looked at as a charity. They can stop looking at you all pitiful.

Because...

Today you're reclaiming your strength back, your drive back, your fight back, and your focus back.

Today you face yourself.

Today you let go of what you've become.

Today you let go of what you've done.

Today you forgive yourself for what has happened.

The devil is knocking but he can't come in.

You haven't laughed your best laugh, thought your best thought, and dreamed your best dream.

You haven't had your greatest day yet.

It's somewhere inside of you. Today you come out of your coma.

Today you awaken to a new, fresh perspective and belief system about who you are and the possibilities for your life.

You're a miracle looking for a place to happen. A testimony waiting to be delivered.

The best is yet to come. Today is the day. My God...today is the day.

Spiritual Teacher

The best spiritual teacher you can have is suffering.

Because eventually the suffering brings about an awakening.

The fiercest souls are built out of suffering.

Many of the strongest and impressive personalities have endured many scars.

Suffering will open your eyes in ways that will blow your mind.

Suffering pulls the artificiality out of you, and awakens your true essence.

Real transformation is born out of suffering. Suffering knocks you out of your stupor.

It pulls you out of your continuous day dream into a world of truth and reality.

It is through suffering you begin to see what others don't see.

If you're going through hell, keep going. Embrace suffering.

You will soon realize the most powerful weapon is the human soul on fire.

Suffering is nothing more than preparation for the revelation.

Family

Ever been related to people you don't relate to?

Breaking the gravitational pull of immediate family members is one of the biggest hurdles many will face in trying to find their authenticity and unique path in life.

You can come from something, but choose not to be of it.

Sometimes being disowned by your family is a blessing.

Like an arrow pulled back in a bow finally let go...to fly at its intended target.

Sure blood is thicker than water, family is important, as well as being loyal...

However, people that say people should respect their family assume that everyone has been treated well by that family.

Respect is not freely given, it is earned. You don't owe anyone respect, you don't owe anyone anything.

Some families can be just plain stressful and so dysfunctional it deteriorates your mental health.

Most often the isolated black sheep of any family is the one that's most awake.

The most enlightened. The one who sees through everyone else's crap.

Sometimes the oddball isn't so odd at all.

Often the realest of any family faces fierce resistance in the truth they speak.

In fact, spit out enough truth, and your own mom or dad will dislike you and resent you.

People don't want to hear the truth because they don't want their illusions destroyed.

Speak it anyway.

Besides, life can be a lot broader than the town you're from, the street you grew up on, and the bedroom you slept in as a baby.

It's ok to outgrow and evolve beyond anyone. Including family.

Silly People

Engaging in meaningful conversation, good productive debate, and healthy worthwhile arguments are really a good thing.

However you lose interest quickly when you realize you're dealing with a fool.

You know, a blockhead, buffoon, ignoramus, imbecile, simpleton, dope, or knucklehead.

A bulldog can whip a skunk any day of the week... but it's just not worth it.

Self-control and maintaining the ability to remain calm and composed when someone is testing your last nerve is literally a superpower.

There are some people that you need to prepare yourself for, prior to any form of communication with them.

Just being within several feet of them and hearing their voice raises your blood pressure a couple notches.

You've got to get primed and ready. Make sure you're in the mood.

Practice your friendly smile and respectful mannerisms, getting them down real good as they will be put to the test.

The more you argue with an idiot, the more you disrespect yourself.

Insecurity is loud. Confidence is silent.

In mastering the fine skill of resisting the temptation to bring yourself down to their level you get quiet, reducing your responses to single word answers.

Only talk to agree, concede, tap out, and surrender to hand over the victory uncontested.

So the fool will shut up and stop talking.

Save your two cents until you have a full dollar.

Better yet, maybe a twenty or a hundred.

Inner Fulfillment

True success is the realization of a worthy ideal, where you are truly at peace.

At peace with who you believe yourself to be, the relationship you have with yourself and God, and the life YOU have chosen to live.

No matter how big the house you build, how much money you make, or how many cars you have in the driveway...there will always be a feeling of dissatisfaction if you are not really following that calling. That strong urge toward a particular way of life.

No matter how much sex you have or how many relationships you have you will never feel loved...if you don't love yourself.

No matter how many friends you have...you will never feel accepted if you don't accept yourself.

You can't get enough likes on Facebook and Instagram to feel validated...if you don't like yourself.

You can't get enough people to tell you you're beautiful...if you think you're ugly.

True contentment and happiness is a matter of the heart, mind, and soul...not external factors or material items.

You will never get to know you as long as you study them.

Nobody wants to look inside. Peel the layers back down to your core and examine what you see.

Happiness is a state of inner fulfillment.

Give to Charity

Some people can't support you in public because of how they've talked about you in private.

You can walk on water and some people will say it's because you can't swim.

You're always going to have people that will put you down so they can feel better about themselves. It's just the way it is.

So they can justify their inaction, excuses, limitations, and incapacities.

It's absolutely, incredibly amazing to think that when you become better or more successful that there will be some people that aren't happy for you. In fact, some will be downright bitter and angry about it.

People don't like when you obtain success outside of them. When you come from the same place they're stuck in and find success...they're not going to celebrate or be happy for you.

The brighter you shine, the better you become, and the bigger your spirit becomes...the more they're reminded of their demons.

It's really all quite alright though. See, it's like giving to a charitable cause.

Making others feel better about themselves at your expense is heartwarming.

You're essentially donating, making a pledge to their self-worth and self-esteem.

If by putting you down, belittling you, mocking you, laughing at you, and ridiculing you, they somehow feel better about who they are, then be happy to keep making donations.

If by calling you names, picking you apart, and pointing out all your flaws, it helps them feel better about their delusional importance and self-image, it's really a good thing.

At your expense, be tickled to make deposits in their insecurity fund. It's really a good deed to assist some people in liking what they see when they look in the mirror.

So, keep shining, keep doing you, keep talking your truth, keep growing, keep becoming, and don't let the chatter of insignificant people stop you.

The only people that take issue with truth are people that fit the description.

And besides, whoever is trying to bring you down is already below you. True winners in life lift other people up. They have no reason to do otherwise.

Love

Love is passed around loosely.

You are disrespecting yourself if you are pouring your time, energy, and soul into someone who loves you conditionally.

If you lose someone's love they never really loved you. If the love was conditional it wasn't really love to begin with.

A parent's love for their children, intimate relationships, marriages, even friendships or any other personal relationships.

Real love has no conditions. Real love knows no limits. Real love isn't about convenience.

If you change, and are therefore not loved because you weren't the way you were before, you were never really loved.

Real love is when they see the bad in you and love you anyway. It's not based on certain unspoken rules and conditions.

Unconditional love is when you're hard to love but they love you hard anyway.

Unconditional love doesn't come through mixed signals. Do yourself a favor and take mixed signals as a no.

They cheated because their expected conditions weren't met, let them walk, it's not love.

The trick is to understand and be wise enough to know when you are being loved conditionally or unconditionally.

Conditional "love" is perfectly fine, just know and accept it for what it really is, don't be blinded by fake love. There's a difference between interest and love.

Love is profound. Don't get it twisted.

Spend your time and energy on those that love you unconditionally, no matter what, not on those that only love you when the conditions are right for them.

True, real, unconditional love bears and endures all things and is worth fighting for.

True, real, conditional love is not.

Are You Ready?

You can't make a person comprehend a message they aren't ready to receive.

Words stop going through one ear and out the other...

When struggle and hardship become disturbing and hopeless.

When you feel alone in a room full of people.

When treading water becomes drowning.

When a slight hiccup becomes utter devastation.

When minor discomfort becomes chronic debilitating pain.

When your life falls apart and you submit to the idea that you don't know how to pick up the pieces.

When you realize you're sleeping with the enemy.

When the doctor reveals the diagnosis.

When you shed tears from time to time for seemingly no reason and don't know why.

When your wants and needs become frantic desperation.

When you destroy your life and have nothing left except the last drop down to the bottom of every bottle.

When a small crack becomes shattered pieces.

When the truth comes out and it rocks your world.

When you're in prison but not behind bars.

When you discover their true colors.

When you were forced to say goodbye to them...forever.

When you're crawling in your own skin and your worst enemy is you.

When you swing around on that barstool and realize it's not fun anymore.

When a vibrant smile becomes a blank possessed stare.

When you're down to your last dollar in your checking account and the shut off notice is in the mailbox.

When your life doesn't look the way you'd thought it would look at that age.

When your back is pinned and the walls are closing in.

When silence is deafening.

These things make words strike a chord, it is then you will pay attention.

When the student is ready the teacher will appear.

Plan B

Plan B is really just an expression of self-doubt.

When you always give yourself a way out you subconsciously move forward with an emergency brake on.

Self-belief says...

"I'm doing this no matter what it takes."

"Whatever the price, I resolve to pay it in advance."

"I refuse to be denied."

"I don't need you to believe in me, I believe in me."

"I can do this I just haven't figured it out yet."

It's particularly hard when there's no immediate display or evidence that what you're doing is amounting to anything.

That's of course when the critics, naysayers, and know it alls with good advice begin to take a victory lap.

You've got to be tough enough and believe in yourself deep enough to continue to move forward even at times you question yourself.

Watch how you talk to yourself. Many times you sabotage yourself with your own negative self-talk.

"What if I put in all the work for nothing?"

"What if everyone is right?"

"I can't do this, I'm not skilled enough, I don't have the training, I don't have experience."

Blah, blah, blah.

When you drown out every voice but your own, delete all negativity, and go at what you want without limiting beliefs...

You will have it.

It's a simple matter of cause and effect. Big in, big out. Little in, little out.

You're never going to have the perfect plan. The time is never right. You will look stupid.

It will become increasingly more challenging. People will try to convince you to give up.

Don't.

It really truly is just a matter of not giving up.

Expectations

There's danger in low expectations. See, you generally get what you expect.

It takes courage and guts to want more. To expect more.

Expectation costs you something, which is why many just decide not to have any.

Not money. Something more profound than that. Something deeper. Something you can't touch or even see.

To always be in a position of readiness to receive something is not easy on a person's mind, heart, and spirit. It costs you peace and comfort.

To say "I expect more out of my life "and "I expect that good things are going to happen to me" when it doesn't look like anything is happening.

When there's no immediate sign, display, or evidence of things coming together.

There's a certain grace given to those who continue to walk when they feel that they can't walk anymore.

When they believe and have faith good will come out of their situation and out of their life.

When you can take a licking and keep on ticking...when life tries to break you, but you don't break...doors will start swinging open.

There will be things in store for you that your ears have not heard, your eyes have not seen, and your mind has not imagined.

<u>Grand Illusion</u>

Things aren't always what they appear to be.

Many feel inadequate, unsuccessful, and like they're not enough because they're comparing themselves and their lives to an illusion.

You never really know just how much of a gift someone has until you unwrap it.

Many people's lives are not as great as they're portrayed to be in real life or on social media.

A false advertisement. Many offer product that they don't carry in their inventory.

All hat and no cattle.

All show but no substance.

The tree stands tall, but the roots don't run very deep.

The container is much better than the contents.

A house of cards, smoke and mirrors, a grand illusion. Acting rich, down to their last penny.

Looking important, choking to death.

Don't emulate everything you see.

Identify the main character traits of someone you admire and emulate for all the right reasons.

Develop and embody the same character traits.

Then you'll find the person you admire and emulate the most is yourself.

Mommy

There are maternal and non-maternal mothers everywhere, from all walks of life.

However we should all have an extra special thank you and appreciation to the mothers who have accepted and consistently maintain the commitment and responsibility that comes with having a child...

That is being a mom.

Becoming a mother does not make you a mom. Consistent motherly actions make you a mom.

Motherhood is hard. You've got to be tough to be a mom. Like a woman of steel...when it comes to her children...

A mom will leap tall buildings in a single bound to care for them.

Become stronger than a locomotive to protect them.

And, be there faster than a speeding bullet when they are desperately in need.

A mom gives unconditional care and support despite her means, and despite being misunderstood or underappreciated at times.

A mom understands it's her attention that's important, not her money.

Even when her children don't make the choices in life she would have liked them to make or acted in ways she would have liked them to act...

Even when her children under appreciate her, shout at her, or hurt her...

She's still there saying "come on in baby and have a seat at the dinner table, you're still my child."

Standing as a beacon, not holding grudges, and being a true role model in making her children realize their mistakes, without giving up on them or hurting them.

When it's inconvenient, she's still a mom. When the circumstances aren't perfect, she's still a mom. When it's burdensome, she's still a mom. When it's uncomfortable, she's still a mom.

A mom's love is selfless and true. Bold and unwavering. Fierce and intense.

It refuses to be denied, and is willing to overcome and withstand even the fiercest resistance, difficulty, or rejection.

Whether you're eight or eighty, a mom's work is never done. A mom doesn't take her COMMITMENT lightly.

So, if you've made it into this elite class of motherhood...

The mommies, mamas, mums, and mammies of the world... I salute you.

You deserve a badge of honor.

You are legendary. You are a rock star.

<u>Right Now</u>

In this moment right now, somewhere in the world...

Someone is on a ventilator.

Someone is taking their final breath.

Someone is saying their last goodbye to this world.

Someone is starving, impoverished, destitute, and lives in a war zone.

Someone has suffered loss and devastation of massive proportion.

Someone didn't wake up this morning.

Someone has just been diagnosed with a terminal illness.

Someone is fighting for their life and peace physically, emotionally, or spiritually.

Someone is praying for what you're taking for granted.

At this moment someone is praying for the problems you have right now.

At this moment someone is praying for the situation you have right now.

At this moment someone is praying for the opportunity you have right now.

At this moment someone is praying to see what you see right now.

At this moment someone is praying to feel what you feel right now.

At this moment someone is praying to hear what you hear right now.

At this moment someone is praying to believe what you believe right now.

At this moment someone is praying for the miracle you have right now.

There's a lot more to the world than you and your life.

You really don't have it as bad as you think you do.

Your "problem" isn't much of a problem at all.

You need a new way of looking at your situation.

You better wake up.

You better step into this moment.

Right now.

What's Underneath

You never really know what's going on with a person and their life underneath the surface.

Things can look good on the surface but be ready to cave in underneath.

Like a sinkhole in the ground, when the surface layer all of a sudden collapses out of nowhere.

What's gradually dissolving and eroding underneath their smile, their hand shake, or their hello how are you.

Their secret fights...voids they have that are creating instability, growing weaker, and moving them closer to sinking in.

Things build up and build pressure until suddenly one day a person loses it, snaps, and no one knows why. No one saw it coming.

They come crashing in, and what was lacking...the emptiness that was under the surface is suddenly revealed.

In regard to building a life...

When you don't build an authentic and genuine foundation of solid rock for your life and who you are...

Sooner or later...

Time will bring to reality of what lies underneath the surface.

What's under your surface?

Bigger and Better

Don't worry about what it looks like right now.

See if you can be faithful and believe with a little...I assure you my friend, you will be given a lot.

Some people get bitter in the battle. Some people get better in the battle.

Some acquiesce, and some say "NO!" and "I WILL!"

Some people go into the battle aluminum and come out solid gold.

Some people go into the battle a dandelion and come out a sunflower.

Some people go into the battle a caterpillar and come out a butterfly.

Some people go into the battle a little bitty drop and come out a tsunami.

Some people go into the battle a kitten and come out a lion.

Some people go into the battle a crater and come out a mountain...

Snowcapped.

Some people go into the battle water and come out wine.

Some people go into the battle a shadow and come out as the light.

Some people go into the battle a puppy and come out a wolf.

Some people go into the battle with knowledge and come out with wisdom.

Some people go into the battle a pigeon and come out an eagle.

Some people go into the battle an essay and come out a novel.

You WILL come out of this...

And when it's all said and done...

It's gonna be bigger and better than you think it is. Keep the faith.

Deception

Lies come in all shapes and sizes.

Harmless little white lies like a child lying about cleaning their room or saying you took the trash out when you really didn't is one thing...

But there are levels of deception that are so profound there are no words for them.

Lies that are strategic, intentional, and designed to purposefully mislead a person to believe something that is not true.

A conspiracy.

Crooked, sick, and twisted behavior.

A web of lies that are carefully crafted and calculated to make you look to the left, so you don't see your life being destroyed on the right. Like slowly poisoning someone little by little until they die.

Where it doesn't matter how badly a person is destroying someone else as long as they remain undercover.

Let's be real about it...

People that can look a person right in the eye, calm, cool, and collective as can be, and be lying through their teeth are disturbing.

To engage in wicked behavior with no remorse or empathy, with a blatant disregard for another person's life, and come off charming as can be, is demented and deranged.

You know the type of person that has those types of character traits and tendencies?

An axe murderer.

Don't let a pretty face fool you.

Not everyone you lose is a loss. It's a blessing.

Free Your Mind

It's unfortunate people give so much power and meaning to a "thought".

I mean, what is a thought really?

Ready for a revelation?

EVERYTHING, really has no meaning. You, at some point, gave it a meaning.

Upset over nothing. Upset over a conjured up "meaning" of something that happened. Upset over a figment of your own imagination.

A made up, invented, and fabricated "meaning" you're holding onto that's destroying your peace of mind and holding you in a jail cell that doesn't really in fact exist.

You don't need bail money, you don't need the key to the lock, you don't even need to stand trial and plead your case.

You just need to eradicate and push out the "thought" that's in your head.

Freedom is just on the other side of letting go.

Perceptions of past events are holding your spirit and soul captive.

A new life can't work its way into your consciousness as long as you are holding onto a mindset that refuses to change.

The enemy doesn't have to tie you up to be bound, he just needs to tie up your head.

With bitterness, jealousy, anger, malice, revenge, vengefulness, and unforgiveness.

Nothing can have power over you unless YOU GIVE IT POWER.

It's not the event of what happened that dictates the direction you will go in, it's your interpretation of the events "meaning" that will hold you back.

A boat doesn't sink because it's in the water, it sinks because of the water that gets inside of it.

Transformation cannot occur until there is a renewing of your mind. Until you refuse to ALLOW what's on the outside to contaminate what's on the inside.

Embrace a mind that is open to everything and attached to nothing.

Free your mind and the rest will follow.

Say No

Say no...a lot.

If you're not careful you will allow people to pull you straight apart.

Bending backwards for everyone until you snap in two trying to please everyone is a losing proposition.

People sign on to a million things and wonder why they don't make any meaningful progress in a singular direction.

Sometimes you just have to be willing to disappear for a while and don't apologize for it.

There's power in saying no.

Not only to people's requests but to what they want to hear or see from you and your character.

People are all about you as long as you say things they like to hear, portray a persona they want to see out of you, and hop, skip, and jump to their every wish.

Cut the strings, draw a line in the sand, and throw up barriers to entry.

Saying no doesn't mean you're cold hearted, that you don't care, that you're a jerk, or that you're selfish.

It means you have to set limits because takers have none.

It means there's only so much of you to go around.

It means you are a limited resource.

It means you need to set boundaries around what needs to take first priority in your life so you can make meaningful progress in a direction you really want to go.

Besides, people that are the most difficult to please are often the ones that are the least worth pleasing.

Do you, be you, some people won't like it, and you don't have to care.

You can't please everyone. You can't solve everyone's problems. You can't be there for everyone all the time.

And...you shouldn't try.

Dope Soul

We all come into the world a little bundle of joy, full of wonder, energy, and excitement.

Many grow up to be miserable, depressed, unhappy, unfulfilled, and that twinkle in their eye...long gone.

Something happens to all of us as we grow up, myself surely included.

LIFE.

We're told to be realistic, get our head out of the clouds.

We're told to go to college and get a "good job".

We're told to do like your mommy and daddy did, they know what's best.

How come you're not married yet? We want grand kids and grandma is getting older!

Why can't you be more like your brother or sister?

Now sweetie, those types of things aren't meant for people like us.

Sell your soul to the company and you can have a big screen TV just like me!

It's no surprise we find ourselves in places as we grow older that we never dreamed of being in.

The miserable job or career we have no emotional connection to, more committed to the "we" than what's best for us.

The marriage or relationship we settled for because biological clocks are ticking and after all, If you're not married with kids or dating someone that means there's something wrong with you.

Living up to all kinds of expectations that were never our own. Concealing our true self and identities to keep temporary people.

We let life tell us who and what we can be.

We allow the comings and goings of this world to make us change our name.

We conform, fit in, stay in line, don't cause too many waves, and try to keep everyone else happy.

We become accustomed to a regime of thought beat into us by the world we grew up in, our families, our friends, our teachers, our bosses, or our spouse or significant other.

The hardest thing in the world is to be who and what you want to be in a world that's constantly trying to make you who and what it wants you to be.

Don't let the world make you change your name. March to the beat of your own drum.

Become the dope soul you were before the world taught you not to be.

Power Within

A lot of people say they want things...

One shows up in conversation, the other shows up in behavior.

There are some people that just have that extra something. You can't put your finger on it. You can't touch it or see it, oh but you can sense it. You can feel it.

They have a bold intensity in the way they approach life as well as everything they do.

It's an intensity that is fueled by something deep inside of them.

Life goes in the direction they PROVOKE it to go. The direction they straight up WILL IT to go.

They don't go with the flow in their life, they create the flow.

They boldly live in the future, and prepare now for what isn't reality yet.

They don't sit back and wait for something to happen. THEY MAKE IT HAPPEN.

They go and get it. They don't wait for it to arrive, they deliver it.

Calling those things that are not as though they were, they're willing to look like a fool.

Getting busy working on something that can't be seen right now.

They have no problem being out of step with their reality to be in step with their destiny.

Where does it come from?

They understand they will not find what they're looking for in other people. They stop looking there.

They start separating themselves. They stop trying to fit in. They stop making homes in other people.

They have experienced the revelation of the powers within.

And with that...they are not subject to life.

LIFE IS SUBJECT TO THEM.

Complaining

Don't like your job? Quit, get a new one.

Can't stand your boyfriend or girlfriend anymore? Cut them off.

Don't like where you live? Move.

Can't stand that loser friend? Become better attract better.

Always broke? Work harder and spend wiser.

No hope for your marriage? Get a divorce.

Can't seem to get ahead? Evaluate and change your priorities.

Sick of being out of shape? Work out and stop eating garbage.

Tired of others doing better than you? Get educated, work on yourself, and work harder. Stop complaining. Nobody cares. Do something about it. You are 100% in control of your life.

Just Words

Words have a tendency to woo us and make us emotional. Make us blind.

Actions speak louder than words. You'll never be misled by an action.

What a person does speaks volumes. The proof is always in the pudding.

People like to talk. They like to pass around loose commitments. They like to throw loving, caring words around easily.

They like to say one thing and do another.

Some of the most rotten people will be telling you one thing and be involved in an all-out campaign to manipulate and deceive you.

People that tell you what you want to hear are a virus.

The person you consider the closest to you on a daily basis that you're convinced is for you and loves you, could be slipping a knife inch by inch right in your back.

Let words go through one ear and out the other. Don't be swept up with words.

Listen closely with your eyes.

Blame Game

I could've blamed a lot of people or circumstances in my life to justify to myself why I should just embrace an average life path, average way of thinking, and a low level of achievement.

I could have blamed my absent parents and my childhood experience.

I could have blamed it on depression, drug, and alcohol abuse due to the fact I was alone, scared, hated who I was, and uncertain about the future.

I could have blamed it on the fact I was a lost kid as an adolescent. Completely misguided.

I could have blamed it on not having a father to teach me how to be a man and handle life.
I could have blamed it on not having a college degree like "successful" people do.

I could have blamed it on the people I worked for in my life and their bullshit political agendas, dictating my ability to move upward while smiling in my face.

I could have blamed the marriage that left me devastated, broken, tattered, and torn.

I could have blamed it on all the people that completely disregarded my life or wellbeing, stepped on my soul, and left me for dead.

No, see I decided not to let the circumstances around me determine the conqueror within me.

I decided to rise above and reposition myself to prosper. I repositioned my life by repositioning my head.

I spit in the face of adversity. Things that should have held me down and killed me forced me to search my soul.

I'm unshakable. Negative words can't move me or disrupt my peace. My mind and spirit are solid as a rock.

The second half of this story will be better than the first. I must maximize the time I have left. No time to look behind me. I must look ahead.

The thing that is in front of you is greater than the thing that is behind you. Believe the future can be better than the past and believe you have the ability to make it so.

Excuses

So many people talk the talk but don't walk the walk.

Drop your excuses.

Success and achievement doesn't care if you feel like it or not.

Success and achievement doesn't care that you just need a vacation.

Success and achievement doesn't care that you're tired, frustrated, and stressed out.

Success and achievement doesn't care that you've had enough, it's just too much.

Success and achievement doesn't care that you have plans this weekend.

Success and achievement doesn't care you're at a disadvantage or someone else has more advantages than you.

Success and achievement doesn't care the football game or your favorite TV show is on.

Success and achievement doesn't care you need a break.

Success and achievement doesn't care you're scared.

Success and achievement doesn't care you have no money.

Success and achievement doesn't care your friends are having a party.

Success and achievement doesn't care you're having marital problems or fighting with your significant other.

Success and achievement doesn't care about your feelings.

Success and achievement doesn't care you don't know what you're doing.

Success and achievement doesn't care your family doesn't support you or care about you.

Success and achievement doesn't care you wish things could be easier.

Success and achievement must be worked for. They have no plans of coming easy. They have no plans of coddling your emotions and feelings.

So, enough talking. Start walking.

Success and achievement are about doing whatever it takes, no matter what. Period.

True Wisdom

Many people ask where I got my "wisdom" and how I know so much about life.

Truth is, my true wisdom is that I understand that I don't know everything. I've made plenty of stupid mistakes in all facets of life. I'm far from perfect and still have a lot to learn.

I'm a person that put a greater demand on myself and on my life.

When I made mistakes or my life wasn't going right I was hungry for the right answers. I spent thousands of hours studying and reflecting.

I diligently looked for the answers then took MASSIVE ACTION to live and think a better way refusing to stay stuck in the same patterns.

Knowing is not enough. Many people know what to do but stay stuck because it's easier than taking the appropriate action.

Admit when you're wrong, admit when you don't know.

Close minded know it alls make it nowhere in life.

Comparison

Never compare yourself to other people. Don't judge a book by its cover or take things at face value. I've learned things aren't always what they seem or appear to be.

Just because you're smiling doesn't mean you're happy.

The big house, 2 brand new cars, and granite counter tops are beautiful. You're not wealthy. You're broke.

You said the vows, had the wedding, and danced the night away. The marriage is suffering and should have never happened.

You have a fancy title, a dry cleaned suit, and look real important. Walking in to that job siphons your soul right out of your body.

Such a close and loving family. Pick up the carpet and see all the crap brushed underneath.

Your life is the bomb on Facebook and Instagram. If only people could see behind closed doors.

You're such an expert. You know so much of what other people should do to fix their issues and life. You can't even fix your own life.

You make six figures. Real big shot. You're suffocating. Your life has you stuck with its hands wrapped around your throat.

Your significant other is a match made in heaven. You need an extra room for their baggage and they're slowly turning you into something you won't recognize in due time.

You are so sweet. Such a nice person. Everyone likes you. If only they knew how bitter, spiteful, manipulative, and vindictive you really are.

Focus on creating a life that can be measured by its face value.

A life where what you see is what you get.

An authentic life is a happy life.

Mirrors

When you look in the mirror what do you see? A reflection of yourself?

Well not really, go deeper.

There's a lot to be said about that reflection.

You want to achieve great success.

You want a better relationship with your family, significant other, children, and spouse.

You want to be respected by other people.

You wish you had more control over the circumstances of your life.

So, what do you see?

What you see is what you get. What you see manifests in your head. What you see manifests in your life.

It's not just your physical reflection in that mirror. What you see in the mirror is what is seen in your life.

Work on the reflection, fix the reflection, and love the reflection. Dominate the reflection. Dominate your life.

Commitment

What's in a commitment?

Many people fail to finish what they start in life. People start things with plenty of enthusiasm until they realize the true depth of the commitment.

A commitment shouldn't be taken lightly, however many people pass them around loosely.

Don't take the job if you're not going to really work it.

Don't start the business if you're not going to put an all-out effort and make the sacrifices to build it.

Don't get married if you're not going to be a husband or a wife.

Don't have children if you're not going to be a parent.

Don't start the diet if you're not going to follow it.

Don't start the friendship if you're not going to be there in times of need.

Don't say you love someone and stab them in the back.

Everyone wants an asset, liabilities get left behind.

So, finish what you start. Half committed just doesn't cut it. Are you committed?

Pessimism

Pessimistic people love to project their shortcomings, fears, insecurities, doubts, disbelief, and lack of courage on you.

I can't help to just smile at pessimism.

Understand the true depth of what someone had to fight to get to where they are before you try to educate them on possibilities.

I know what I've overcome. I know what's in me. I define myself and my abilities through experience. I would've never discovered what I had in me had I not gone through struggle, tragedy, and adversity.

I am an insufferable optimist. I simply can't focus on why something can't be. I see potential and possibility everywhere.

I never ask why, but always demand why not.

Problems are a temporary inconvenience, not a permanent definition of where my life is going.

Repeatedly rising to the occasion in life does something to your character. When you've seen the bottom, you have a better appreciation and very deep sense of gratitude for higher ground.

You develop an innate strength that runs deep to your core.

Before you voice your pessimistic views, understand they fall on deaf ears. You're talking to a true survivor. A warrior. Highly skilled to fight on the battleground called life.

Have such a strong belief in yourself that you can shut out the noise of other people.

Fighting

Life is a fight. From the day you're born you come out crying and screaming.

I've had many fights in my life. None of which I'm ashamed of. They serve as the foundation to this indestructible mindset.

I was a neglected youth and didn't have parents that were there for me in times of severe need. No family that valued togetherness.

Living hand to mouth, I've lived a life fending for myself. A do or die, sink or swim kind of life. I battled with severe depression. Drug and alcohol use to escape my reality.

A devastating conspiracy of lies and manipulation I thought was a marriage. Inexplicable pain and turmoil.

No college degree, not really skilled in anything. Job after job, career after career, getting nowhere. Never seeming to ever be able to get ahead. Hopeless and afraid.

I've experienced feelings and emotions I wouldn't wish on my worst enemy.

Sometimes it's hard for me to even make sense how I got out of my own life alive to be where I am. Well and free.

I experienced an epiphany, an awakening that set me free.

The biggest fight you'll ever fight isn't your family, your personal or intimate relationships, your depression or substance abuse, your job or your career, or your finances.

The biggest fight you'll ever fight is between your own two ears. If you can fix it in your head, you can be well and free.

YOUR MIND IS THE BATTLEGROUND.

Disruption

People don't like disruption. They don't like to be uncomfortable. They don't like their beliefs to be challenged. They don't like to disrupt their "normal".

Disruption is essential to growth.

To "see the light" is to understand or realize something that was long doubted or not understood before.

"Seeing the light" makes you change your unpleasant behavior or opinions in a radical way.

When you're in the darkness, you have no vision. Your eyesight adjusts to the darkness. The darkness becomes comfortable. The darkness becomes your "normal".

Light is disruptive.

When you're consumed in the darkness, sudden light is blinding. It's painful and uncomfortable at first. It takes time for your vision to adjust. It takes time to start to see clearly.

Turn the light on.

Support

Ever notice how people that don't even know you support you more than people that do?

It makes sense really. Many people you know are still stuck where you once were. Stuck mentally and spiritually in the same place.

They're still dealing with and living the same miserable circumstances.

They still haven't made all of the key decisions they know they need to make to change their life. They're still making excuse after excuse to validate their limited belief systems.

They're still crippled by what everyone in the world thinks about them and how they would be perceived if they just did what they really wanted to do.

They're not happy for you. You came from the same place they came from and you made it out. You did what they cannot do.

You remind them of their limitations. You remind them that they're lying to themselves. You represent what they could be if they just had some balls.

So, many of these people don't like you very much. They love to talk about you though. It makes them feel better and bigger to tear you down, which leads to the most important point of all.

People you know can't support you in public because of what they said about you in private.

So, don't worry about anyone that isn't happy for you. They most definitely aren't happy about themselves either.

Just give them a good smirk and keep it moving.

Do Work

Where is your life going? Do you ever really stop to think about that?

If you're complaining that your life isn't where or what you want it to be than do something about it.
Either work to strategically change direction or stop complaining.

People get so distracted in life and wonder why they never really get anywhere. Nothing changes.

They get all excited and pumped. "I'm going to do this!!" 12 months later...

Get unbalanced. Get unsocial. Get to work.

Throw your TV in the dumpster.

Cancel your dinner plans for the next 3 years.

Stop the desperate search for a date or hookup. Search for a better life.

Friends want to go out tonight? Sorry you have to work.

Weekends. Work.

Burn your season tickets.

Put your significant other in check or get rid of them.

Smash your video game system into pieces.

Sit the family down and explain mommy/daddy is going to be working long hours.

Vacations, I don't think so.

Cancel your membership to the jelly of the month club.

It's about creating the proper habits. You think this is unnecessary?

A little of this here, a little of that there. It won't hurt right?

One decision compounds into another, subconsciously you become completely distracted and off course.

Years pass by, nothing changes, don't wonder why.

Don't worry though, this post will still be here for you to read again.

Genuine Smile

Back in my corporate days there were many perks to my job. I had a good position, the money was good, I had a brand new car off the show room floor, I could've put a down payment on a beautiful home with all the fixings, wore fancy clothes, and I could afford to do things a lot of people couldn't. All of which was not granted to me. I worked very hard for it.

Everyone I worked with had something they were working for. A reason why they came to work every day. Goals and desires.

My reason was very different. I wanted a genuine smile.

The fact that the smile I displayed outwardly didn't truly reflect what was going on with me inwardly was unbearable to me.

I gave up the position and made less money, I traded in the car, I didn't buy the house with the fixings, traded in the fancy clothes for a t shirt, and I didn't do any of the things I could afford to do.

I sacrificed it all and leaped out into the unknown, searching for what I so desperately wanted.

Life hasn't been easy since the suit and tie, but fulfilling and oh so worth it. I found what I was looking for.

I found my genuine smile.

Changes

There are moments in life that simply change you forever. There are severely painful moments. There are severely lonely moments. There are severely eye opening moments.

In these moments we wonder "why me?" and "how could this happen?"

It's not the moments that define who we are or how our lives turn out, it's our perception of those moments.

My mind and spirit have been crafted by these moments and it's in hindsight I realize their value.

Interestingly these moments were brought on and dictated by my perception of something someone else did to me or how they treated me.

I battled with myself because of someone else.

Don't let other people's actions influence your one chance at life. Don't let other people's actions or words shackle you from living your highest and best life.

The clock is ticking and time is running out. You've wasted enough time playing the victim and feeling sorry for yourself.

Life is happening now. What are you going to do with the time you have left?

Are you really going to live your whole life in defeatism based on other people or are you going to say screw them and triumph?

The most fulfilling thing you can do in life is become a person so beautiful, so grounded, and so massively successful, in spite of these other people and what they said or did.

Become so successful and vibe so high, you don't have to say a word. Those that afflicted you will hear you loud and clear.

Don't say "why me", say "try me". Success is always intentional. Success is the best revenge.

It Is What It Is

You get what you expect.

Raising your expectations takes tremendous courage, therefore many don't do it.

Most people lower their expectations to match their reality, rather than bring up their reality to match their expectations.

When you settle you get stuck. Stuck in a life that's just ok. Stuck in a life you don't really want.

"It is what it is" right?

Wrong. It is what you expect it is.

So what do you expect? You can't obtain something you don't expect to get.

Your job, "it is what it is."

Your mind, depressed, "it is what it is."

Your marriage, "it is what it is."

Your physical fitness, "it is what it is."

Your house or apartment, "it is what it is."

Always broke, pay check to pay check, hand to mouth, "it is what it is."

Friends and family aren't supportive and bring you down, "it is what it is."

Girlfriend or boyfriend, good enough, "it is what it is."

Your life, "it is what it is."

It's time to make "it is what is" not good enough.

It's time to take the bull by the horns. Don't expect anything, demand it.

Anything or anyone that can't rise up to meet those demands will be left behind.

Life is too short to settle for less than the very best you can strive for.

But wait, what if you raise your expectations and get disappointed you ask?

Shoot for the moon, because even if you miss, you'll land among the stars.

Feeling Happy

There's many places in life that can make you "feel" happy.

Friends, acquaintances, coworkers. Definitely! Until they demonstrate they were just temporary people.

Immediate family, absolutely! Unless they're separated, isolated, and never together.

Parents, for sure! Unless they're divorced and too busy trying to get their groove back.

Cars, a condo, and a fancy title at work with perks. You know it! Golden handcuffs definitely make you "feel" happy.

Marriage, you bet! Unless you're married to a twisted individual.

In laws and extended family, tons of "happy" feelings there! Unless you're dropped like a bad habit. On to the next guy or girl.

Dating person after person. Feeling "happy" indeed!

Vacations, partying, all kinds of recreation. Can't argue with that! Until you "return to reality."

But, where's the place you can find that real deep, unshakable, true happiness that's not easily disturbed, fleeting, or taken away?

I found and cultivated it in the last place I ever thought possible.

IN ME. It's an inside job.

Torn

Have you ever been pulled apart?

Torn between two worlds.

Torn between who you are, and who you want to be. Torn between where you are, and where you want to be.

You can imagine it, dream it, conceptualize it, understand it, know it, and want it. But, you can't seem to realize it.

Your ideal you and ideal life is alluring and enticing, pulling you in one direction. Your current life reality is pulling you back.

There's a constant tug of war going on in your life.

Commitments you've made in your life in many different areas to many different people that have created expectations.

Expectations you be someone and remain somewhere that just isn't serving you anymore.

Commitments that represent who and where you are, not who and where you want to be.

It's a lopsided tug of war. Several against one. So hard to win. So hard to hold on. So hard to keep up the struggle.

So many keep pulling and tugging, stressing and straining, until their hands bleed and their spirit is shattered.

Set yourself free. Let go of the rope. Stop holding on.

Some will be angry, some will be sad, some will be hurt, some will be broken, some will be bitter.

You will be you. You will be free.

Broken

There's a secret tribe that exists among broken people that have survived and overcome.

Initiation comes through pain and suffering.

It's a community of commonality rooted in overcoming severe trauma, turmoil, heartache, selfdoubt, and despair.

A clan of diesel spirits that shine a blinding light onto those around them.

Superb fighters, warriors, that have fought the good fight and triumphed.

They speak a language that can set you free.

In the wilderness of life, they occupy a sacred territory that is impossible to invade or conquer.

They were once lost, but then found.

A group of grounded individuals with indestructible personal foundations.

The tribe empathizes in a way that is deeper than most because they've had the sickness before.

Revealing their scars to the world, gives others the permission to heal their own wounds.

Many haven't asked for or wouldn't have chosen inclusion to the tribe. Nonetheless, affiliation is embraced and accepted.

Their scars have equipped them to perform an important task of healing others in a way that transcends beyond normal comprehension.

The tribe isn't easily understood by those that have never really been through tough times, or a tough life, and survived.

So if you're lost out in the world, tattered and torn, beaten down by life, and don't know where to turn...know there's an open spot in this society.

Come on into the tent, have a seat, let us teach you the ways of the secret tribe.

Hands on Me

I was born a blank slate. I had no concept of me, who I should be, what I thought about anything, or what I thought my life path should be.

Until the world got its hands on me. It had much different plans for the direction of my life. The world was convincing me to be far less.

That broken home and sorry excuse for a father.

Message taken.

Scrounging for money, paycheck to paycheck, living wherever I could.

I understand.

Mommy has needs of her own, sorry son, you're on your own now.

Understood.

Afraid to go to sleep for fear I wouldn't wake up, the emergency room, and the blood all over my kitchen.

I'm listening.

Like a puppet on a string in corporate, be like this guy, you'll make lots of money and be "wealthy."

I hear you loud and clear.

Happily married? Maybe, but unfortunately the baby wasn't mine.

OK point taken.

I mean what am I doing? I must be crazy. Who the hell do I think I am?

The world was doing such a good job of conditioning me to be a depressed, low down, average, and an extremely limited human being.

The world had me in the palm of its hand. Teaching me who I was and what I should believe is possible.

Life was convincing I'd have to say. Took me down some pretty convincing roads.
Life whispered in my ear, "Your not going to be anything in your life."

I whispered back to life and said, "You're."

Kick Me

Try to kick me while I'm down and I'll break your leg.

People wonder how and why I have such relentlessness and just keep coming hard.

Because I've been through something.

You can't scare me away with trouble. I've danced with the devil more than once.

It's impossible to ware me down. I just will not take no for an answer.

I don't care how long it takes. I have aggressive patience.

What most won't do, I will, enthusiastically.

I refuse to settle for less than the absolute most I can squeeze out of this life.

I understand one day it'll end. I'll have no regrets.

I'll have a smirk on my face when I'm taking my last breath to venture into the afterlife because I'll be content.

Content in knowing I put it all on the table. Bet all my chips. Maximized my time on this earth claiming mine.

I'll rest easy knowing I wasn't afraid.

I went for it.

Prisoner

You don't have to be locked up behind bars in prison to be doing time.

Working a job you hate. Sunday night you start to get anxiety at the thought of waking up Monday morning. Just doing time.
You're in a relationship with someone, it's not what you want, and it's not what you need. Just doing time.

You're married to someone that is present, but not connected. Just doing time.

You're stuck dwelling on the past. Things that have happened and mistakes you've made. Unable to get out of your own way. Just doing time.

Influences from family and friends on your life. Living how everyone else thinks you should live. Living a life you don't want. Just doing time.

Stuck in a rut. Self-sabotaging beliefs about who you are and what's possible for your life. Just doing time.

Feeling sorry for yourself. Years go by. People that have done you wrong or hurt you are long gone. You just will not let it go and move on with your life. Just doing time.

Life isn't something that just happens to us and we must just sit helplessly and endure it, it's something that we must proactively create.

So, at what point do you start striving to live the highest and best life possible?

At what point do you stop making excuses and stop complaining about circumstances that are totally in your power to change?

At what point do you become consciously aware of the fact that you have a limited amount of time on this earth and you're completely wasting it?

There will come a day when your life is going to end and you're just doing time until it comes to pass.

You're living a life sentence on death row. Just doing time.

Transformation

Transformational thinking results in transformational living.

Say what you will. Do what you will.

I am untouchable and unshakable simply because no one can penetrate and manipulate my thoughts.
I own my thoughts. I dictate them. I am the master over them.

You control your thoughts or your thoughts control you.

Your life is a reflection of what's going on in your head. It's that simple.

Where you are right now is a direct reflection of what you think.

Your circumstances aren't holding you back, it's how you're processing them.

You can't control the behaviors or voices of others, but you can control how you think about it and feel about it.

You can't be any better than you think.

You can't live out on the outside, what's not lived out on the inside.

Many are convinced otherwise, but you CAN control your mind.

You can choose the way you think about a situation.

There are many people that are doing more, with less than you have, because they think they can.

What you think, you become.

Steps

Life is like a staircase. It takes you through steps.

In each new phase I was tripping and falling on the steps trying to figure it out. Trying to find my way.

I learned to respect the steps.

I needed to grow into and become the person I am today to have the character and capacity to receive what is in store for me.

I simply wasn't ready, life was first teaching me the steps.

I wasn't mature enough in my character and my thinking at younger ages, but I'm ready now.

I've made mistake after mistake and put myself in many undesirable circumstances, but I'm ready now.

I tried and tried to do the best I could simply to fall short over and over, but I'm ready now.

I lost my way many times, wandering in directions I thought were leading me to my promise, but I'm ready now.

I was controlled by the wills and minds of others, but I'm ready now.

I felt sorry for myself because of how other people left me and tore me down, but I'm ready now.

On my knees, begging for the answers as to why my life was a failure. I was confused, but I'm ready now.

Self-sabotaging and destructive thoughts pinning me against a wall, but I'm ready now.

I was concerned with the thoughts and opinions of insignificant people, but I'm ready now.

I hated the man peering back at me in the mirror, but I'm ready now.

Today, I look behind me, down at the long staircase of steps I've climbed.

I'm grateful for the steps. After all, what is the purpose of steps? Steps take you to a higher level. I'm ready now.

Not That Easy

Sometimes you can be so invested in something it's just absolutely impossible to change it isn't it?

You know, it's just not that easy. I mean it's easier said than done. You just don't understand, it's more complicated than that.

These are just other ways of saying, I'm afraid, I don't believe in myself, I'm uninspired, I lack self-respect, I'm weak, I can't control my thoughts, I can't control my emotions, I'm making excuses, my life is controlling me.

If something or someone is no longer serving you and holding you back from realizing your highest and best life, cut it loose.

It doesn't matter how long you've been married. Look they're not going to change already.

It doesn't matter how long you've been working that job. Your boss doesn't "care" about you as much as you think. Don't miss out on what can be best for you.

It doesn't matter how long you've been friends with that person. 4th grade was a blast but you have different values now.

It doesn't matter your girlfriend or boyfriend is going to be upset and throw a tantrum. They can take the spices they paid for out of the spice rack on their way out the door.

It doesn't matter that it's your mom, dad, sister, or brother. No, they don't know what's best for you. You need to know what's best for you.

Until you get rid of the things holding you down, you will never grow.

People that make it in life and live to their fullest potential look around for the circumstances they want, and if they don't find them, they create them.

It's that easy, it's that simple, and it's that uncomplicated.

Rules

There's so many rules in life.

Be an exception to those rules.

Step out of bounds.

Color outside the lines.

Operate outside of the box.

Think and act different than the majority.

Be a unique individual.

Don't fit in.

Don't go with the flow, create the flow.

Take your own advice.

Believe in miracles.

Hear your own voice, not that of others.

Give up good, run after great.

Be alone.

Rattle some cages.

Take the road less traveled.

Don't settle, create the life you want.

Epiphany

Come to yourself.

Don't let the routine of life creep into your mind.

Don't allow who and what you're surrounded by all the time to take your life and your character in a direction that you don't even realize is happening.

Ever ask yourself, "how did I get here?"

I surely have.

Your job, relationship, marriage, friends, family, and other associations rub off on you. Unaware, you start to become what and who you're surrounded by all the time.

Afraid, codependent, and lost, you hold on tight, and when you lose these things you're left with no understanding of who you are anymore.

"Come to yourself", become aware this is happening or has happened.

"Come to yourself", remember who you were before external factors dulled your shine.

It's time to become conscious.

It's time to break out of that sleep walk.

It's time for an eye popping, head spinning, heart racing, tear shedding, sweat breaking, nerve wracking, radical awakening.

Good morning sunshine, welcome to the real you.

Behind the Scenes

It's the work put in behind the scenes that counts.

When no one is watching.

When the "feeling" goes away.

Just you, and the voice of encouragement is your own.

There's a fire within that roars.

You think about your life and what it could've been, might have been, and should have been.

Believe you're greater than where you came from. There's more in store for you that goes so far beyond your past life circumstances.

It's not about what you say you're going to do, it's about what you actually produce. The proof is always in the pudding.

Many say they want success but few really do the work necessary to get it.

Your level of success is directly related to your level of sacrifice and tolerance for pain to obtain it.

The more you put in, the more you get out.

Cause and effect. There is no if or maybe.

Creation

The best way to predict the future is to create it.

Everyone has a personal testimony.

My testimony, I truly believe, is a miracle.

Who would have ever thought I'd be on the life path I am today.

Everything in my past from the day I was born should have confirmed a much different path.

Broken home, absent parents, troubled adolescent, drug and alcohol problems, manipulative cheating wife, corporate politics dictating my future holding me down, severe depression, no college degree, no family that values togetherness.

I should not believe I'm worthy, deserving, or capable to even have the audacity to think I can reach ultra-successful heights.

I should possess an average mindset and expect average possibilities.

It's about your resolve. It's about resilience. It's about changing your story.

I didn't let the chaos around me dictate the conqueror within me.

See it doesn't matter what life throws at you. It doesn't matter who left you. It doesn't matter what problems you face.

WHAT MATTERS IS WHAT YOU INTEND TO DO ABOUT IT.

Your reality is a manifestation of your INSUFFERABLE, and IMMUTABLE conviction around what MUST be.

Demand more from yourself and from your life.

Decide what it's going to be and resolve to make it a reality.

You have to believe you are better. Make the rest of your life the best of your life.

So, I ask you, what you are going to do about it.

Not Good For Me

Truth is, not all people are good for you.

When you choose a unique path, you can never be common in your associations. Choose your associations wisely.

You can't surround yourself with blindness and expect to see.

Listen carefully with your eyes.

Who you are depends on who they are. Treat people accordingly.

People are either lifting you up or they're bringing you down.

Delete relationships that make more withdrawals than deposits.

Givers have to set limits, because takers have none.

Protect your energy, not everyone deserves it.

Not every action requires a reaction. Silence speaks louder than words.

Some people will try to break you, shake you, manipulate you, cheat you, use you, and abuse you.

How firm you stand will be what makes you.

Be so emotionally strong you're able to shut down every voice but your own.

Your elevation may require your isolation.

You may feel like you stand alone, but someday you will stand out.

You are the Chief Executive Officer of your life. Hire, promote, and fire accordingly.

Own Worst Enemy

What's holding you back?

Wait, I can answer that for you.

The answer is you, your thoughts, and your perceived limitations.

Somehow you've built these invisible walls around you.

Life is an equal opportunity experience. It's what you decide to make it.

Some come into the world with everything given to them and do nothing.

Some come into the world with nothing given to them and build empires.

There is always plenty of abundance around us, it's our mind that creates limitations.

It's not your boss or your job.

It's not your education.

It's not your history.

It's not because of what happened to you when you were a kid.

It's not your girlfriend or boyfriend.

It's not your husband or wife.

It's not your kids.

It's not your siblings or extended family.

It's not your living situation or the town you live in.

It's not your bank account.

It's not your mom or dad.

It's not your depression.

It's not because of anyone or anything else under any circumstance.

It's YOU. You are a prisoner in your mind.

There are people with your exact circumstances doing exactly what you don't think can be done because they THINK differently about it.
What you think, you become.

What are you thinking?

On the Verge

Ever feel like you're on the verge of something?

On the verge of something big. On the verge of something awesome.

You can't even explain it to other people, they wouldn't understand.

Every day and every ounce of energy you can feel it getting closer and closer.

On the verge of a massive breakthrough.

On the verge of a major shift.

On the verge of a new level, a new life.

On the verge of a new mindset.

Busting out of, and breaking old habits, routines, and ways of thinking.

On the verge of a new you.

Like a caterpillar breaking out of its cocoon, you're on the brink of a radical, unrecognizable transformation.

You're on the verge of a new identity in mind, body, and spirit.

Butterflies give up their caterpillar ways and tendencies.

It's been a struggle, but you've been on the verge.

Fly butterfly. Fly.

<u>Thankful</u>

Gratitude. It's what will keep you going.

When you begin to start coming into your own, and live out your highest and best life, there's a gratitude that gives you a spark, an energy, that's unexplainable.

But mostly, there needs to be a greater level of gratitude for all the lessons that have been getting you ready. Morphing you into who you needed to become first.

A deep gratitude for where you've been. A gratitude for many of the uncommon things people are usually grateful for.

Be grateful for being weak, taught you an indestructible strength that remembers where you've been.

Be grateful for being stupid, taught you a new found wisdom.

Be grateful for the closed doors in your life, taught you were you don't belong.

Be grateful for the people that hurt you, taught you the type of person you don't want to be.

Be grateful for having a lack of vision, taught you how to see clear.

Be grateful for the hopelessness you've felt, taught you to make demands on life instead.

Be grateful for being brought to your knees, taught you to stand with an unshakable firmness.

Be grateful for being afraid, taught you what miracles can happen when you take action in spite of it.
Be grateful for being spineless, taught you how to be bold and conquer life.

Be grateful for being in those dark places, taught you a shine that disrupts the darkness.

Be grateful for frowning, taught you a genuine smile.

Be grateful for being broken, taught you how to become properly fixed.

Be grateful for being pulled apart, taught you how to be made whole.

Be grateful for being unappreciated, taught you how to really appreciate.
Be grateful for being stuck, taught you to claim your freedom.

Be grateful for your life, you only have one. It's a gift. Make the most out of it starting right now.

Judgement

Imagine if people worried more about fixing themselves rather than criticizing the people around them.

Next time you find yourself judging or criticizing someone else negatively, stop in that moment and reroute it onto yourself.

People don't like to face themselves too much. Their judgement and criticism makes them feel better about their own shortcomings and incapacities.

If it makes you feel better to tear someone else down you are the epitome of a pathetic human being.

Many know exactly what other people should do or need to do to fix their lives but can't even fix their own.

Many don't practice what they preach.

Many point out others imperfections and they are about as faulty and incomplete as it gets.

Nobody is perfect. We all have issues. We all have imperfections. We all have things we need to improve on. Including myself. It's easy to criticize and judge others, try looking in the mirror.

Other People

One of the biggest prisons most live in is caring about what other people think.

It's extremely hard to be who you want to be in a world that's constantly trying to change you.

When you know who you are, you know who you are not.

When you have no sense of who you are, you become whatever others say or think you should be.

Don't change who you are or become something you're not to keep friends, save marriages, maintain intimate relationships, keep your parents happy, or commit to the "we" of your job or company.

It's time to stand up to life. It's time to stop living in a way that doesn't serve you.

Unfortunately, you will have to disappoint some people.

As long as you are a facade, you will never attract the life you really want.

You don't get in life what you want, you get in life what you are.

Just like your life is a reflection of who you are, your future will be a reflection of who you become.

Time

Time is taken for granted. Many don't value time.

When you think or feel like you have an overabundance of something you tend to use a lot of it, not thinking it will ever run out.

It's only when you start to run out of something that you value it more and start using it more carefully.

There will someday be a final year.

There will someday be a final week.

There will someday be a final day.

There will someday be a final hour.

There will someday be a final minute.

There will someday be a final second.

People waste time like it'll never run out.

We are all present in a specific time span. Think of those that came before you and those that will be here when you're gone.
Soon we will all be washed away. Life will go on without us.

Don't live and die not knowing what could've happened.

What could've happened had you took the risk, had you made the move, had you took the action, had you spoke the words, had you went for it, had you not been afraid, had you not cared what other people thought, had you stood up to life, had you did what was best for you, had you followed your heart, had you not doubted yourself, had you not talked yourself out of it again and again.

When faced with death, you see, you really don't have anything to lose.

See... you thought you had time.

Dumbing Down

Don't ever dumb yourself down. Make people come up and get it.

Make people rise to reach to your standards. Don't lower your standards to accommodate someone's shortcomings.

Demand more from your life and from people and don't apologize for it.

You generally get what you expect. What you allow will continue.

Know the difference between what you're getting and what you deserve.

With people, demand assets, leave liabilities behind.

Vibe so high, toxic people get confused and don't even know how to approach you.

You are the common denominator of the few people closest to you on a regular basis. Divide and conquer.

Valuable items cost what they cost, there's never a discount. Don't put yourself on sale in the bargain basement.

When you become the highest and best version of who you are, everything in your life will fall into place.

Stop trying to fit in. Create your unique, authentic identity.

Your life will become a direct reflection of who you are. Become extraordinary.

Brutal

Most of us are unaware that our inner conversations dictate the circumstances of our life.

My self-talk is brutal.

Brutally honest.

I NEVER let myself off the hook.

I never lie to myself.

I never tell myself something is ok when it's not.

Everything in your life that's not quite where you want it to be is directly linked to the story in your head about every aspect of your life.

YOU dictate that story, no one else.

Hold yourself accountable, accept no excuses, and be your toughest critic.

Forget where you came from, it doesn't matter. That story is over. This chapter is about where you're going. Is your self-talk brutal?

Let Them Go

If someone can walk away from you, let them go.

Don't beg people to stay in your life, be your friend, love you, care about you, or want to be with you.

When a person is really for you, they'll do all of these things without coercion, convincing, or begging.

There shouldn't be conditions to someone's interest in you.

When someone makes you an option, help them narrow down their choices by deleting yourself from the equation.

They have time, you're just not a priority.

How you allow yourself to be treated, uncared for, left behind, cheated on, used, abused, manipulated, and taken advantage of is a direct reflection of your self-worth.

When you have no self-worth, you don't believe you deserve better from people.

You devalue yourself when you chase people and allow them to walk all over you like a doormat.

Know your worth and unapologetically put people in their place. Don't be cute about it, make sure they know what's not going to be allowed or accepted.

Get rid of and delete anyone that has a blatant disregard for you, your life, and your worth. Show them the door and kick them in the ass on the way out.

Understand that how a person treats you is a reflection of who they are not a reflection of who you are.

Don't ever take it personal, it's not about you. However, leave people alone to do the pathetic things they do.

You will never find your worth in other people. You must find it within.

When you view yourself as valuable, so will the rest of the world.

Feelings

Everyone has something that if you think about it hard enough it'll make you cry.

Some experiences you just never forget.

Feelings that crushed your soul, tormented your mind, and destroyed your life and wellbeing.

The pain was so immense and the mental torture so hellish, you were sure it would never subside.

I've felt feelings that make me uneasy to even think about. Feelings that literally brought me to my knees, made me cry in the middle of a crowded night club, and led to self-harm and infliction.

My lack of understanding, confusion, and maturity caused me to blame my circumstances, my afflictions, the people in my life, and my past.

There comes a point in life where you vow that you will never feel the way you once felt ever again. I certainly did.

Something needed to change.

I didn't start by changing my spouse, where I live, my significant other, my friends, my habits, my job or career, my family ties, or my finances.

I started by changing my MIND.

I needed a new mind.

A new perspective. A new way of looking at my situation.

As long as you don't change your mind, the same experiences will perpetuate over and over.

Life is after your mind.

After your peace. After your joy. After your will. After your resolve. After your security. After your self-image. After your well-being. After your heart. After your consciousness.

If you can drive it out your head you can drive it out of your life.

Had Enough

There comes a point in a person's life when enough is enough.

Pushed far enough, beyond your threshold of tolerance, your eyes suddenly become wide open and your blindness starts to become 20/20 vision.

What are you tolerating in your health, physical appearance, intimate relationships, marriages, jobs and careers, businesses, friendships, family relationships, etc.

It's not ideal, but it's not painful or bad enough. It's tolerable, so you just leave it alone and live indecisive and miserable because it's easier than facing the truth and doing something about it.

Stop tolerating and start dominating.

It takes guts and courage to raise your standards and expectations for your life.

Your lack of belief is holding you down.

Belief in yourself, belief in what's possible for your life, and the belief that you can obtain it.

The only thing holding you back is the belief that there is something holding you back.

Lose the stories you're telling yourself as to why you can't live a better life.

Dominate your life. Today. Tomorrow. Forever.

Progress

Not everyone will be happy for you when you begin to make meaningful progress in your life.

The closer you get to excellence in your life the more people and friends you'll lose.

People prefer when you're average operating at a low level because it makes them feel comfortable in their own incapacities.

People see your success, or the fact that you're striving for success, as something they either must compete with, or something that somehow diminishes their shine or their ability to succeed.

People that aren't growing, trapped in their limited, bitter, contaminated state of mind and being, will not join you in this change. In fact they will literally think you're crazy, that you think you're better than everyone else, and that you've "changed".

When someone says "you've changed", say "thanks, I hope so!" and keep it moving.

True winners in life lift other people up and are happy to see others make progress. They don't see others successes as something to be bitter about, but something to celebrate.

They don't see others successes as something that somehow diminishes their success or ability to succeed, but as something that inspires them to be better as well.

People that don't take inspiration from successful people, or people that are at least striving for something greater will stay where they are.

GUARANTEED.

Don't worry about people that aren't happy for you, they most likely aren't happy for themselves either.

Let them go.

Even if you have to walk it alone. Let them go.

You may have to stand alone in your journey, but someday you'll stand out.

Unhappy

So you're down and out and unhappy.

Changing your life begins by changing the story in your head.

It begins by changing the meaning around your situation. Your life is a byproduct of what you're thinking. Nothing in life has any meaning except the meaning you give it.

When you change the way you look at things, the things you look at change.

You're not defeated and victimized. You're not unhappy, weak, or without control to change your life.

You've just convinced yourself you are.

Rise above, take your problems, obstacles, afflictions, heartaches, and struggles by the balls and make them understand who the hell they're dealing with.

As long as you sit around defeated and unconfident, you will never attract the better life you seek.

You don't get in life what you want, you get in life what you are.

You will never attract positive outcomes as long as you are a ball of self-defeated, victimized, negativity and doubt.

You're only held down or stuck where you allow yourself to be.

You need an insufferable belief that you are greater than your circumstances. You need to believe that no circumstance or person is going to hold you down.

Taking your life back is fully in your control as soon as you want to stop feeling sorry for yourself and accept it.

Stop playing the blame game.

Are you really going to sit around dormant and stagnant because of what someone said about you or did that made you believe you are somehow less of a human being or not worthy or capable of living an extraordinary life?

Screw them. They don't own your life.

You define you. You create your reality. You can't change what happened, what someone said, or what someone did, but you can change the direction your life is headed.

So you're down and out and unhappy?

Good, the stage is set for greatness.

Go and take it.

Appearances

Don't judge a book by its cover.

Sometimes the container is better than the contents.

Many advertise product they don't carry in their inventory.

You can be a cover model but have a character and personality that's rotten to the core.

I've been involved with people that are seemingly the sweetest most sincere human beings, but will lie and cheat then tuck you in and kiss you good night.

There are people that look raggedy and drive a beat up used car with more money than they know what to do with.

Picture perfect house, spouse, and kids. House is two payments behind, you're not in love anymore, and it's a struggle to even walk back in the house.

All the money in the world, "ballin", and absolutely miserable.

Big office, big desk, big name plate, big salary, big shot. Little fulfillment and real happiness.

People with handicaps or chronic illnesses that have the strongest hearts, minds, and spirits you'll ever encounter.

People that look bold, rugged, and rough around the edges, but are the kindest hearted people on the planet.

Some appear to be happy and live the perfect life on Instagram and Facebook but never post the bombs that are going off in their head.

Best friends and people that are seemingly for you that will rob you blind and slip a knife in your back.

There are many that possess such a big mouth with a big and bad persona, but are scared of their own shadow and weak in spirit.

There's many that are quiet, reserved, and sometimes unnoticeable but have the strength and spirit of a lion.

You don't always see what you get. You never really know someone like you think you do. Get the facts and judge people accordingly.

Uninspired

Weak and uninspired people always say something is "easier said than done" or "it's not that simple."

Follow the same people around for 24 hours and watch their actions. Identify their priorities. Examine their level of effort.

It's simple really. What you put in is what you get out.

Big in. Big out.

You can control your actions, priorities, and effort. They define what you are and what you will be.

So next time you think something is easier said than done, just step aside and think it.

You're in the way of the people that are doing it.

Ears

The biggest most profound fight you'll ever have is the fight in between your own two ears.

When it really comes down to it, it's a fight you must fight alone.

When you've come out of a battle with yourself and survived, you walk with a different kind of step.

You see with a different kind of vision.

You live with a different kind of confidence.

See, no one really knows the depth to which you had to fight to be where you are, or to be who you are today.

When you've fought a tough fight and overcame tremendous adversity you just really don't care what other people think.

When you've climbed out of hell and created a life that you battled for internally and externally there's not much that can shake you.

You develop a deep trust, love, and respect for yourself that no one can penetrate or break down.

People can say what they want, criticize how they want, and judge how they want, but who cares.

You've earned your stripes and wear them boldly and proudly.

They don't understand the feelings you've felt, the things you've experienced, or the turmoil you've endured.

If people knew the depth of the fight, they would understand why you're so fierce in protecting the gates to your world of sunshine and prosperity.

Only magical shit has the right to enter.

Defining Moment

Everyone that ever makes a drastic life altering change has a defining moment.

A critical moment of disgust and distaste towards that thing that you're about to change. "I refuse to be treated like this anymore."

"I hate this job."

"I'm done with being out of shape."

"I'm sick and tired of being sick and tired."

"I don't want to do this anymore."

"I'm done settling."

"There's more to life than this."

"I refuse to feel like this anymore."

"I deserve better than this relationship."

"This company doesn't appreciate me."

"I've had enough, I'm done."

Change occurs when you view your current life, situation, and set of circumstances as such misery that something breaks.

Change goes from a should to a must.

You will get what you HAVE TO HAVE.

You will get what you want when it's not just a passive thought, but an obsession.

When you become fed up and your need for change becomes a MUST HAVE OBSESSION, you will have it.

There's nothing that can stop a determined heart and soul that seeks change.

Decide, commit, and change your life.

Be obsessed or remain the same.

Inaction

What's the real reason many don't take action to change their lives?

The unfortunate truth is, when you really get down to it, it's because of other people.

Many live other people's ideas of what their life ought to be. Your thoughts aren't your thoughts and your life isn't your life.

There's too much invested in your current life.

The roots run too deep.

Afraid of being a "sell out" to your company or group of friends.

Afraid of letting your family down doing something outside of what they consider "success" to be.

More committed to the "we" of your environment than what's best for you.

Afraid of the endless criticisms and backlash you'll receive because everyone else knows what's best for your life.

Can't let the family down!

What will everyone think if you get a divorce or break up your relationship?

So, you dumb yourself down to fit in so your sociological needs are met, so everyone likes you, and so everyone approves of your life.

Put a smile on and no one knows your soul is twisted and there's bombs going off in your head.

You live in a constant state of inner conflict and quiet desperation. Aren't you meant for more?

<u>Standards</u>

Raise your standards.

Everything in your life is a depiction of the standards you hold.
A persons standards says a whole lot about them.

Raising your standards takes courage and hard work to maintain.

You'll lose people that can't elevate themselves to meet higher standards.

This is why so many settle for lower standards than they really desire.

Many don't even have standards.

They're unhealthy and out of shape.

Date and have sex with whoever is available to avoid being alone.

Always look a mess.

Live in squalor.

Never try to educate themselves.

Keep loser friends.

Get married and have kids because the biological clock is ticking.

Consistently operate below their potential in everything they do just to get by.

Talk and act "cool" like an idiot.

Show me your standards and I'll show you your life.

Your life is far less than what it could be because you're not demanding more.

Success is always on purpose and intentional.

You get what you expect. Nothing more, nothing less.

Driven

When you're driven whatever lies in front of you will get destroyed.

See there's a difference between kind of wanting something and being driven to want it.

Most people have their brakes on. What if you fail? What if you look stupid? What if you put all this work in and you don't succeed?

Problem is you lack belief. Obtaining what you want in life is easy. Convincing yourself you can obtain it is hard.

You talk yourself out of more things than anyone else ever will. The hardest person in the world to convince is yourself.

And when your belief becomes a conviction, there's absolutely nothing that will stand in your way.

A person that is driven to obtain something, backed by an insufferable conviction that they can obtain it, is a person that can and will have whatever the hell they want in life.

It might not happen quickly. It might require months or years of dedication. It might make other people think you're crazy. It might require you to go to hell and back.

But it will be damn worth it.

If you want to be an anomaly, then you need to start acting like one.

Expectations

You can't expect from other people what you don't even expect from yourself.

We spend so much time analyzing and figuring other people out, envying other people, looking for love and respect from other people, and looking to other people to fill a void.

What about you? You're a person?

Figure you out, analyze you, look in the mirror for love and respect, and envy yourself.

Look in the mirror to fill a void.

So many people come and go in and out of our lives. People lack consistency.

Truth is, life is lonely business.

Many things we go through we must ultimately suffer it alone, within, in our own hearts and minds.
No one can save you but you. No one can make it better but you. No one can overcome or ease pain, heartache, turmoil, struggle, and depression but you.

Be good to yourself. Take care of yourself. Love and respect yourself.

The one person that will always be consistent, be there for you, never let you down, build you up, encourage you, and love you, is you.

You have a long life to live with that one person who will always be there, looking back at you in the mirror every day, pleading for you to open your eyes and love them back.

That person is you.

Memory

What will you be remembered as?

Many of us never really stop to think about it.

I want to be remembered as the underdog that never lost hope.

The person that went left when the majority took a right.

A person whose dogged determination build an empire.

A success story that was never supposed to happen until I willed it into existence.

A victor in the battle of life that overcame the odds and became what no one would've ever expected me to be.

A beautiful, well rounded person despite the uneducated, tiny opinions of tiny people that thought they knew me.

A person that took the deepest, most profound feelings of turmoil, hopelessness, fear, and heartache, packaged it up, and delivered a life of massive success.

A person that lived on his own terms, built the life HE wanted, and made no apology for it. A person whose actions backed up the words coming out of his mouth.

A person that didn't live like a puppet on a string. Shackled and chained by no person or entity. A free thinker, mentally independent. Owner of his own thoughts.

A success, regardless of where he came from, who left him, who hurt him, who lied to him, and who walked all over him like a useless doormat.

A person that lived in a higher state of consciousness, a free spirit, unmoved by the chatter of insignificant people.

A person that took the chances, risked everything, sacrificed greatly, and won.

A person that helped others realize that they don't have to be defined by what people think and say, they can be defined by what they think and say about themselves.

You're writing the story of your life every day, make sure it's worth reading.

Tested

You never really know how strong you are until you've been tested. Until you've been tried.

Devastation and heartache can ignite a fire in you that you never knew could burn.

Your lowest lows can bring you to your highest highs.

It's easy to be happy and optimistic when everything is going right.

It's when all hell is breaking loose and there's no evidence of any light at the end of the tunnel is where the magic happens.

It's the down moments that create the warrior. When fighting is the only option you have, you get a taste of just how strong you can be.

It's in the dark places that great spirits grow.

You need a good fall to know where you stand.

It's not allowing the chaos around you determine the conqueror within you.

When you're battle tested you're dangerous.

Life can try you, test you, and take its best shot.
You've been there, you've done that, you've gotten back up again and again, torn, tattered, and still standing.

Nothing can diminish the shine of a diesel spirit that has been tested.

Thank you. Thank you for the down moments. The tests.

I discovered strength I never knew I had.

See, if you can take it, you can make it.

Opinions

Everybody has one.

Someone's opinion doesn't have to be your reality.

Too many people have opinions about things they know nothing about.

Interestingly many opinions are rooted and shaped around that individual's view of the world.

Their perspectives, beliefs, and views projected onto you.

If you shape yourself around their opinion, you're life and circumstances will miraculously look just like theirs.

In a lot of cases, that's a scary thought.

If you wouldn't trade places with someone why would you take their opinion?

The vast majority would be better off being opinionated about themselves or their own life.
My life and mentality is a mess, but hey, here's my opinion about yours.

Relying too much on other people's opinions can greatly stunt and inhibit you.

Value your own opinion over the opinion of people that think they know more about what you should say and do, or who you should be.

Opinionated people make gross misjudgments. Let them misunderstand and judge you based on what they think they know about you.
Those that have time to opinionate and judge you or your life have lost focus on their own life.

It takes all my time to mind my own business. Mind my own life. You shouldn't have time or the mental energy to delve into someone else's life.

People know your name and what you've done, but don't know your story or what you've been through.

So, take opinions with a grain of salt. The ONLY opinion that matters is the opinion you have of yourself.

Courage

It's radically courageous to walk by faith and not by sight.

Blind faith, a trust in the process, that with extreme commitment and sacrifice you can and will overcome.

You keep picking up the pieces even though you can't see how they'll fit back together.

You can't see the whole staircase but you still take the first step.

No complete blueprint of how it's going to work out but you just keep building.

Without all the proper ingredients in the recipe you still imagine the taste of victory.

No answers, but you keep asking the questions.

You've fallen to your knees but your spirit won't stop standing.

Every part of your being wants to stop, but you just keep starting.

Everything around you is falling apart but you just keep putting it back together.

Your faith may be blind, but you can see something no one else can see.

There's a light at the end of that tunnel of darkness. You can't see your hand in front of your face, you're bumping into things, and you're scared to death.

But it doesn't matter, you're walking by faith, not by sight.

Gift of Life

The best definition I've been able to find for a miracle is an extraordinary event manifesting divine intervention in human affairs.

I truly feel there has been divine intervention in my life.

A distinct moment I will remember forever that woke something lying dormant inside me.

A lifeline that picked me up off my knees, dried my tears, gave me the information I so desperately needed to live a better life, led me in the right direction.

I began seeing signs on a regular basis of the universe working in my favor.

My life could have and should have taken a very different path.

I believe life itself is a miracle. I didn't always see it that way which is why I wasted it, abused it, and allowed people to control it and walk all over it.

Too many take it for granted just as I did for a good portion of my life.

In the bible, Jesus says he came so that you may have life, and live it more abundantly.

Whatever you believe, whatever your religion, wake up and know that life isn't something to waste.

As you go blindly through the motions of Christmas, remember the real gift given to you has nothing to do with the expensive material items under your tree.

Not a new watch, or a pretty necklace, or a gift card to your favorite store.

The real gift given to you is your life.

A gift that keeps on giving every single day.

Don't waste another single day of it.

Truth

When a person lives in truth it irritates people.

To people living a lie, truth is a bitter pill to swallow.

Truth is a threat to the beautifully crafted illusions they've created.

When you live in truth, people living a lie look at you like you're the crazy one.

Like you've lost your mind and belong in a mental institution.

There's something wrong with anything that contradicts their delusions.

People living in truth don't care they have nothing to hide. People living a lie need to cover up their life, handing out blindfolds.

If you're disgusted by those that are living lies there's a solution that will surely eradicate them from your life.

Start speaking and living 100% complete truth.

They'll go running for the hills.

It's like a vampire seeing the sunlight.

So if you're one of the rarest breed of human, someone that speaks and lives truth, congratulations.

You've escaped the shameful life of slavery living lies creates.

You're not the crazy one, you know the truth, and the truth has set you free.

Sorry Not Sorry

Did you ever have to forgive someone that wasn't even sorry?

A person that did you so wrong and acted like it was nothing at all?

That is the definition of strength.

You forgave them for you, not for them.

You forgave them because it costs too much not to.

You forgave because bitterness and animosity does more harm to your soul than revenge or payback ever would.

You forgave because you have love and respect for you and your life, even though they didn't.

You forgave because you refused to be defined by what someone did to you. You understand it was a definition of their character, not yours.

You forgave because you will not let what's on the outside contaminate what's on the inside.

You forgave because your future depends on it. The best revenge is massive success. You're going to make the rest of your life the best of your life.

You forgave because you're truly grateful for the life lesson, in that you would've never known how strong you were until you had to accept an apology you never received, and forgive someone that wasn't even sorry.

Get Real

I'm a realist to my core. I don't see the world for how I wish it to be or how it ideally should be, but for how it is.

I've come up from where I've been, accomplished what I've been able to accomplish in my life, and haven't even scratched the surface because I'm not stuck on stupid.

It was, and continues to be because of the positivity and good of people around me, an extremely positive outlook and mindset, and an indomitable will.

You can't find another person more positive and optimistic than me.

However, here's the real truth.

Your perception of people, and the world we live in, is a direct reflection of just how far down the rabbit hole you've been.

Your experiences, or lack thereof, where you've come from, what you've seen all shape your perceptions and views.

The world can be a very tough and unforgiving place. Life will body slam you and beat you into submission. People will use you, manipulate you, take advantage of you, and hurt you. The unfortunate truth is bad things happen to good people.

To believe all people are good, no one will ever hurt you, and we all just live in a world frolicking around sniffing daisies, admiring rainbows, and playing with butterflies is a cute and fluffy notion, but far from reality.

Pain, friction, trauma, extreme struggle, and heartache wisen you up. They knock you out of your stupor.

I'm talking about the on your knees begging and pleading kind of pain, friction, trauma, extreme struggle, and heartache.

The hopeless, distraught, unnerving kind of turmoil life can deliver.

Those that have been there know what I'm talking about.

Does this mean, you walk around a ball of negativity, full of hate, thinking there's no good in the world, thinking everyone is bad and out to get you, thinking no one or nothing good will ever come into your life, and thinking you always have to be on defense?

Absolutely not.

But when the harsh realities of life surface, and they will...bring it, I'm ready.

Are you?

Doors

Be thankful for closed doors in your life.

Every door that closes does so for a reason.

Closed doors force us out of where we don't belong. They force us to give up what's not meant for us. They force us to move in a different direction.

When a door slams and locks shut, many just won't accept it and let go. Many try to bang on the door to be let in again. Some try to pick the locks. Some even are able to jar it back open a bit to peek in only to be reminded why it was shut in the first place.

Behind that door was a place you felt comfortable. What was behind that door gave your life normalcy and some sort of stability.

Life made sense behind that door.

Your whole world was behind that door.

Some never move on, just living right outside of the closed door, looking, wondering, upset, bitter, and miserable.

When enough doors close on you in your life, it's easy to just give up completely.

Whether you realize it or not we all have a set of keys within us that will open other doors in our lives.

The bravest and boldest among us, those that refuse to be denied, simply install and create new doors in their lives.

The longer you wait to start trying your set of keys on other doors, you will forever be stuck.

It may take many attempts, putting your keys in different locks, but eventually one will open.

You'll never know until you start trying.

It's when new doors open and you see what's waiting for you behind it that you understand why some had to close. See it's not the closed door that is the problem. It is your closed mind.

Resolution

New Year resolution... get a new mind.

Don't take an old mind into a new year.

If you continue to think the way you've always thought, you will get what you've always gotten.

You are only confined by the walls you mentally create around yourself.

Your soul and spirit suffers when every single day looks exactly like the day before.

How predictable is your life?

All growth occurs outside of your comfort zone.

Give up the label or definition that you or others have attached to who you are or how your life should be lived.

Don't settle for that which is comfortable, life is an equal opportunity experience, you get to create what you want to become.

In order to create what you want to become, you need to get comfortable being uncomfortable.

Leave a known hell to step into an unknown heaven. Step out into the unknown and do something new.

Give up familiar and get unfamiliar. Don't keep the peace, get unpeaceful.

Shake things up. Moves things around. Turn your whole life upside down.

Challenge your normal. Challenge the way it's always been. Challenge the way you've always thought.

Challenge others that are defining you in a certain way. Own your life.

When you change the way you look at things, the things you look at change.

Don't pull off the highway of life and park, sitting idle watching the world pass you by. Come down off the nose bleed section of the bleachers and get in the game of life.

Change your story. Choose to live by a different narrative. Begin to change the definition of who you are and what you're doing with your life.

You think there's always tomorrow, or next week, or next month, or next year.

The clock is ticking on your life experience.

Time waits for no one. There's no pause or rewind button on life.

Wake up.

Get Tired

Screw this. I got tired.

You gotta get tired of watching other people just like you walk through doors while you just sit there and stare.

You gotta get tired of fake friends that can't support you in public because of what they've said about you in private.

You gotta get tired of your own piss poor attitude and constant negativity.

You gotta get tired of eating dirt and accepting failure as a way of life.

You gotta get tired of the limited, self-defeating story you keep telling yourself as to why you can't get in life what you want.

You gotta get tired of the advice from people that don't know what they're doing either.

You gotta get tired of people asking you how you're doing but keep walking and don't wait for an answer.

You gotta get tired of fake people talking negatively about others then posting pics of themselves with their arm around those same people, smiling like they're friends.

You gotta get tired of being an option and not a priority.

You gotta get tired of not wanting to go home to your husband or wife.

You gotta get tired of your monotonous predictable routine you call life, living the same day for 70 years and calling it a life.

You gotta get tired of people throwing the word love around with no substance or commitment behind it.

You gotta get tired of being what your friends, family, and job want you to be and become your authentic self.

You gotta get tired of the image that stares back at you in the mirror.

You gotta get tired of settling, knowing full well what you deserve.
You gotta get tired of the wealthy facade of keeping up with the Joneses.

You gotta get tired of being insecure and jumping from relationship to relationship.

You gotta get tired of being sick and tired.

When you get tired, you MUST live different.

Stop making excuses for yourself, your life, and the people in your life.

You gotta get tired.

Emergence

In order to emerge where you're going you have to disrupt where you've been and what you've thought.

You have to disrupt your normal, your peace, and your comfort.

Emergence takes guts.

Emergence into the manifestation of a new you and a new life will require you to challenge and reconsider your current beliefs, philosophies, and perspectives.

Complete metanoia. A transformative change of heart and mind.

Not just a passive, maybe change of mind, but a radical, disruptive change of mind.

A change of mind that disrupts your soul.

A change of mind that pushes you to question everything you ever thought you knew about yourself, your life, people, and the world we live in.

A change of mind that turns old beliefs into new, fresh convictions.

A disruption that causes a sense of unease inside.

A beautiful unease.

It becomes so quiet in your head you can hear a pin drop.

People you used to know and things you used to enjoy no longer interest you or serve you.

A higher state of consciousness that pulls you away from the normal, typical society.

You're woke.

You're free.

You've gained vision in your third eye after a lifetime of blindness.

You've emerged, gladly leaving the world as you once knew it behind.

Right and Left

Two completely different people. Two completely different minds.

Guy on the left, conformity. Guy on the right, freedom.

Guy on the left, fake, a fraud. Guy on the right, authentic, what you see is what you get.

Guy on the left, smiling on the outside, screaming on the inside. Guy on the right, not smiling on the outside, jumping for joy on the inside.

Guy on the left, concerned about fitting in with certain people. Guy on the right, not concerned about who likes him, rather if he likes them.

Guy on the left, asleep and completely controlled by his subconscious mind. Guy on the right, conscious mind dominating his life.

Guy on the left, quiet desperation. Guy on the right, load roar.

Guy on the left, a product of the shit advice given to him by all the people that surrounded him. Guy on the right, a product of the superb advice he sought out himself.

Guy on the left, prim and proper as required. Guy on the right, prim and proper however the hell he wants.

Guy on the left, a prisoner in every aspect of his life, career, marriage, finances, you name it. Guy on the right, a free warrior living life on his terms, manifesting abundance in every aspect of his life.

Guy on the left, successful appearance, fully loaded brand new vehicle, six figure income, and nice condo. Guy on the right, gave it all up, took several steps back to take giant leaps forward, delaying gratification.

Guy on the left, living a life designed by others expectations and agendas. Guy on the right, living a life he created and really wants.

We all have the ability to completely change our stories of who we are and where our life is going.

It's your life. Claim it before your time runs out.

Unliked

If everyone likes you, you're not doing it right.

The unfortunate truth is that some people will like you and some people won't.

Albert Einstein said, "Great spirits have always encountered violent opposition from mediocre minds."

No matter what you say or what you do, there are some people that are just going to have an issue with it and with you.

You can be the most beautiful, kind hearted, giving, and hard working person on the planet and there will be someone, somewhere, for some reason, that will not like you or take issue with you.

Not everyone will always like what you have to say, what you believe, your views, your perspectives, the decisions you make, how you live your life, or how you see the world.

It's perfectly OK.

If you want to avoid criticism, say nothing, do nothing, and be nothing.

Some develop perspectives and viewpoints based on limited facts, massive assumptions, and are so incredibly closed minded it's impossible to engage in a productive conversation with them.

People always and only see things from their level of perspective.
In some cases that level is very limited and small.

When you realize that, you simply just stop explaining yourself and let people believe what they want to believe.

Those that even have the time to delve into, or negatively criticize your life have lost focus and vision on their own.

Let them criticize the you they think they know, not everyone deserves to know the real you.

Never dumb yourself down, dilute your personality, or dull your shine to accommodate those that don't like you.

Remember, don't lose sleep over people that don't like you.

They most definitely don't like themselves either.

Say a prayer for them, after all, they need it.

After Your Mind

Life is after your mind.

If life can tie up your head, life will surely hold you down.

It's not what happens in life, it's how you process in your head what happens in life.

Life is out to worry you to death, make you doubt yourself, and make you want to give up.

The warfare is in your head.

Life doesn't have to physically tie you up to be bound, life just needs to tie up your head.

Tie up your head with low self-esteem, worry, and self-doubt.

You can have a healthy heart and body but be sick in your head.

You can have a high IQ and score high on your SAT test and go home not being able to cope with life.

You can be big and strong with 20" biceps and be an emotional train wreck. The fight you have to fight is in your head.

Happiness, freedom, self-respect, and peace all begin in the mind.

Don't worry about changing your job, your address, your spouse, your significant other, or your friends.

First start by changing your mind.

What's in your head will be what's in your life. Fix the mind and the rest will follow.

Test Days

We all have our days.

Days you feel off. Days you don't feel very shiny. Days you feel down.

Test days I like to call them. Anyone can be happy, inspired, confident, and motivated on days you feel great and everything seems to be going your way.

It's the test days that really define our trajectory in life.

Days you discover not how bad life is, but how strongly you've been created.

Having a bad day tests your resolve or lack thereof. How you come out of and ultimately handle these days, again and again, will make or break you.

Bad days are not a sign of weakness because they are when you're fighting your hardest. Bad days are when you're really building your strength. Bad days are when you're growing mentally.

You will have them. No one is exempt. You're not going to feel good every day. Accept that fact, it's just a part of life.

You have to take the good days with the bad.

Some days it's like your heart and your mind are barely hanging on the edge of a cliff.

It's about not creating a permanent place to stay in that spirit and mindset.

It's about your resolve.

You've gotten through all of the bad days you've ever had in your life and survived. You've made it this far.

This too shall pass.

Tomorrow is a new day. A new opportunity.

Some days will just be better than others, but don't quit. Fight back.

You've just got to fight the bad days to earn some of the best days of your life.

A bad day doesn't mean a bad life. A bad day only lasts 24 hours.

Let the bad days go and resolve that tomorrow you will greet the new sun with confidence that this new day will be the best day of your life.

Cheaters

The reality of life is some people aren't meant to be together in a relationship or should have never gotten married in the first place.

Sometimes, you realize you're two different people, just have different values, you grow apart, and you're just two perfectly imperfect humans.

All fine and good. That's life, nothing at all wrong with that.

Normal, sane, and stand up human beings come to terms with and accept these facts, respectfully dissolving, dealing with, and leaving their current relationship to move on. They reflect, and eventually start a new relationship more suitable for them.

Unfortunately there are those that take a different route.

You know, someone that likes to text even when you're lying in bed right next to them.

Getting a side piece and living a double life is never a proper course of action.

Seems like a simple enough concept, however there are many that don't seem to grasp it.

As a victim of adultery, I know first-hand how sick, manipulative, and absolutely twisted those that are unfaithful can be.

Infidelity isn't a lack of love, it's a lack of respect for another human beings life.

No person has the right to manipulate and walk all over another person's life in such a way.

You may think, "What's wrong with me?" and "how could they do this to me?"

Know that there's nothing wrong with you.

It's always about them. You may not have been perfect, you may have made some mistakes, you both may not belong together, but know this, and you did nothing to cause or deserve it.

Don't internalize someone's pathetic behavior.

Cheating is a choice made by something missing in them, not you. It's never a mistake, it's a decision.

A person that can look you in your face, be lying through their teeth, then happily smile and sleep like a baby is twisted.

Finding out the truth, and finally losing a person like this is not something to cry about, it's a blessing to your life.

You will be better for it, they will not.

They weren't stolen from you.

Know that they weren't valuable to you or your life anyhow.

As they say, one person's trash is another person's treasure.

What Would Life Look Like?

What would your life look like if you didn't care what other people think?

What would you attempt to do if you were guaranteed not to fail?

How many more chances would you take if you knew you only had a limited time left to live?

What would you attempt to do if you weren't afraid?

These questions will haunt you later in life when it's too late to ask them.

When it's too late to realize the only thoughts that matter are your own.

When it's too late to take that chance or make that attempt.

Life doesn't wait for you to grow up, or become ready, or get out of your own way.

The days, weeks, and years pass quietly, unnoticeably.

Regret later in life will be all that remains from a life not fully lived.

Look at the thing everyone's telling you not to do. Ponder the chance or attempt at something you've been putting off. Pinpoint exactly what you're afraid of.

Then just do it.

One shot. One at bat. One chance at this game.

No do over. No rewind button. No second chance. No time to waste.

Better make the most of it.

LIFE IS HAPPENING NOW.

What do you intend to do with it?

So I ask you, what would your life really look like?

Depressed

I believe depression is a manifestation of life's experiences.

A final destination of sorts, where the happenings of life culminate into a tragic self-fulfilling prophecy of turmoil and despair.

I've been there, I've contemplated the point of living, and I've drowned in the deep sea of depression.

I've sat still for hours, dazed, confused, staring, lifeless, motionless, and careless.
My contaminated mind drove abusive and hateful behavior towards myself and my own life.

You didn't believe you were worthless, ugly, unlovable, stupid, incapable, and limited until the world told you.

The purity and uncontaminated innocence we have as children is a beautiful concept.

As children, we have no life experiences, are trusting, and expect the best in people. We are always active with imagination, playfulness, and curiosity.

We develop big dreams and aspirations, never thinking they're not possible or that we can't achieve them.

We don't know enough to understand that we actually get to choose our own perspectives, beliefs, values, and attitudes about life.

What the world shows us and demonstrates to us is our reality, our truths.

Life gets its hands on you and molds you like clay.

As adults we lose our sense of purity and innocence.

Don't let life or the world make you change your name.

Adulthood is a complicated process of learning and unlearning many of the things you know to be true about life and about yourself.

A boat doesn't sink from being inside the water. A boat sinks because of the water that gets inside of it.
What's gotten inside of you?

Break free from the clenched grip life has on your mentality, on your views of the world, and on your beliefs about what's possible for you, your life, and yourself.

Don't shape yourself around the comings and goings of the world.

Put away childish things and decide who you're going to be and how you're going to think.

Life is one big delivery room.

You're constantly being birthed from one stage to another. Each stage you come out a different person with new experiences and new beliefs.
Become reborn into the you that you know you want to be, you need to be, and that you're destined to be.

Let today be your new birthday.

Let today be the celebration of a soul that has consciously chosen to recapture its purity and innocence.

Let today be the beginning of a new path and a new mindset chosen by you. Molded by you.

Go back, coddle, and show the child you once were that you've become the man or woman he or she really wanted you to be.

You were never supposed to be depressed and hopeless in life. You were born to shine.
As soon as you start looking at life as the gift it truly is, it will become one.

Self-Respect

You've got to earn the right to respect yourself.

Self-respect is not just given to anyone.

Self-respect comes from making the hard decisions in life.

It comes from choosing not to take the easy way out.

It comes from chasing your full potential, not settling back into a life of comfort.

It comes from facing yourself, not liking what you see, and doing something about it.

Self-respect comes from how you treat other people.

Self-respect is reserved for those that take the chances in life no one else wants to take.

Becoming someone you're proud of. Becoming someone of value. Becoming someone of strict principal.

Self-respect is granted to those that stand up to their demons and force them into submission.
Self-respect is merited based on how you stand up to life. How you overcome and rise above.

Self-respect is obtained through how you allow people to treat you, use you, and manipulate you.

Self-respect is given to the man or woman not concerned with fitting in, choosing their personality and their life.

Self-respect comes to those that demand and expect it from life.

Self-respect is a choice that takes guts.

Take a long hard look at yourself.

Are you earning self-respect?

Calluses

A callus is a thickened and hardened part of the skin created by friction.

Callus your mind like you callus your skin.

Life throws a whole lot at you.

Build a mind that can handle whatever life throws at it.

It doesn't matter what life throws at you when you have a mind that can withstand things, and has a high tolerance and threshold for pain.

There are people dealing with your same issues and problems with ease.

They handle the same problems with ease because they are psychologically and mentally fit for the fight.

Life is no match for a mindset that is well equipped.

Weakness in your head transfers and manifests into weakness in your life experiences.

Build a mentality that dominates your thoughts.

If you don't dominate your thoughts they will dominate you.

Strength of mind is built like a muscle. It must be developed through friction, through struggle, through pain.

People become too domesticated, tame, comfortable, and avoid struggle. They avoid pain.

Create friction, struggle, and pain. Force it.

Weakness is a choice. Choose strength.

Life will exploit your weakness and use you, hold you down, and beat you into submission.

But only if you let.

Self-Discipline

Anybody that knows me well will tell you I have an extraordinary ability to implement focus and extreme self-discipline into my life, much of which I developed through competitive bodybuilding.

They're literally like my super powers, and two very important reasons I've been able to bounce back again and again, break bad habits, and come up out of a rut.

There's a highest and best version of each and every one of us.

Maximizing your full potential is a habit of setting your standards for yourself high and consistently raising that bar.

It's up to you to set that bar for yourself.

Many set the bar so low they can easily just step over it with little to no effort.

How you do one thing is how you do everything.

If you have any fraction of an ability to not want to do something, and still do it, watch how much progress you make in all facets of your life.

In your fitness, health, career, finances, relationships, it doesn't matter.

You always get what you expect.

You can't tip toe through life. Make demands on your life and yourself.

Strive to become the best you that you can possibly be.

Your life is always a reflection of the height of that bar. You can't grasp anything you're not reaching for.

Your life becomes better when you become better. Your life becomes better when you feel better about yourself.

Those that develop the ability to dominate their mind, body, and spirit develop the ability to dominate their life.

Stop simply coping with life. Start dominating. Dominate yourself.

<u>Too Late</u>

Some things are just too little, too late.

Too late, too limited, too scarce, too inadequate, too insufficient to be effective.

You want to be a mom or dad now, the children are grown, they don't need you to buy them a tricycle now, I'm sorry it's just too little too late.

I know you've had a revelation and want to be a better husband or wife, it's over, I'm sorry it's just too little too late.

I know you've got a little bit to pay, the bills are too far behind, a day late and a dollar short, you've got to be shut down, it's just too little too late.

I know you're here to help now, you were supposed to be a friend, where were you when you were really needed, I'm sorry it's just too little too late.

I know you're sorry and want to fix things, it'll never happen again, you've learned your lesson...I'm sorry the damage has been done, it's just too little too late.

Opportunity of a lifetime, should've jumped on it while you had the chance, one day it's here, the next day it's gone, unfortunately now it's just too little too late.

You now value diet, exercise, and self-care, unfortunately the deterioration in your health is too deep, I'm sorry it's just too little too late.

Your minor problem has turned into a catastrophic situation, it can't be saved now, you should've taken more action when it was minor, I'm sorry it's just too little too late.

You finally know who you are, finally don't care what people think, and are ready to live the life you've always wanted, free, on your terms...

Unfortunately you've waited an entire lifetime to live a life. You're old now and don't have much time left to live.

I'm sorry it's just too little, too late.

Intentions

Success is always intentional.

You don't win an Olympic gold medal by accident.

Successful people set a target, and then succeed on purpose.

Success is a matter of cause and effect, not a matter of happenstance. There is no what if or maybe.

Success, the effect, is a product of the right actions done consistently, the cause.

Success is a reflection of who you are. It's a reflection and a measure of just how much you're willing to believe you can obtain something.

A measure of your heart and will.

It's not just given to you because you want it, or because you like it.

Success has a price tag many aren't willing to pay. It's too expensive. Many settle for what they can easily afford.

Every action has an equal and opposite reaction. Big in, big out. Little in, little out.

Behind every huge success are countless hours of blood, sweat, and tears spent privately, before you see it publicly.

Successful people can literally see the end result so clearly, so vividly, and so consistently, that it's literally thought into reality.

Success is a habit, a lifestyle, a mindset, an oath, an obsession.

You can't see what you're not looking for, can't grasp what you're not reaching for, and can't realize what you're not dreaming.

Whatever you want, whatever you're aiming for, whatever decisions and life changes you're thinking about making, whatever that thing is you need to deal with...

Don't be cute about it. Don't tip toe and tap dance around it.

Square up, clench your fists, assume the fighting position, and beat that thing into submission.

Take life on.

Go after what you want like your life depends on it.

Because it does.

Good to Great

When you're asked how things are in your life, is your response "they're good" or "they're great?"

Good is the enemy of great.

As long as things are "good", there will never be a compelling enough reason to change.

Your desire to change must exceed your desire to stay the same.

"Good" things in your life aren't painful enough, distasteful enough, or miserable enough to cause that desire.

Good is not good. Great is good.

Good is comfort. Great is uncomfortable.

Good is fear. Great is guts.

Good is an excuse. Great is being honest with yourself.

Good is settling. Great is what you really want.

Good is a lie. Great is the truth.

Good is an act. Great is authentic.

Good is a dumbing down. Great is leveling up.

Good is fake. Great is real.

Good is what you get. Great is what you really want.

Good is achievement. Great is reaching your highest potential.

Stop settling for good. Stop settling for just ok.

So, how's things in your life?

Be Quiet

There's so much noise in the world.

In order to engage in self-discovery you need to be quiet.

You've got to get quiet in your head.

Shut out the noise of other people and listen to your own voice.

Go in a room alone and sit in silence.

We spend so much time surrounded by and listening to other people and things that are demanding our attention.

The world is constantly trying to grab, dictate, and influence your thinking.

Bombarded by the news, advertisements, friends and family, significant others, companies you work for, propaganda, politics, etc.

Before you know it, and without even realizing it, your thoughts are no longer your own thoughts.

Your actions become based on what you've been brainwashed to believe.

Many people are brainwashed and don't even realize it.

Control what gets into your head. Don't allow anyone or anything to control your mind.

Force solitude and silence. Force the world out of your head.

Discover your own thoughts and let them guide you.

You will never discover who you are and what you really think when you're constantly consumed by the world around you.

Demand your own attention. Trust yourself.

Become the loudest voice you hear.

Learn to hear the sound that goes beyond the sound of the noisy world.
It's the sound of yourself.

Definition

There are some that will just always define you and see you a certain way.

It doesn't matter what you do, how you change, how better you become, or how successful you become.

Stop trying to convince people to change their mind about you. It doesn't matter how other people see you.

Success will not be based on how other people see you. Success will ultimately be based on how you see yourself.

Let people think what they want, say what they want, mock you, laugh at you, smirk, and joke so they can feel somewhat better about their existence.

Had I limited myself by what every single person thought about me I would still be weak, still be average, still be limited, still be doubtful, still be questioning myself, and still be stuck.

JUST LIKE THEM.

Break away from the pack. Leave the herd. Forget the flock.

Define yourself.

People that doubted you, spoke down on you, disrespected you, didn't believe in you, and labeled you.

Crush them every single day.

Keep rising, keep climbing, keep growing, keep winning, and keep shining.

Keep smiling.

Let success speak volumes. Don't tell the world who you are, show them.

Smash their definition of who you are into pieces with the definition you create for yourself.

Be bigger, be bolder, be wiser, be stronger, be smarter, because people that pretend to not even see you are watching. Give them something to talk about.

What If?

There's one simple question that stops many in their tracks.

"What if?"

This simple question can hold you back or help you grow.

It's all in how you choose to ask it.

What if you put in all that work and you don't succeed? Oh but what if you put in all that work and you succeed beyond your wildest dreams?

What if you trust people again and they let you down? Oh but what if you trust people again and they prove trustworthy?

What if you take another chance to love and you get your heart broken again? Oh but what if you find the love of a lifetime?

What if you invest the money and lose it all? Oh but what if you invest the money and it grows and multiplies?

What if you take the chance and it doesn't work out? Oh but what if you take the chance and you get what you're after?

What if by deciding to become better you lose some people? Oh but what if you decide to become better and doors start opening and you level up?

What if you become who you really want to be and find yourself alone? Oh but what if you become who you really want to be and attract a crowd?

What if you take the risk and fall flat on your face? Oh but what if you take the risk and you fly like an eagle?

What if you plant that seed and nothing happens? Oh but what if you plant that seed and you grow a harvest?

What if everyone's opinion is correct? Oh but what if you prove everyone wrong and prove yourself right?

What if you stopped limiting your potential by asking "what if?"
Imagine what "ifs" would exist then.

<u>Understanding</u>

People that never change don't understand people that do.

If you knew me then, you don't know me.

Unless you know me now you don't know me at all.

I'm not the same person I was 5 years ago, 1 year ago, or even 5 minutes ago.

See, I caught a glimpse of something.

When life gives you a glimpse....an opportunity to step into a higher, better situation and expression, run towards it.

Don't walk, don't stroll, don't be cute, and don't be afraid.

RUN.

When life reveals greater things, lose lesser things.

When you run towards your destiny, you automatically distance yourself from your history.

Your history doesn't have to define your destiny.

The best way to change your life is to change your life.
When you reach for something greater, you become something more, because in order to handle something greater you have to become something greater.

Those timid souls that are the same person they were 5 years ago, one year ago, or 5 minutes ago ignore the glimpses of life.

Dead set on limited possibilities based on what is and what was.

No....see, I ran.

I caught a glimpse.

<u>Right Track</u>

How do you know you're on the right track in mind and spirit?

When people tell you that you've changed.

When you start losing friends.

When you become the isolated black sheep of your family.

When you bask in solitude.

When you start questioning everything that is and ever was.

When you lose interest in fitting in.

When you genuinely don't give a damn what anyone thinks about you.

When people think you've lost your mind.

When you start demanding more from life.

When you see souls everywhere instead of faces.

When you feel out of place in places and with people that once fit like a glove.

When you're disgusted by and have zero tolerance for fake people.

When you begin to distance yourself from old habits and old ways that you have nothing in common with anymore.

When you get your sense of identity from something much deeper than social reputation and seeking approval.

When you crave the truth like an addict.

When you become consciously aware of everything.

When you never get angry anymore because you understand everyone's reasons for doing what they do.

When you refuse to allocate time or energy to anything or anyone that is not helping you grow, level up, or serving your transformation. Be different, step out, break free. Are you on the right track?

Same Places

Ever wonder how you always seem to end up in the same place over and over no matter how hard you try or how much you try to change?

You've changed everything. Everything is different, new, upgraded, and improved.

Only one thing you forgot.

There's one element to really changing your life that many overlook and flat out ignore.

If you don't change the mind, and therefore who you are, the same experiences will keep perpetuating themselves over and over.

You can change your address, your spouse, your girlfriend or boyfriend, your job or career, your friends, your hair color, your makeup, your clothes, your routine, your diet, even your name.

But if your mind doesn't change the outcome will be the same.

That relationship was toxic, you deserve better and raised your standards. New relationship, you saw the signs and ignored them, but after all, you're lonely and they're so fine.

The complications that got you fired, demoted, or kept you at a low level in your first two jobs or careers will get you fired, demoted, or keep you at a low level in the third.
You can take the person out of the ghetto, but you can't take the ghetto out of the person.

Your new spouse is way better than your old spouse. Unfortunately you are the same person in the new marriage you were in the old marriage. Good thing you kept the attorney's number.

New makeover, gorgeous on the outside. Damn you're fine! Still ugly as can be inside.

You're ready, you're leveling up, and you're getting around new groups of people. Discomfort and rejection dumb you back down to comfy status. Call your homeboy.

New year resolution, new diet, new routine. Great, problem is this is the seventh attempt and it's just one bite.

When you take an old mind into all of these new life changes, upgrades, and makeovers, you're kidding yourself.

Change your mind, change your life.

Disassociation

Disassociation is critical to elevation.

Because of the uniqueness in the thoughts you want to think and the path you want to take, you can no longer be common in your associations.

Some people only love you or have interest in you how they met you.

Unfortunately sometimes, you can't relate to people you're related to, or you love someone you don't like.

Not acting in your own best interest creates animosity towards those that are unknowingly holding you captive in places you don't really want to be, living a way you don't want to live, and dealing with circumstances you don't want to deal with.

Whenever you depend on someone else to give you what you can't give yourself, you are at the mercy of that person, which creates an inner conflict that will drive you out of your mind.

When you change, develop as a person, lose interest in certain things, or want to live a different way it creates conflict, friction, and resistance.

There will always be conflict and resistance between extraordinary thinking people and ordinary thinking people.

There's just some people you'll be forced to let go of, distance yourself from, and stand up to so you can move beyond your current circumstances into the life you have in your heart and in your head.

Never stay where you know you don't belong.

Make the tough decisions, have the uncomfortable conversations, and start acting in your own best interest or you will never be truly fulfilled. You will never be good for anyone.

If you think growth and change is painful, try staying somewhere you don't belong with relationships that don't serve you.

You have one life and it will someday reach its final hour.

It's time to go. Even if you're not sure of the destination.

It's time to go.

Competencies

Most people only want to do what they know well.

What they've developed a level of competence in. What people might know them for.

Redirection creates a discomfort and vulnerability most can't handle.

Most people's egos are so large that they stop themselves from doing new things for fear they'll look bad if they fail.

Most convince themselves something doesn't work or that it can't be done because there's no real commitment to stay the course.

They don't REALLY want to do it.

Protecting their ego and image is more important than finding success in redirection.

One foot in, one foot out, right from the start.

When it gets hard they take the back door and go back to doing something they know well. Something that's familiar and comfortable.

They go back to their default setting.

I didn't know anything about real estate when I started. It was totally unfamiliar.

I was uncomfortable and I was vulnerable.

I got taken advantage of for what I didn't know. I felt stupid at times and made plenty of dumb mistakes.

A single investment in a two family house is now a real estate company consisting of 26 properties.

I didn't quit. There was no plan B.

No safety net. No way out.

You must make a commitment in advance that you will not give in to the struggle.

Struggle is inevitable. No one is exempt.

You can completely reinvent yourself and your life at any point you make the decision.

Drop the inflated ego, you're not as important as you think you are.

The wise person knows that he or she doesn't know anything at all.

Growth cannot occur until you give up your inflated self-image.

Develop a life that just doesn't look good on the outside, but feels good on the inside.

No Response

No response is a response.

In fact, it's the most powerful response there is.

Silence can speak louder than the loudest scream.

Be grateful when someone is giving you the gift of their verbal and mental energy.

When a person pleads with you, and goes above and beyond to communicate with you, it means they care.

It means they are putting an effort into you. Whether it be to rectify a situation or a relationship.

They're trying to give you a chance.

When someone gets quiet on you...know this.

They're done. They've given up on you.

It has been determined that communication with you, and dealing with you in any way, is the equivalent of bashing their head against a brick wall.

Matter of fact, bashing their head against a brick wall is actually more enticing and probably a better use of their time and energy.

So, when you're no longer receiving a response to your ignorant, uneducated, and irrational attitude, behavior, and overall communication...

Take a look in the mirror.

Where Are You?

You're wondering why you're not further along in life than you thought you'd be?

Here's just a few reasons why that could be.

You collect liabilities not assets.

You will not sacrifice immediate short term pleasures to invest in your future, trading time for money and material items.

You value the opinion of what other people think about what you're doing with your life than your own.

You're a people pleaser and haven't mastered the fine art of saying no.

You follow the rules, are conditioned, and brainwashed by society. You'd rather fit in than stand out.

You keep up with the joneses. How you appear to your friends and family is more important than how you appear to yourself.

You keep doing what you've always done expecting a different result. An undisciplined life is an insane life.

You won't confront people and situations in your life that are holding you back.

You're taking advice from people that don't know what they're doing either.

You feed your brain garbage on a daily basis.

You let your boss and parents dictate your life.

You work 9-5 doing something you hate then "relax" after hours and on weekends.

The story in your head is an excuse you conjured up to feel better about the fact you aren't realizing your full potential.

You'd rather look successful than be successful.

You won't feel the fear and do it anyway.

You think you're smarter and more important than you really are.

You're looking for some secret or magic formula to obtain success.

You won't take personal responsibility for your circumstances, you're waiting for someone to come save you.

You over analyze everything. Better to be a hot mess of decisive action than a perfectly organized coward.

You've developed a habit of quitting everything you've tried that didn't come easy.

You suppress instead of confront each and every point made above.

<u>Who Are You?</u>

Who the hell do you think you are?

Who do you think you are thinking you can do that?

Who in the world do you think you are striving for something like that?

Like it's really going to happen?

How did you get so smart? You think you know it all?!

You think you're better than everyone else!?

Who do you think you are trying to emerge from the back and step to the forefront?

Thinking you're some kind of leader, a boss, a bad ass?

Thinking you're some kind of talented or gifted person?

Who the hell do you think you are having such high standards?

You think you're something special??!!

Please...give me a break. I mean really. Come on now. Who do think you are!?

You may be struggling to find yourself.

You may be struggling to emerge.

You may not be where you want to be in many aspects.

But I'll tell you who you're not...

You're not the person asking those questions.

Thank God for that.

The real question is...who are you not to be?

Get What You Want

So you got what you wanted.

You wished for it, begged for it, pleaded for it, and did everything in your power to get it.

You just had to have it!

Sometimes in life you get what you want, then don't want what you get.

You force your way into it...then cry to get out of it.

Sometimes when you get what you want you realize it's not really all it's cracked up to be.

A living hell can come disguised as everything you've ever wanted.

Sometimes getting all you prayed for is more of a punishment than a blessing.

It's not what it seemed. It's not exactly how you envisioned it when you were trying so hard to get it.

You get it, and don't know how to handle it, or what to do with it. It's more than you can handle. More burden than fulfillment.

The grass starts looking a lot greener on the other side of the fence.

Be careful what and whose grass you admire.

It might be grown from the same seed as the grass you tried so hard to get in the first place.

Be careful what you wish for...because you just might get it.

Obsession

Improving your life requires obsession.

A beautiful obsession.

It's an all-out campaign.

It needs to be an act of war and the battleground is your head.

Laser focus.

Water, focused into a waterjet, can cut metal and rock.

The sun's rays, focused through a magnifying glass, can create fire.

You, focused and obsessed, can move mountains and walk on water.

Not a walk in the park, but an all-out sprint.

Obsessed, not just interested.

Don't wait for life to come and get it.

Deliver it.

Commitment at the highest level, failure is not an option, results are demanded and required.

Abrasive effort.

This isn't a tap dance recital, you're a bull in a china shop.

Eyesight better than 20/20. You see the invisible.

No fancy degrees necessary, they don't teach this in a classroom, you're willing this into existence.

Life kicks you while you're down, you break its leg.

You're not going with the flow, you're creating the flow.

Most won't, but you will. Enthusiastically.

The chaos around you will not determine the conqueror within you.

No directions needed, you're paving your own way.

Life shouldn't have accepted the fight, it doesn't know your heart.

Be obsessed or be average.

Heart

Take the advice of very few people.

Many people's advice always stems from their perceived limitations.

They can't or won't do something so then you can't either right?

Wrong.

Don't allow their limitations and incapacities to become yours.

See, you're not them.

They don't understand what kind of man or woman you are.

They don't understand all you're willing to do to make that thing a reality.

They don't know your heart.

They don't know the true depth of your indomitable will to survive and succeed.

For you, it goes beyond a mere interest. This is an obsession.

There are no should do's or maybes in your world, only must do's and hell yeahs.

They don't understand you are not them. You are you.

Let them keep their excuses and believe their own incapacities.

Do the thing others say you cannot do.

Prove others wrong and prove yourself right.

Soon enough people will see what you saw all along.

What Do You See?

There are many people that look but don't see and hear but don't listen.

Changing your mind, beliefs, and outlook in your situation is a process.

It requires a dedicated commitment.

Just like anything else in life that requires focus and hard work to build and maintain, the same stands true with your mind.

What you put into your mind is what you will get out.

Try putting chocolate milk into your gas tank. Sounds funny, but that's what people do with their mentality.

What you mentally consume dictates your thoughts, beliefs, perspectives, and philosophies.

Your thoughts, beliefs, perspectives, and philosophies dictate your habits, values, and actions.

Your habits, values, and actions manifest and create your current reality. Your current life.

Over time you've developed your current state of mind and outlook.

It can be undeveloped, torn down, and rebuilt like a house.

As a man or woman thinks, so then will he or she become.

Period, end of story.

Break the Cycle

Be exceptional.

All the people in your family are dysfunctional, except you.

All your friends aren't doing anything with themselves or their lives, except you.

All your coworkers have no desire or aspiration for bigger or better things, except you.

All your acquaintances accept their lives for what it is and think they can't change it, except you.

All your siblings are stuck in defeatism and playing the victim because they can't let go of their childhood issues, except you.

Break away from the pack.

Be an exception to the rule. A trend setter. A rule breaker.

Many people let their past define how their story is going to end. Except you.

Ingredients

Success in anything really boils down to two main ingredients.

First, what are you willing to give up and sacrifice? Many like the idea of being successful, but very few really are willing to make the necessary sacrifices in time, money, and commitment.

When expressing the desire to reach a specific goal, habits and actions don't match the words that come out of most people's mouths.

It's not about what you say you'll do, it's about what you're actually doing.

A tree is judged by the fruit it bears, not by the fruit it talks about.

You can tell exactly how successful a person will be by looking at how the spend their 24 hours.

The more things you put between you and your goal, the less likely and harder it will be to obtain.

A few years of obsessive sacrifice and commitment to something with zero distractions will guarantee a catastrophic shift in that direction.

Second, you need a high tolerance and threshold for pain. How much can you withstand and still remain in the fight?

People quit when it gets hard. Period. End of story.

Road blocks, self-doubt, limiting beliefs, frustration, setbacks, obstacles, resistance from friends and family.

Everyone eventually reaches a breaking point. The point where most people pack it up and throw in the towel.

Resilience, perseverance, whatever it takes, commitment, resolve, and a never say die attitude. These are the characteristics most lack.

The characteristics of success. Who are you?

The lack of these two elements is precisely why many just aim low and set easily obtainable, average goals.

People don't fail in life because they aim too high and miss. People fail in life because they aim too low and hit.

Processing

You will forever be stuck in a rut, eating dirt, depressed, and held back until you do one very simple thing.

Change the way you process what's going on in your head.

There's a voice speaking to you every day all day. Sometimes it's loud as hell, sometimes it's a whisper you barely notice. It's always there, you can't stop it no matter how hard you try.

However, you CAN control it.

People that go on to realize great success and freedom are no different than anyone else, except in one distinct way.

They process their thoughts, feelings, and emotions differently.

If you don't get a grip on your thoughts, feelings, and emotions, they will use you.

You can literally think the life you want into existence.

Don't believe this idea?

Your beliefs become your thoughts. Thoughts become actions. Actions become habits. Habits create your values. Your values dictate you entire existence.

Think it's just not possible? Think it's easier said than done?

There lies the problem.

PROCESS DIFFERENTLY.

Too Soon

Don't quit too soon.

Keep plugging away even when there's no evidence of success.

Inch by inch, step by step, you will have traveled miles.

Small, seemingly inconsequential actions eventually lead to big results.

Whatever you want in your life, you have to stick with it long enough to see the benefit.

Massive success is a culmination of productive actions made over a long period of time.

Actions made consistently and whether you feel like it or not.

Have blind faith and keep plugging away.

Soon the small insignificant brick you laid will be a wall.

Pulled

When you're pulled to do something you don't need an alarm clock.

People are tired, unmotivated, and seek escapism because they are not inspired.

When you're working towards an abundant life of fulfillment and a worthy ideal you don't need to escape.

If you "need a break from life" it's time to stop planning your Saturday night and start planning your life.

It's time to save your money shopping or "getting lit" and invest in your future.

Monday mornings aren't the problem, it's your job that sucks.

You don't need a vacation, you need a new life.

Sacrifice a few years of your life with intense sacrifice, focus, and commitment to something, and you'll be surprised at how drastically your life can change.

When you're actively creating the life that you want, that you're passionate about, you'll have no lack of energy or motivation.

Delete distractions, throw your whole self at something you want, and live the rest of your life fulfilled.

Just Visiting

We are just visitors passing by in a moment of time. Soon our visit will run out.

Someday you will go far away from here. What will remain of your existence?

People prefer a known hell rather than an unknown heaven.

You're not always going to have all the answers and the perfect plan.

There's never going to be a right time.

When you act in spite of fear and uncertainty, walk in faith and not by site, doors just start opening. The universe conspires to make it happen.

Resolve to pay the price in advance, no matter the cost.

Big life decisions. Big life changes.

When you believe in yourself to do what is required no matter the cost, you'll make it happen.

Trust yourself. Bet on yourself.

You may not have all the answers laid out in front of you. But the one thing you do know is what you will do to see it to fruition.

You DO NOT have an unlimited amount of time. It is running out.

The only thing that's going to matter later in life are regrets.

THE THINGS YOU DIDN'T DO.

There's no rewind button on life.

Your life is happening right now as we speak. Stop wasting it.

Seconds and minutes are precious. Time is a precious commodity.

JUST DO IT ALREADY.

True Happiness

There are people that seemingly have it all, but deep down, are extremely unfulfilled and discontent.

It's hard to explain at times. It's just a nagging feeling that something isn't right or is "missing."

There are a lot of elements to life that certainly help in the pursuit of happiness.

Elements that are like the fruit on a tree. Everyone loves the fruit and wants the fruit. The roots are way more important. Nobody wants to focus on the roots.

Where there are no healthy roots, there is no fruit.

People can't make you happy.

All the friends in the world can't make you happy.

A trophy spouse or significant other can't make you happy.

Shopping and material objects can't make you happy.

Sex can't make you happy.

Money can't make you happy.

High career status can't make you happy.

Vacations can't make you happy.

Being famous can't make you happy.

You have to go deeper. You have to go to the roots. Forget the fruit.

Cultivate it on the inside. Happiness is a perspective. A philosophy you live by. A choice. A conviction.

The more you look for happiness outside of yourself the less of it you will have.

Create a life of fulfillment and gratitude. The less you need the more you will have.

Take care of your roots and you will have a lifetime of good fruit.

Mind Wounds

The healing of an emotional or mental wound is similar to the healing of a physical wound.

You can't speed it up, but eventually it will subside.

It will never be forgotten as you develop an emotional scar.

The scar serves a new very important purpose. A purpose the normal unharmed skin could not.

Where there was once just normalcy, now there is a useful protective barrier.

A battle scar can tell an amazing story of strength, but only if you let it. Don't see it as a weakness.

Life is a fight. Wear your battle scar proudly.

Thinking

Make no mistake about it. Highly successful people think differently.

Success is a mindset. You must learn it by consuming material and content that will cultivate it.

You are not succeeding in life because you are not upgrading your thinking.

What are you feeding your brain?

You care so much about upgrading everything else in your life, but don't upgrade your head.

Candy Crush Saga, please no.

Reruns of Seinfeld, just stop.

Celebrity gossip, oh my, no.

Howard Stern on your morning drive, come on now.

Don't keep up with the Kardashians.

ALWAYS sharing pointless memes and posts, what's going on here?

Religiously following the latest shenanigans of your friend Claire or Cousin Jimmy on Facebook, OK, enough is enough.

You get the point. Ditch the distractions. Ditch the crap.

Just like you are what you eat, you are what you think. Be real careful about what you think.

The Pack

When you break away from the pack you will not be celebrated.

When people are stuck they don't like to see you break away and succeed.

They want to be validated.

Your failure validates their lack of courage, and justifies their extremely limited mentality, and timid comfortable existence.

The more successful you become the less and less you will hear from the pack.

A lion doesn't lose sleep over the opinion of sheep.

Thanks for asking....yeah I'm still winning.

One Life

Whenever you want to do something, it's guaranteed there's someone that is not going to agree with what you are going to do.

You're letting the possible thoughts and opinions of other people dictate your one life.

ONE LIFE.

It's YOUR one life.
When you're 90 years old and full of regrets what's going to matter then?

Your mom's limited opinion of how you need to live your life?

Your dad's expectations because he's a self-proclaimed genius?

Your spouse's idea of keeping you in a restricted box?

Your significant other's jealousy over your success?

Your "commitment" to your boss and the "we" of the company?

Losing your best friend Sally that doesn't even have a job or any aspirations in life?

Have the tough conversations needed. Your life depends on it.

It's not selfish. It's not disrespectful.

You can't pour from an empty cup. Do you.

Until you're happy with your life you can't be your highest and best self to or for anyone else. Including yourself.

The Who

Learning the x's and o's are easy. Learning to become a person with a solid foundation of the necessary character traits to thrive and succeed is not.

Success in anything in life requires you to be a certain type of person, regardless of the how to.

Everyone is so concerned about and you can find tons of advice on how to do something. Valuable information you obviously need to learn and know.

However, without addressing who you need to become in order to realize meaningful and sustainable success is a totally different story.

Regardless of the how to, do you possess the necessary character traits to succeed?

Are you emotionally and mentally prepared for hardship, stress, uncertainty, sacrifice, doubt?

When things don't go right, you don't have immediate answers, and most importantly, when things get hard and don't come easy, what then?

It's not enough to simply know how.

Many people fail in just about anything they do, not because they didn't know the how, but because they didn't know the who.

Most Won't I Will

Doing something I know many people will not do gives me life. It's where my happy place is.

I've taken on many projects that have been abandoned by most.

Projects that are too much of a struggle. Too much work.

Projects where some have tried but couldn't cross the finish line.

I'm enthusiastic and obsessed to progress where others have tried and given up.

Where others have shied away, I show up with enthusiasm.

Where others have had enough, I say give me more.

Where others see the impossible, I see possibility everywhere.

Where others see problems, I see solutions and opportunity.

Where others see too much work, I see a playground of prosperity.

Take the road less traveled. Go where it's empty.

When you find yourself doing the same thing as the majority you have a serious problem.

Many only want easy. I beg for hard.

The more you are willing to struggle, the greater your success will be.

Do what is hard and your life will be easy. Do what is easy and your life will be hard.

Just like life, great things come through struggle and pain.

Good Affliction

I've had many unfortunate circumstances and experiences in not only my life, but in my business. I don't look at any of them as sad or unfortunate. I'm certainly not bitter, I'm better.

That's not just a fluffy, cute little self-affirmation. It's a convicted belief that is fact.

My life is proof of it.

I've been able to rise above, dig my life out of the gutter, and build a successful real estate business because I don't have the interest, the time, or the mental and physical energy available to be bitter. Bitterness is unproductive. Bitterness is a waste of time.

Affliction hasn't just made me better, it's made me unstoppable.

I can withstand things in life and business many cannot. Plain and simple.

I've withstood things and continue to withstand things due to the fact that I have a tremendous resolve and a relentless tenacity to overcome.

I have a resume of overcoming challenges and adversities. Therefore, in life and in business, I am not easily deterred. I am not easily discouraged.

I can rise to the occasion. I am just absolutely insufferably relentless. I will keep coming again, and again, and again, and again. I have a deep resolve and a dogged determination to never give in.

Frankly, I'm prepared to literally die before I would fail in bettering myself, my life, and my business.

I would have given up a long time ago if not for my afflictions.

Sad and unfortunate? No, no, no. More like hell yeah and thank you very much.

You Suck

You can't do anything with a person that doesn't see anything wrong with their actions.

It's amazing how blind some people are. They just do not see the error in their ways. They have a perfect answer for literally everything.

They can tell you with absolute certainty why something failed, why something didn't work, why they fell short of hitting the mark in something.
It's never their fault either. They did everything correct. They couldn't have done any more than they did.

The problem is never them. The problem always lies somewhere else outside of them.

Many times they'll blame you for their shortcomings. It's your fault they suck. You should have done something different or better so they won't suck. You're the reason.

Talking to these kinds of people is like bashing your head against a brick wall repeatedly.

So, very simply, I stop talking to them. I leave them to bask in their bullshit. I leave them to live their delusional existence, believing their delusional excuses.

It's my fault you suck. I got it. No worries. Talk to you later, I'm busy.

Chief Executive Officer

Many people live a life they don't really want. They live someone else's life based on someone else's views. Their thoughts aren't their thoughts. Their views aren't their views.

Many times you end up with a certain mindset or in a place in your life you don't even know how the hell you even got there.

The influences are subtle. Over time they add up to undesired circumstances.

You may need to cut off some people in your life. Mom, dad, husband, wife, girlfriend, boyfriend, brother, sister, best friend, coworkers (your job), etc.

This doesn't mean you don't love them with all your heart. This doesn't mean you don't care for them tremendously. This doesn't mean you're a cold hearted person.

You can love someone and care about them but be forced to let them go.

If there is a person that is inhibiting you from being or becoming your highest and best self, living your highest and best life, based on your definition, it's time to take a serious look at that.

Don't "keep the peace". You're the CEO of your life. Hire and fire people accordingly.

Less Then You Expect

It takes courage to elevate your expectations. It takes guts.

Further, it takes even more courage to NEVER settle for less than what you expect.

Sadly many people don't do it. They put themselves on sale in the bargain basement.

They take the closest guy or girl available to them so they don't have to be lonely. Nobody is perfect of course, but they're good enough.

Changing jobs is hard. You know your current job so well, everyone looks up to you and you're good at it. It's just easier to stay where you are. Who wants to start all over?

You're so invested in that career. So much time spent, so many years given. It sucks you're not appreciated, but you can't possibly switch direction now.

Your biological clock is ticking, mom and dad want a grandchild, you HAVE to be married with children, and time is running out! Settling at its finest.

You're the man or woman in your career, top dog, highly respected. You have seniority. You're a top producer. You're being bought and shackled with golden handcuffs. It's fine though, your image and the money to fund it is more important than your screaming soul and sense of true fulfillment.

It's too hard to stand up to the criticism and resistance of your boss, coworkers, family, spouse, significant other, and friends when you need to be more of who you really are or make a big life change. It's so much easier to just stay being who they want you to be. After all you don't want to be a sell out or lose people because of it. You might be alone and you already have quite the collection of masks.

Everyone else has so many advantages and opportunities you just don't have. They're so lucky. After all, who are you to think you can have a much better life? Stay broke, stay average, stay limited. All the reasons of why you can't are totally justified.

You generally get what you expect. People that live the lives they want look around for the circumstances they really want and if they don't find them, they change them and create them. No matter how difficult the decisions and actions might be.

Headspace

Those "other" people. Sleepwalkers. Those that look but don't see, and listen but don't hear. The uninspired. The close minded cowardly critics. Those timid souls that live a beautiful lie to escape an ugly truth.

Some people are so unbelievably determined to stay stuck in their current state of mind. Refusing to change. Refusing to see things differently.

Some are aware and just too afraid or stubborn to change, and many simply have no selfawareness at all.

Not you. You're different.

You're part of an elite class. Your eyesight is crystal clear. You don't walk in your sleep. You live life with a ferocious, determined soul, conquering and slaying your truths.

Your mind is open to fresh ideas and concepts. You don't just hear, you listen and receive. Your need to change is as strong as your need for oxygen to breath.

For you, an epiphany and awakening aren't just mere words in a dictionary or fluffy delusional concepts. They're life. They're self-fulfilling prophecies that have delivered you from the grip and stronghold of what those "other" people think.

Know who you are. Embrace who you are. Love who you are. Don't be convinced otherwise. Don't let small minds infect your life.

Guard your head space like your life depends on it. Because it does.

Fight Back

Every day the voices in your head are telling you a story. A story about who you are and what's possible for you in your life.

Sometimes these voices are deafening. They're haunting. They're convincing.

Pay very close attention to the people around you on a regular basis. Pay very close attention to the type of environments you allow yourself to be in on a regular basis.

Who told you you're not capable, not worthy, not smart, not attractive, not courageous, not strong, not powerful, and not good enough?

Who told you it's not going to work, give up hope, it's destined to fail, you're in over your head, you can't do it, it's a stupid idea, and it's not worth it?

Voices in your head. What are they saying? How did they get there? No you're not crazy, whether you like to admit it or not, everyone has them.

You didn't believe these things until someone, including yourself, you're someone, told you and planted it in your head.

Don't believe everything you think. Destructive, self-sabotaging thoughts will kill you. They'll stop you dead in your tracks.

It's time to fight back. It's time to get angry. It's time to declare all-out war. It's time to shout back and take control. It's time to edit the story in your head.

Quitter

Here's the truth.

You're a quitter. You give up easily. You lack resiliency and grit. You want all the benefits of high achievement but don't want to do the obsessive work over a long period of time to obtain it.

You fall back easily. You convince yourself why something isn't going to work and switch direction. Your head has a library of bullshit stories. Your resume is eight miles long.

Trying isn't enough, you must do. Results are the only thing that matter in life. No one cares about your sob story about how hard you tried and it just didn't work.

High achievement comes to those that grind it out at one thing. High achievement comes to those that remain undeterred in the face of challenges and obstacles.

How you handle the breaking points will define your life.

You can't be constantly starting over and think that you will achieve great success.

Bad Memory

Sometimes having a poor short term memory is a good thing.

Inevitably there will be times in life where things aren't going as planned.

What's done is done. Forget about it. It happened. It's a situation. What are you going to do now?

Dwelling on mistakes or failures, worrying, and focusing on what you can't change or control will get you nowhere. Have a strong sense of resiliency to immediately start to fix the problem and begin to move in a better direction.

Identify the things that you have control over and increase your level of effort there. You can't change what happened, but you can greatly diminish the damage, stop the bleeding, and begin to move in the right direction with obsessive, focused effort on the right things.

Key word, obsessive. You might have to be willing to disappear for a while to get on the right track.

Fix your life, focus on what you can control, and go all in with obsessive effort.

Still People

Still people are an absolute drag on your life.

Still bitter. Still limited. Still blaming. Still angry. Still close minded. Still pathetic.

Still, still, still, still.

Still people have an extremely limited perspective. Still people do absolutely nothing to develop themselves or evolve.

These are the same people that always "put you in your place". Remind you of how they knew you. Remind you of who you used to be, how you used to think, and ways you used to act.

They're stuck mentally and spiritually and completely reject or don't even understand the concept of personal growth. They do absolutely nothing to improve themselves. The concept makes as much sense to them as rocket science does to a 1 year old.

Get rid of still people. You've got places to go. You've got people to see. You've got things to do. You've got to continue evolving into the best and highest version of yourself.

Life waits for no one.

You want all of the best things life has to offer and must become the right person necessary to be able to obtain it.

Be in a perpetual state of constant self-improvement. It's OK to become a totally different person than you were 20 years ago, 1 year ago, or 5 minutes ago.

Keep becoming. Don't be still. Keep it moving.

Insanity

Doing the same thing over and over and expecting a different result is the definition of insanity.

Identify the steps you took and the contribution you made to be in the set of circumstance you're in.

Blaming someone else will get you nowhere. It's your life. Handle it.

Take responsibility for it. Take responsibility for your actions. Promise yourself you will NEVER be in the same situation again because you will identify and not repeat the same actions and steps that put you there.

Stop whining, figure out where you went wrong and begin to take steps to change it for the better. Ruthlessly, unapologetically, and immediately.

Never Knew

There have been many times in my life I was playing a part. Playing a part to fit the mold of my environment. Playing a part to agree with and live out the ideologies of those around me so I can be accepted.

These were some of the most miserable and soul sucking times of my life. Conflicted on the inside about who I really was, how I really thought, how I really wanted to live my life. My reality made me sick. Being someone I wasn't or didn't care to be made me sick.

Going against the grain in life is hard. People will reject you, criticize you, laugh at you, and belittle you. Leave these people alone to play their parts.

It's time for you to introduce yourself to the world and start playing the part that was designed for you. The role of a lifetime. The perfect script. It may not be popular but it's right. It feels amazing. And frankly, who gives a shit what the people you knew think about it. You'll have plenty of new supporting actors and actresses auditioning for the new story of a lifetime. Your lifetime.

You're not crazy, you didn't change, and you didn't lose your mind. They never really knew you.

<u>Highlight Reel</u>

Some people are so amazing.

They never seem to struggle.

They have such a beautiful and supportive family.

They're so happily married.

Their significant other is the bomb. So attractive.

They never seem to feel pain or turmoil.

They're always smiling. Amazing smile.

Their children seem so perfect.

Their career is so wonderful. They look so important.

They're always having fun. YOLO.

Their life is just absolutely amazing.

I wish I could just be them. Oh how great my life would be.

Bummer I'll just have to settle for the reality of me and fantasize watching their highlight reel.

Beautiful Mind

A beautiful life begins with a beautiful mind.

A mind that is open to everything and attached to nothing.

Operating through imagination not limitation.

Programmed as intended on purpose, not unknowingly by accident.

Awakened, it houses a vast array of truth setting its owner free.

A garden that plants seeds of knowledge, sprouting crops of wisdom.

Dominated by conscious thought, not subconscious dormancy.

Serving the greater good, revealing itself through an outward projection by the person that uses it.

Clear, present, and hopeful, it's not consumed with its memory, but glimpses of the the future.

It's not easily tampered with. Calm and at peace like a still pool of water, no matter how much anyone tries to jump in it.

Firm and unwavering on convicted belief that is unique and uncommon to the majority.

Free, wandering but never lost.

As a man or women thinks, then so shall they be.

Think beautiful my friend.

Tight Places

Have you ever just got tired in a tight place?

A place where you're closer than you were but not quite there yet.

Not knowing if you've got the push to keep going and get to the next level.

A place where you just keep saying the same prayer over and over, seems like nothing is happening, nothing is moving.

Between a rock and a hard place.

Pressure.

Places that make you wonder will I make it through this.

People you run into daily don't even realize you're in a tight place.

That you're smiling from a tight place.

Working from a tight place.

Living in a tight place.

When you feel like you're going to snap, and think, "God if just one more thing happens"...

Uncertainty and anxiety of not knowing how things will turn out are enough to eat you alive in a tight place.

You begin to distance from others because you look around and realize no one is going through it but you.

Other people don't connect with what you're going through.

Know that you've been given that tight place...to be given a promise.

See, you don't ever get promised the obvious. What you know or expect for sure.

A promise is only made when something comes against you that gives you doubt.

When you are in trouble.

The promises of God come and are made in tight places.

What's not empty can't be filled.

What's not broken can't be fixed.

Keep your head up and keep walking, otherwise you'll never know the promise you've been given...

In the tight place.

Final Chapter

The story of your life is continuously unfolding day by day.

Each day, you're writing another a page.

Sometimes we get caught in a chapter where every word and sentence just make no sense, your mind is blank, you lack inspiration, and you're lost for words.

Nonetheless, turn the page, get to the next chapter, and don't burn the book.

See, as we turn the pages we learn a bit more about ourselves and our lives.

The words that should be written become clearer.

We come to understand that at any given time the page we're on is not our final destination.

That as long as we keep rewriting what we've already written, the story will forever stay the same.

Because although it may be uncertain how the story will end...

It's a long way from what you're writing now to that final chapter, and a lot can happen along the way.

Turn the page with fear. Turn the page with uncertainty. Turn the page with faith.

And most importantly make sure you're holding the pen.

There's a happy ending in store for those that do.

And, although the entire book may not have been a masterpiece...

The final chapter will forever hold the bookmark to your life's eternity.

See, it's not how the story started that's important, it's how it's finished that will stand the test of time.

Impressive

I mean the way you flipped that person off! They'll never cut you off again I'm sure! Incredible strength.

The way you threaten to beat up every guy that is within five feet of your girlfriend. Savage.

So beautiful you are, that ugly attitude problem showcases it perfectly.

Your wife bows to the king. Divine.

Big shot boss, you don't need to earn respect, demand it! Now that's a role model.

Whoa! You really told them! Pure beast. Amazing.

The only people that take issue with the truth are those that fit the description.

Anger is not impressive.

It can't be stated any simpler than that.

Stay humble....bro.

Change Direction

Many lack vision because it's hard to be a dreamer.

A dreamer sees what shall be, but is forced to wake up every day and deal with what is.

Tormented by something they can see, but is invisible to the naked eye.

To constantly be surrounded by people that major in minor things...but you've got a major mind.

People that just don't see the way you see. People that don't hear the way you hear.

It's easy to feel isolated, like you're on an island...but I suggest to you that this is divine independence.

Life is short. Take the island and burn the boat.

See, you have to run the risk of being controversial and not have the support you need to do what you've been called to do.

A rebirthing, cut the umbilical cord of public opinion.

Let god be true and every man a liar.

God will bless you whether people like you or not.

Start a riot.

Start doing things people don't understand until later.

Do great things. Do exploits.

Be influential.

Raise some eyebrows.

You're doing something right when average minds do not think highly of you.

Nobody in history achieved greatness because everybody agreed with them.

You will always be limited if you need people to agree with you or agree with what it is you're going to do.

You can be the most beautiful, giving, well rounded human being on the planet and there's still going to be someone, somewhere that's not going to like you or agree with you.

You're never going to make everyone happy...you shouldn't try.

One thing is for sure...

If you don't change direction you might end up where you're heading.

This Time

My whole life I've had people let me down.

Inconsistent people. Broken promises. People that betrayed my trust. People that used my vulnerabilities as a tool to use, manipulate, and make me feel unworthy or not good enough.

With each experience, the hardest thing in the world was to let my guard down, open myself up, and become vulnerable again.

The past I came from and the fear it created caused me to fear vulnerability.

It caused me to question or give up on new prospects of love and joy in my life.

The ability to open and let newness in was canceled out by the fear that what happened before will happen again.

But I've come to realize the beauty in vulnerability. Vulnerability creates possibility.

The possibility of something good.

I realized that my strength was in my ability to let my guard down. To trust myself, know myself, and be grounded in myself enough to take a risk and know if it didn't turn out the way I wanted I would still be OK.

Having the courage to let someone in so deeply, running the risk that they could hurt me badly, to hopefully find that they will actually give me everything that was always lacking in everyone else.

I've learned that giving up the fierce need to protect myself from what could go wrong or what might go wrong, allowed me to wipe the slate clean of past experiences and give everyone new, a fair chance.

I've learned that the reality is every person is different and so are their values and intentions.

That until I became open to the beauty of what could happen, I'd always be stuck in what did happen.

If I kept allowing past experiences to leak into new ones I would forever cancel out the possibility of something potentially good working its way into my life.

I've learned not to sabotage my life by what happened to me "the last time".

I've learned to let "the last time" go.

"The last time" is no indication of "this times" outcome.

To not allow "the last times" of my life to prevent me from living my best "this times".

When you let "the last time" go you give "this time" a chance.

After all, beautiful new beginnings are often disguised as painful ending.

<u>May You?</u>

It's not about finding the light, but learning how to see in the dark.

Adversity is your greatness teacher.

I've learned far more from my adversities than I ever could from my successes.

I would have never known what was in me or how blessed I really am until I had something to measure it by.

Adversity allows you to measure the extent to which you've been blessed.

When other people would have been destroyed and swallowed up by what you overcame you know you're blessed.

If you think you're not blessed because you have adversity.

You are wrong.

May you have the courage to break the patterns that are destroying you.

May you have the courage to do what you know is right.

May you have the courage to disappear and come back better.

May you have the courage to be alone.

May you have the courage to decide what life you really want and say no to anything that doesn't fit.

May you have the courage to walk through hell like you own the place.

May you have the courage to set your past on fire and leave it behind.

Sometimes bad has to get worse before it gets better.

But I'm a witness and I assure you...

Your strength is made perfect in your weakness.

Keep your head up.

Be Too Much

Decide in advance to lose people.

This is fact...

Many people are not aware of their own BS.

They don't like to hear truth because they don't want their illusions destroyed.

When you vibe high, your presence alone is going to make some uncomfortable.

People will reject you not because there's something wrong with you, but because there's a lot wrong with them.

You remind them of what they lack.

Not only the guts to face truth, but guts to actually do something about.

People tell themselves these lies and contrive delusional truths for comfort and convenience.

False realities they really truly have just talked themselves into believing.

Building habit and routine around things they think they can't change.

Never evolving beyond this BS story they've written for their life.

See...that's probably getting on someone's nerves right now.

Someone who's stuck with a mind that refuses to change.

Don't ever let limited thinking people convince you to dumb down to their level.

The more you're misunderstood, rejected, criticized, scoffed at, talked about, and not accepted...

The more you're moving in the right direction.

People that are highly successful in life do not ever make excuses for anything.

Period.

They face what they have to face, fix it, and get on with it.

Elevation requires separation. You're summed up by your associations.

Even if that means moving alone.

Eventually the right people will find you.

As long as you remain limited, you're only always going to attract limited people.

Keep it moving.

Reciprocity

Listen to people closely with your eyes.

Without reciprocity no relationship will ever reach its apex because there's no real investment.

Stop pouring yourself into people that struggle to give you a single drop of themselves.

Traveling a million miles for someone that won't even cross the street for you.

There's a level of responsibility one must have in any relationship. You cannot have relationship without reciprocity.

There's a lot to be said about one very simple little thing that most people oddly seem to miss...

Effort.

If a person is really interested in you or cares about you they'll show it...through effort.

A give and take. A fair exchange. A matched effort and reciprocated interest.

If someone looks at you as an option, make it easy for them and delete yourself from the equation.

People are busy. We all have a lot going on. No doubt about it. There's just not enough time in the day.

If they don't call, you should understand.

If they don't text, you should understand.

If they don't have time to see you, you should understand.

If you forget about them and move on...they should understand.

Here's the truth...

People make time for what they want to make time for.

For what they deem to be important.

People always have time...it's just that you are not a enough of a priority in their life, so none of that time is allocated to you.

Any relationship without reciprocity will die.

Sometimes a person's heart, mind, and life are a busy road...and you can't read the mixed signs and signals.

Stop traveling the wrong way down a one way street.

Move on.

<u>Living a Lie</u>

When your dream is born through someone else's desire you can be destroyed trying to fulfill it.

Stop for a minute and think about what you're doing, what you're chasing, what you're plugged into, and what you're striving for.

Where did your dream come from? Who put it there? Who influenced it?

Inheriting other people's dreams and trying to please and appease what their wishes for your life are is a losing proposition.

Sometimes you will have domineering and overbearing people speak into your life. They start pointing you to what they think you should do, steering you in a direction that isn't what you want, or are called to do.

If you allow someone to live vicariously through you you'll never be free.

You could be rich, live in a house on the hill, have it all...but be miserable, full of resentment, unfulfillment, and dissatisfaction.

Chained, locked up to the prison of their idea. A slave to their imagination.

You become frustrated doing something you really don't want to do. Living up to what they want to see out of your life, not what you want out of your life.

It is stressful to live a lie.

It's not what they want you to be, it's what you want you to be.

Cut the strings. Start moving in ways that are natural to you.

Become someone no one thought you should be...because you know in your heart what you could be.

Nah...Bigger

You can often be given a tremendous gift and not feel gifted at all.

Often times when we're given a great gift we're left in disarray, not joy.

Misperceptions and misinterpretations cause us to run from it.

It's not the gift itself that causes us to be doubtful and fearful, but the wrapping paper it's wrapped in.

Great gifts are often wrapped in terrible circumstances, problems, anxiety, and worry.

Like the person you thought you couldn't live without leaving you, getting cut loose from a job, afflictions, rejection, shut doors, and struggles.

But who knows what's in a gift until the gift is unwrapped.

Fear not.

Don't let fear cause you to give up prematurely on yourself or life, robbing you of sure recovery and redemption.

Robbing you of a gift that is being used to bless you.

There's some hidden magic working in your favor. You can be blessed in an unlikely place.

Don't be afraid of the gifts God gives.

He has set an open door before you.

It's up to you to walk through it.

Eventually you will celebrate the very thing you used to cry about.

Know that when you are given a gift from God, it worries you before it blesses you.

You thought you lost out on something big...

But it was just God saying....nah, bigger.

Belief Protection

Pay attention to those that don't clap for you when you win.

Then show them the door.

Delete negativity like your life depends on it.

People will try to tell you that you can't do something because they can't do it.

Never let other people put their limitations on you.

You won't even attempt to do something if you don't really believe it's a possibility.

Belief drives activity.

Your entire existence is a manifestation of belief.

You don't need anyone else to believe in your aspirations and dreams.

You need to believe in them.

Protect those beliefs. You can't surround yourself with blindness and expect to see. Letting blind people proof read your vision is a losing proposition.

Hot Mess

I'd rather be a hot mess of decisive action than a perfectly well organized coward.

Many have such a fragile ego they won't risk looking foolish.

Won't risk people seeing them stumble, trip, or fail.

They always need to be in a position where their viewed to be highly competent.

They'd rather get sweet kisses on their rear end than criticized for stepping outside of the box.

You will never accomplish anything extraordinary far beyond your current situation if you refuse to become vulnerable in success.

Everyone that starts something new doesn't know what they're doing.

It's through trial and error you gain wisdom.

Through new found knowledge and know how mistakes become less and less.

Your ability to make wise productive decisions that move you in the right direction begin to compound.

You begin to dominate.

But first, there's tuition you must pay in the school of success. The school of hard knocks.

A price you must pay for what you don't know.

The price of your ego, your pride, your sanity, your peace, your confidence, and most importantly your fragile image.

Failure and defeat are a mindset. They can only exist as long as you accept them as your reality.

If you're waiting for the perfect time, the perfect plan, or for everything to line up you'll be waiting a long time.

The perfect time does not exist.

The perfect plan does not exist.

Overnight success does not exist.

There's no secret sauce or or magic formula.

There are some people that want to do something with their life.

They don't want increase, they expect it, and do whatever it takes to obtain it.

Regardless of how they look to other people in the process.

When you make excuses for your limitations you get to keep them.

But here's the good news...

No opportunity is ever lost.

Other people will always take the ones you don't.

Like a Seed

Burying a seed looks exactly the same as planting a seed.

You can't tell the difference it's really all just in your perspective.

It's very easy to confuse the two.

It's all in which you choose to accept.

When you plant something it is intended to come up better than it went down.

It is intended to go through a metamorphosis and transformation from the experiences it will go through in the dark.

A seed has to be buried in a dark place before it can flourish.

A planted seed has its destiny hidden and concealed in the ground. Only in time will it's destiny be revealed above ground.

In order to be revealed you must water it.

See, if you accept that you have been buried to die...you won't do much watering.

In order to grow the seeds environment is very important. The elements that surround it will dictate its ultimate destiny.

Like a seed...

It is good that you have been afflicted.

It's good that you have been placed in a dark place.

It's only a matter of time your concealed destiny will be revealed.

With time, proper watering, the right elements and environment...

Your harvest will be full.

Don't give up just because you're in a dark place.

It's in the dark places great spirits grow.

Self Talk

Thoughts become things.

Right now, each moment, all day, you are telling yourself a story.

There's a narrative you live by.

Chronicles of BS.

A fairy tale. You created the main characters, the setting, and the perceived ending.

If you can change the direction of the way you think then you can change the direction of the way you live.

Something needs to go off in your head.

You need a miracle in your head.

Transformational thinking.

You don't need more money, a significant other, a spouse, a new job, a house, a car, more friends....

You need to get out of your own head.

You need new thoughts.

You can't get enough people to tell you you're pretty if you think you're ugly.

You can't get enough people to tell you you're successful if you think you're a failure.

You can't get enough people to like you or approve of you if you don't like or approve of yourself.

Allow new truths to replace past experiences, thereby changing your mind.

You have to be willing to break old thought patterns, old systems, and develop a new normal in your head.

Anything you focus on you can change. You don't have to be anything you don't want to be.

It's time to tell the negative committee in your head to shut up.

Your self-talk determines your self-worth.

Don't believe everything you think.

It might just magically appear in your life.

I Do

For better or for worse...

Until death do us part...

Ummmm...yes, I do...

But only as long as there's more better than worse.

Only as long as I could show my friends a 14 carat ring instead of the 1/2 carat because they all got 13.99 carats.

Only as long I remain as happy as I was walking down the aisle...everyday...forever.

Only as long as people know my dress was expensive.

Only as long as everyone lets me off the hook...I know he or she was my side piece, but I'm marrying them for heaven's sake.

Only as long as I love coming home every day...otherwise I'll probably start dating someone else...but I'll stay married don't worry.

Only as long as everyone is in agreement with it...I just want everyone to be happy but myself.

Only as long as he or she makes me happy and whole...after all I'm half a person and not emotionally secure otherwise.

Only as long as our guests are more impressed with the venue than the true love we share...after all we drained our entire savings to make this happen.

Only as long as everyone we know makes just as big a deal about our wedding in 20 years as the day we got married.

Only as long as we never have to worry about money, have a white picket fence, 1.5 kids, and a Golden Retriever...that's what our friends John and Betty have.

Only as long as he or she remains EXACTLY the same person they were on our wedding day.......forever.

Ok ok! Anything else?!

Well no...I mean what else could there be? Our life is going to be perfect.

I now pronounce you husband and wife.

You may now kiss the bride.

Congratulations.

Ignorance

Ignorance...the lack of knowledge or information.

An incomprehension of things you'd be better off comprehending, but unfortunately do not.

People only see things and understand from their level of perspective.

When you understand that you stop explaining your position and stop arguing.

Although unbeknownst to them, you understand it's not their fault.

You understand that a person can't think higher than the level they're exposed to.

Some just have a limited perspective based on a limited world view.

People always respond according to their capacity, which in the case of ignorance, is narrow minded, misguided, and very small.

People just respond at the level that they're on.

They talk on the level that they think.

This is absolutely, without a doubt, perfectly ok, if you have one very simple thing working for you...

Awareness.

Awareness that you do not know what you do not know is the highest form of intelligence there is.

Being aware that you are misinformed will cause you to seek the correct information in regard to the subject matter you speak so definitively and firmly about...

Awareness creates enlightenment.

So, if you have an illusion of knowledge, please know that your ignorance is not bliss.

There's nothing bliss about conscientious stupidity.

In The Arena

There are some people that want to do something with their life.

The credit goes to the person in the arena.

The person that has the guts to get in the game of life.

The person that puts it all on the line and dares greatly.

You will never be criticized by someone doing more than you. You will only be criticized by someone doing less.

It's easy to point out how the person that's taking the chances and making the moves could've done something better.

Never base the chances or risks you take based on what someone will think of you if you fail.

Perfection is the enemy of progress.

I'd rather try and fail than to have never tried at all.

I'd rather try and not get it, than stay stuck, staring at the starting line my whole life.

Let people talk, don't let the chatter stop you, because eventually you will make it happen.

People don't understand what you're doing and why you're doing it, and it doesn't matter.

Eventually they'll see.

You may look stupid and incompetent for a short period, but eventually you'll figure it out.

See who's laughing then.

Just keep going no matter what anyone says.

Forget being realistic. The more unrealistic the better.

Work while they play. Grind while they sleep. Hustle while they relax.

In silence. No need to speak.

Let your success make the noise.

True Identity

People define you where they met you.

As long as you stay on the step where they met you, you're ok.

But the moment you step forward people have all kinds of issues with your transition.

It's hard to be open when you've been closed all your life.

When you've played a specific role or part everyone defines you by.

Taking off the mask and revealing your true identity creates friction.

Friction most can't handle.

Friction that is so uncomfortable most hurry up and quickly put their mask back on to ease the discomfort.

To blend right back in with the status quo and the expectations of others.

A redefinition of character and persona come at a price.

There's always a journey in between where you're going to be and where you are right now.

Some will respect that journey some won't.

Not everyone you start with will be with you at the final destination.

You can't change people that lie to themselves. You can only change how you associate with them.

When you surround yourself with people that lie to themselves, you'll become a fake person just like them, because energy is contagious.

Consciously choose your circle and if you can't find one that fits, better to be alone than drift off from your authentic self.

Let it all go, become the truest reflection of who you are, see what stays.

Learn to hang out with your soul.

People are going to judge you no matter what you do. Live for yourself.

Angels

Sometimes angels are sent into our lives.

People, pure at heart that speak into our life without saying a word.

Touching us in ways that are not physical.

Showing up to fill voids, guide us where we need guidance, and move us in ways we need to be moved.

Speaking truth into our lies.

Giving hope where we had no belief.

Blazing a fire where we had no flame.

Provoking visibility where we had no sight.

Providing direction to a wandering soul.

Loving what needed to be loved.

Attentive to what has been forgotten.

Infusing light into our darkness.

Lifting us higher. Moving us forward.

Guiding what's misguided.

Creating certainty in our uncertainty.

It's through our vulnerability, lack of pride or ego, and openness in our heart and mind we let them touch us.

You are always manifesting someone, and someone is always manifesting you.

Don't ignore a symbol when you asked for a sign.

Don't waste your angel.

It's Radical

Truly letting go is radical behavior.

You've got to be tough to truly just stop caring.

To rather be hated for who you really are than liked for being fake.

Stop trying to explain your side of the story to make sure the facts are right.

Stop trying to change people's minds about you.

Let people believe whatever story they want.

Stop fighting for closure, chasing answers, and asking for explanations.

Stop trying to get people to understand where you're coming from.

Stop chasing people, if they walk let them walk.

Stop investing in half committed relationships.

Stop pouring into half ass people.

Don't allow someone to treat you poorly just because you love them.

Sometimes solutions aren't so simple, and goodbye is the only way.

You have to remove your expectations from things that don't work.

Life is better lived when you just let things be and center it in what's going on in the inside not the outside.

Your life is ALWAYS a direct reflection of how you see, understand, respect, love, pour into, and chase yourself.

Focus on yourself and your inner peace.

Watch everything fall into place.

__Remember__

You've got to go through it to get to it.

Success does not come without struggle.

You're always going to have struggles. But, there are good struggles and there are bad struggles.

Sometimes the good struggles you have cause you to have amnesia.

Something that sucks in the moment causes you to forget how much you should really be grateful.

Don't forget the hard times of your life.

Remember the bad struggles.

Remember when you were lost and confused.

Remember when you thought you couldn't go on living.

Remember when you hated waking up every day doing what you were doing with your life.

Remember when you were strung out.

Remember when the struggles you used to have were the types of struggles you would've gladly traded for the struggles you have today.

There was a day you prayed for these struggles.

Don't get it twisted. You're blessed.

Be thankful for the opportunity to deal with what you've been given to deal with.

There was a day you prayed for what you have now.

Often times things worry and burden you before they bless you.

It's all part of the process.

Not Yet

The right thing at the wrong time.

Even a good thing is a bad thing if it comes at the wrong time.

Sometimes God blesses you in his ability to say, "no not yet".

The perfect opportunities, the perfect person coming into your life, the blessings you asked for...but you aren't the you that you need to be to handle what you've been given.

I've always been eager and had the instinct for increase, but I've learned to pray to not be given more than I can handle.

When you don't know how to handle what you got, you trip and stumble on the steps.

Sometimes you're setback and forced to go back and redo some of the steps you missed.

Life takes you through steps and stages to prepare you for what's already ready...you receive a blessing on credit that time makes payment on.

It's the things you discover along the way that make you able to withstand the process once you get there.

It's the you that you become so you can handle what you have to handle, and keep what you've been given.

Trust the timing of your life. Failure and hardship are blessings in disguise.

Eventually you'll be able to stand flat footed and know that was then and this is now.

Thank you for the steps. Thank you for the lessons. Thank you for giving me the understanding. Thank you for opening my eyes to see what I needed to see.

Though I doubted I still believed you.

Thank you, thank you, thank you for giving me double for my trouble....

I'm ready now.

Cheap Copies

Be who you are supposed to be. Who you were destined to be.

Uniquely made by your creator, you're a designer original.

When God made you he threw away the mold.

You were born to stand out and stand apart.

Don't be a cheap copy of a good original.

You lose resolution and clarity anytime you make a copy of something.

You don't see tribute bands in the rock and roll hall of fame.

No one can do you like you do you.

As long as you try to be like someone else you will never realize YOUR truest potential.

A potential reserved for what you were called to do.

Don't talk like they talk, don't think like they think, don't go where they go.

If you're going to walk a unique path you need to be a unique person.

If you want to be an anomaly, you need to start acting like one.

If you don't stay true to you, you'll always be living in someone else's shadow.

Studying them so hard you don't study you. You know other people more than you know yourself.

You were not created to be them, you were created to be you.

If you blend in like camouflage, you've got a serious problem.

Be yourself, everyone else is taken.

__Precipitation__

Sometimes your situation can be doing better than your soul.

Everyone can see evidence of success but can't see the soul attached to it.

When your soul is empty you can be winning outside but be weeping inside.

What you want shows up in your spirit before it shows up in your life.

But what happens when you see something in your soul that you don't see in your situation yet?

Your spirit will forever be in a drought until you become a rainmaker.

You have to see things that are not, as though they were.

See the ending finished in advance, then work backwards to get there.

Don't avoid the storm, become the storm. Create your own precipitation.

Trust and walk out into the water. You just might find yourself dancing and singing in the rain.

Competency

Experience doesn't necessarily bring competence.

If you don't learn from experiences and move forward in a smarter improved way, experience means nothing.

Competency is a result of the lessons from past mistakes, sticking with you, and showing up in the form of improvement.

Competency is an acquired skill through trial and error.

A know how developed through conscious understanding of stupid and dumb mistakes.

Stupidity is the enemy of competency.

Stupidity is kryptonite to competency.

5 different jobs in 12 months, 5th marriage, 6th attempt at business, begging someone for a 4th chance, second half of your life just as screwed up as the first half.

It should be expected that the more you do something you gain a level of proficiency, ability, and skill.

Competency.

A new attempt should benefit from the dumb mistakes of the prior attempt.

So when you do something for the third time, the same way you failed to do it the first and second time...and expect a different result...

You've gained experience but no competence.

But hey, the odds are in your favor, the third times a charm.

Plugged In

Be careful what you're plugged into.

You don't have any power because you're not plugged into the right things.

Lights don't turn on unless they're plugged into power.

Your light isn't on because you're not plugged in power.

When you're plugged into nonsense, drugs, alcohol, women, men, sex, a go nowhere job, go nowhere friends, mindless entertainment...

Vices, urges, impulses, and temptations...

Your light will be constantly flickering, close to going out completely.

We all need to be reenergized at times, but many pick the wrong outlets.

You were meant to shine, but until you plug in...in the dark is where you'll stay.

Same Mind

Getting a new spouse isn't going to matter if you're still the same selfish, ignorant, and narcissistic creep you were in the first marriage.

I know your new boyfriend does the dishes but you're still the same liar and cheater you were in your last five relationships.

The same problems will exist in that ocean front property just as they did in that little house in that crappy neighborhood.

New uniform, new title, new office...same laziness, still no work ethic, still think you know it all.

Forget them, you got some new friends...only problem is you're still the same back stabbing, fake loser you were before.

Beautiful, love the hair color, those highlights are the bomb! Who did your makeup?! Oh wait, you're still ugly as all hell on the inside.

You can change your spouse, your significant other, your address, your job or career, your friends, your hair color, your makeup, your clothes, your routine, your diet, even your name.

But, if your mind doesn't change the same experiences will perpetuate themselves over and over because everything outwardly changed, but nothing inwardly changed.

A brain transplant comes first, everything else second.

Becoming a new person is only done by changing your mind.

"Daddy"

Hey "dad".

I know you're busy and have other priorities to tend to, I'll make it quick.

Just wanted to say I'm not a kid anymore. I'm a grown man now.

Hey "dad".

I thought you would like to know...

I've done good for myself and became a good man.

I know you'd be proud...

After all, you did say once I'm the type that does whatever it takes to get whatever I want...and boy were you right.

You really knew me.

Hey "dad".

I'm so different now, I'm unrecognizable...but it's me...you know the son you made but didn't create.

I'm almost done, wait a minute, just one last thing.

I just wanted to give credit where credit is due...

Hey "dad"...I did it without you.

Energy

To look beyond what is against you and toward what is within you...

The energy is the same.

It takes the same amount of energy to be...

Pessimistic as it does optimistic.

Angry as it does happy.

Fearful as to be hopeful.

Hate as to love.

Worry as to have faith.

Why wouldn't you choose the latter?

The energy is the same.

Focus on what you have the ability to control. Forget what you do not have the ability to change.

Develop the wisdom to know the difference.

Build the courage to take action on optimism, happiness, hopefulness, love, and faith.

Choose to use your energy in a way that serves the manifestation of the best you that you can be.

It'll show up in your life.

The energy is the same.

I'm Sorry

Sticks and stones will break my bones...but words can never hurt me...and they better be some big sticks and stones.

People who are hurting like to tear things down because of their own pain.

If they loved themselves they wouldn't be hurting you or trying to tear you down.

Hating you because they hate themselves.

I'm sorry your life sucks.

I'm sorry you hate your boss and your job.

I'm sorry your wife is a ball and chain.

I'm sorry you shouldn't have married your husband.

I'm sorry you're not living up to your potential, stuck in a life you don't want.

I'm sorry your significant other would be better off being your insignificant other.

I'm sorry you're afraid to take your mask off.

I'm sorry you're broke pinching pennies.

Most importantly, I'm sorry you're too weak and afraid to actually do something about any of these circumstances.

Look...feel better about yourself at my expense. It's ok.

I'm rich in what you lack so it's the perfect partnership...self-awareness, self-satisfaction, self-respect, self-love, and self-esteem.

I don't mind giving you a loan. I've got plenty to lend. We have a deal.

You take your miserable existence out on me, interest free, and you feel better about yourself for a brief moment.

Don't thank me, no really, it's the least I can do.

Trashy

Sometimes life gets trashy. Filthy, dirty, and disgusting.

Our life becomes a dump that people use at free will.

All the things people did to you. All the ways people treated you. All the things people said about you.

The pain, the hurt, the fear, the lies, and the manipulation.

How much can one person take?

You can feel it building up.

If just one more thing gets thrown on top...

Broken promises, feeling useless, feeling unappreciated, feeling uncared for, feeling unwanted, feeling left behind, feeling abused.

Thrown away, disrespected, discarded....

Treated like you don't matter, like a piece of trash.

Your current situation isn't your final destination.

There's treasure in the trash of your life.

Search until you find it. Look until you see it.

Somewhere in that trash there's some useful things.

You'll find things you can put back together, bring back to life, re purpose, and use a different way.

I know it seems like every affliction, every struggle, and every hardship just keeps piling up.

But, I assure you my friend, if you dig deep enough in the trash of life...

You'll stumble upon stuff that looks like garbage at first glance. But then you realize...

There's some treasure in this trash.

Places

Certain places can hold a particular meaning in one's life.

Going back to a place that you haven't been to or seen in a long time can be a wonderful growth experience.

To see everything exactly as it once was, exactly as you remember it, completely unchanged.

Everything is the same.

The only thing that's different is you.

The person you were the last time you were there is long gone.

You can visualize and see yourself right where you once were. Exactly who you once were.

It's almost an uneasy feeling really. Sort of in a good way, and in a bad way all at the same time.

Good in that through this place that has remained unchanged, you realize just how beautifully you yourself have altered.

But bad in remembering something that place once represented in your life that you would rather have kept stuffed down deep in your memory.

And as your visit once again comes to an end, you're off to continue living and alter some more.

Leaving, watching that place become distant, another piece of your past is added to the timeline of your life...

Through that place that remains unchanged.

<u>Where You Stand</u>

There's something to be said about just knowing where you stand.

Knowing the whole truth.

You can't ever know where you stand when you're not dealing with a stand up person.

A person that can't just say what they really mean or how they really feel.

If you don't like me, great I can deal with that, don't smile, hug me, and act like you do.

If you don't love me, awesome. Don't be reaching around my back holding someone else's hand while I have my arm around you.

If you don't really have my back, super. Don't let me call for you when I'm in a time of need and hear crickets.

Don't tell me how wonderful and amazing am, then slip a knife in my back when I turn around.

You have to choose me or them? Don't choose me.

All these mixed signals, I'll just take it as a no. See ya.

I'd rather a "take it or leave it this is where we stand" slap in the face than be kissed with a lie.

If you ever feel like you have to guess or question where you stand with someone, drop them and stand alone.

If you don't know where you stand you'll fall for anything.

Let them play games with someone else.

Stop standing and start walking.

<u>Real Soul</u>

Many don't acknowledge their soul as a real thing.

A living breathing thing that needs to be nurtured and cared for, much like anything else.

What do you feed it? What to you teach it?

Do you exercise it? Build it? Strengthen it?
Care for it?

What if it breaks?

Just like you put a brace on a broken leg you need to put braces on a broken soul.

Surround it with structure and strength.

With stability and support.

An environment that accelerates healing.

A new situation that removes all possibility of further trauma.

Your soul will be good to you if you be good to it.

Develop a good soul tie and spiritual association with your own soul.

It all starts with you, and you'll be much better at attracting other beautiful spiritual associations.

You'll know a beautiful soul when you feel one.

Focus and Magnification

What you magnify you get more of.

Where there is focus there will be growth.

Concentrated attention.

Massive effort, thrown in one singular direction.

You'll always find what you actively engage in looking for.

Don't say you want something and do nothing to try and find it.

Don't say you want something and put no focus there.

Don't say you want something and exert no kind of effort to actually obtain it.

Nothing in life will ever work unless you do.

Throw your whole self at...

One thing, one course, one trail, one direction, one path, one calling.

Be obsessed.

Role with the punches, ride the waves, and take every punch.

Don't switch, get distracted, diverted, rerouted, or redirected.

Where attention goes, energy flows. The results always show.

Namaste

I forgive you.

Now take a hike.

Lose my number.

Never come back.

You're deleted.

Hasta la vista........baby.

We're done.

Don't get this forgiveness thing twisted.

It's not about you, it's about me.

See ya....ta-ta....arrivederci.

Until we never meet again.

I accept what happened. It's all good.

We're good really.

I'm in a great place spiritually...

Now stay the hell away from me....Namaste.

Don't Have To

Humbleness is a sign of confidence.

Don't walk in the council of the wicked or ungodly.

Tiny, minor, little itty bitty, proud, arrogant, and self-righteous men and woman.

Get rid of all dead wisdom.

Wisdom from how you were raised.

Wisdom of this world.

Wisdom from where you came from.

Wisdom from some of the people around you.

You don't have to treat your wife the way your dad treated his.

I know you want to be a big shot like your boss but truly great men and women don't need a title, because they understand the title doesn't make the man or woman...

The man or woman makes the title.

You don't have to be mean, bitter, and hateful because your siblings are.

You don't have to treat your kids the way your parents treated theirs.

You don't have to get drunk, high, or get into trouble because your friends do.

You don't have to think you're limited and worthless because your spouse or significant other told you so.

You don't have to believe what the majority believe.

You don't have to walk where the majority walk.

You don't have to do what the majority do.

Take the advice from very few people.

Pay closer attention to the person giving the advice than the advice itself.

Don't allow anyone worse off than you to counsel you.

Some ties need to be broken.

Never be more proud over how you got it...

Than WHO gave it to you.

It Takes Courage

Do you have the courage to act outwardly what you see inwardly?

Or will you live always on the edge.

Just on the verge.

In the land of could've, would've, and should've.

It takes courage to be successful.

It takes courage to be blessed.

It takes courage to go against the grain.

It takes courage to leave your hand down when everyone else is raising theirs.

It takes courage to go where you've never gone before.

It takes courage to drive down a one way street.

It takes courage to be educated, knowledgeable, wise, and exceptional.

Because once you do people will try to talk you back to their level.

"You remember where you came from?"

It takes courage to level up.

In this weak, watered down, mediocre world we live in today...

After all you been through, did you come this far and go through all you went through to fit in with normalcy?

You have to have courage to say...

COME HELL OR HIGH WATER ...I'M GOING AFTER MY STUFF.

My God...you've got to have the courage.

I Am

I am.

What you put after this statement runs your life.

You set yourself up for whatever you say.

It's the basis for the narrative you live by.

The identity you've accepted as your reality at one time or another.

You're born with no I am.

Somehow you go from a blank slate to...

I am ugly. I am incapable. I am unlovable. I am limited. I am broke. I am inferior. I am not enough. I am cursed. I am hopeless. I am scared. I am not worth it.

Along the way something happens.

People.

When you don't know who you are, you become whatever other people want you to be, think you should be, and tell you to be.

When you know who you are, then you know who you are not.

Be who you want to be. Own your I am.

Who do you say you are?

Turn every other I am into I was.

I Still Grew

I didn't get water, I didn't get sunlight, but I still grew.

People that grew up with unconditional love, close knit families, well off families, and good circumstances see the world different than those that grew up without.

I didn't have what they had.

I made it anyway.

I stopped grieving off of what I didn't get and celebrated the fact, in spite of it, I still made it.

It's not where you come from. It's what you're made of.

Dirt under my fingernails, tears in my eyes, confused, and even a bit crazy...

I made it anyway.

Those that left, those that forgot about me, those that used me, those that lied on me and to me, those that took advantage...

There's no one you should be so angry at that they're worth messing up how your story is going to end.

I made it anyway.

Broke, busted, and disgusted.

Alone I was believing. Afraid I was believing. Betrayed I was believing. Let down I was believing.

I'm not where I'm going to be, thank God I'm not where I was.

I didn't come this far to only come this far.

The rest of my life will be the best of my life, and when it's all said and done.

I'll get a wink and a nod from the man up above...I had what I needed all along.

I made it anyway.

What Now?

So it happened. What now?

You gotta fight, declare all-out war.

Literally step into the ring and put up your fists. This is a fight.

You can't let anything break your spirit.

This isn't a fight with people. I'm talking about a fight no one can see.

You have to fight to reclaim your mind from the strongholds of affliction.

Demons. You can't change what you won't confront.

It's painful. But you can't feel sorry for yourself.

You've got to get angry.

It's said anger is a bad thing...not this time.

Get livid. Get pissed off. The deeper the fury the better.

Cry about it. Fall out with it.

Develop an attitude problem.

Show life what you're made of.

You got sucker punched so you lay down and cry? No you get up and open a can of whip ass.

So you lost a battle, doesn't mean you can't win the war.

Use the affliction and pain as fuel to overcome.

It didn't kill you, your life isn't over.

You don't know what you got until you've been under fire, until you've been tested.

Affliction is an opportunity to do a great thing.

Seize the opportunity.

Pruning

Certain losses are important to the development of who you are.

A fruit tree needs to be pruned to be more fruitful.

Pruning influences the direction a plant grows.

Prune your life.

The dead wood of your associations, connections, and influences.

Cut away what's getting in the way, what's keeping you in the shade, in the dark.

After all where there is more light, the fruit is more abundant.

You might have some dead limbs and branches in your life that aren't serving any purpose.

Not adding any value to your overall health and well-being.

Growth is promoted through a scaling back, a cutting away...

It frees you up. Gets you moving in the right direction.

Sometimes when you lose certain people you're gaining much more than you think.

Always judge a tree by the fruit it actually bears.

Make sure you're in a position to bear it.

Bear it abundantly.

Words

Words have power.

If negative words have the power to bring you down, positive words have the power to lift you up.

You can always determine just how much powerful words really stick to a person by the way their mindset and actions start to change.

Not words that go over your head, but words that graft like skin into your soul, becoming one with you.

Language and actions are a direct measure of the level a person has really received messages intended for them to hear.

Powerful words, when truly received...

Send chills down your spine.

Provoke tears from your eyes.

Moves you so profoundly that your actions drastically shift.

Goosebumps are common.

You'll develop new desires. What used to interest you no longer does.

Your face begins to glow with beams of truth.

Eyes wide open, shoulds and coulds become musts.

Your normal is disrupted. Your routine obsolete.

It's disturbing, but desirable.

People you've known for a long time begin to look different to you, including yourself...not in a good way.

There's a heightened awareness of everything.

A sixth sense beyond sight, smell, hearing, taste, and touch.

You wake up, and start wiping the crust out of your third eye.

You crave getting up from the popular table to go sit by your damn self.

Black and white becomes every color of the rainbow.

Your show horse becomes a unicorn.

Your telescope becomes a kaleidoscope.

You must break the mold. You must be different.

You thirst for knowledge. That thirst is never quenched.

You realize you've been in a coma, even though you're wide awake walking around.

Powerful words, ingrafted, can save your soul, lift your spirit, and heal what can't be seen, only described.

Words are like gold, sift out what's useful and discard the rest.

Look for a nugget everyday...

Soon you'll be sitting on a goldmine.

Incarceration

It takes guts to walk away from the visible in the direction of the invisible.

Don't let the counterfeit experience of being good prevent you from the pursuit of greatness.

Sometimes you can become incarcerated by a title.

People begin to define you by it, you're known for it.

Meanwhile no one really knows you hate it.

Jobs, careers, hobbies, talents, certain lifestyles, and even relationships.

You can be really good and talented at something you hate.

Don't live in the prison of a label people want to define you by.

If you would rather be doing something else...then do it.

Walk away from comfort and try to become something you don't know how to become.

Get out of step with your reality to get in step with your destiny, your calling, the thing you really want to do.

In the end the only thing that's going to matter is the regret of the chances you didn't take.

Sure some may be shocked you hate what they think you love...

But many are the same people that pretend to love what they really hate.

They don't live your life, or have to live with the torment, stress, and anguish of living a lie...you do.

Don't base your decisions on those that don't have to deal with the results.

One life, live it how you want.

You may lose a lot but gain something you never imagined you could have.

Decide what kind of life you really want... and then say no to everything that isn't that.

Forget titles, they're only meaningful to insecure people.

I've Been Thinking

What you think does make a difference.

Your circumstances don't matter...as long as you just keep thinking.

Thinking of better days and greater outcomes.

Thinking you're greater than your circumstances, nothing can hold you down, and that you refuse to be defined by what happened to you or where you come from.

Thinking the conqueror within you is greater than the circumstances around you.

See, my life hasn't been picture perfect...but I've been thinking.

I looked at the man in the mirror and didn't like what I saw.

But I've been thinking.

On my knees, depression.

But I've been thinking.

Drugs, alcohol, up all night dancing with the devil himself.

But I've been thinking.

Pregnant wife, baby wasn't mine.

But I've been thinking.

Daddy got new kids forgot about the two he made.

But I've been thinking.

Couldn't be a corporate puppet.

But I've been thinking.

Almost went bankrupt, insurmountable mountains to climb.

But I've been thinking.

Mommy is perfect, I was a bad boy.

But, in spite of all that, I've been thinking...

Yeah...yeah...I've been thinking...

I'm on the verge of something.

Something is about to happen.

I kept thinking I'm right on the edge of the biggest breakthrough I've ever had in my life.

Yeah, I just kept thinking...until I finally became what I thought.

I could've given up, I could've laid down and died.

I know you've been dealt a bad hand, are going through hell, and sometimes cry yourself to sleep.

But it's hard to hold a person down that'll just keep thinking.

You can be tied up spiritually, emotionally, and even physically.

But if your mind is loose...no matter the circumstances...just keep thinking my friend.

Emotional Dumpster

Misery loves company.

Don't allow people to lay guilt trips on you because you don't want to lay in the same sewer they lay in.

There's a difference between being there for someone and being their emotional dumpster.

You can be a kind, nice, and a caring person but be strong enough to not let people drag you down.

Help people, be there for them, but don't allow them to become a major hindrance to your own life.

Just because you don't want to lay in the same sewer as another person doesn't mean you don't care.

Even Jesus called people out and redeemed people but didn't go in to get them or stay where they were.

Help people when you can, but don't allow them to be an anchor keeping you limited so they can have fellowship in misery...and you can have failure.

You can lead a horse to water...but you can't make them drink. If a person isn't trying to help themselves you're not going to be able to help them.

Setting yourself on fire to keep someone else warm is a losing proposition.

Especially when someone is looking for a twin flame.

The Same Place

Ever wonder how you always seem to end up in the same place over and over no matter how hard you try or how much you try to change?

You've changed everything. Everything is different, new, upgraded, and improved.

Only one thing you forgot.

There's one element to really changing your life that many overlook and flat out ignore.

If you don't change the mind, and therefore who you are, the same experiences will keep perpetuating themselves over and over.

You can change your address, your spouse, your girlfriend or boyfriend, your job or career, your friends, your hair color, your makeup, your clothes, your routine, your diet, even your name.

But if your mind doesn't change the outcome will be the same.

That relationship was toxic, you deserve better and raised your standards. New relationship, you saw the signs and ignored them, after all, you're lonely and they're so fine.

The complications that got you fired, demoted, or kept at a low level in your first two jobs or careers will get you fired, demoted, or kept at a low level in the third.

You can take the person out of the ghetto, but you can't take the ghetto out of the person.

Your new spouse is way better than your old spouse. Unfortunately you are the same person in the new marriage you were in the old marriage. Good thing you kept the attorney's number.

New makeover, gorgeous on the outside. Damn you're fine! Still ugly as can be inside.

You're ready, you're leveling up, and you're getting around new groups of people. Discomfort and rejection dumb you back down to comfy status. Call your homeboy.

New Year resolution, new diet, new routine. Great, problem is this is the seventh attempt and it's just one bite.

When you take an old mind into all of these new life changes, upgrades, and makeovers, you're kidding yourself.

Change your mind, change your life.

Who Told You?

You're stuck because you care what they think.

A miserable life is a product of valuing someone else's opinion and point of view, about you and your life, more than you value your own.

People screw you up.

Who told you you sucked?

Who told you you were ugly?

Who told you you can't?

Who told you you're not capable?

Who told you you're not smart?

Who told you it's a bad idea?

Who told you you're not living right?

Who told you you're stupid for leaving that job?

Who told you it can't be done?

Who told you?

Your life will dramatically shift when your opinion about you becomes greater than the opinion of your spouse, your parents, your significant other, your siblings, your cousins, your coworkers, your best friend, your acquaintances, your boss...

Basically everyone on earth.

When you seek approval from you first, and everyone on earth second...

You will be free indeed.

Ultimately what you say about you is going to make or break your life.

Anything in your life that's built or based on inauthenticity trying to appease and please someone else will eventually collapse.

You've wasted enough time trying to change certain people's minds about you that are dead set in seeing you one way.

Those people with a mind that refuses to change.

They're a liar. Truth is what YOU say.

Get yours. Stop explaining who you are. Eventually they'll see.

And if they don't, they don't...you have to get busy living.

Sometimes you've just got to leave people alone stuck in their tiny point of view.

You're not here to be who they want you to be, you're here to be who God wants you to be.

I Like It

The fear of failure blocks total commitment.

Always one foot in and one foot out just in case it doesn't work out.

Half committed just in case things don't go as planned you have a way out.

Always keeping your options open just in case you need a backup.

But being half committed in anything yields half committed results.

People are afraid to go all in.

They think they're all in but there really not.

It's scary pushing all your chips to the center of the table.

You've really got to be sure right?

Me?

I like to increase the dose from least to most.

I like to take the same hand someone else is losing with and win with it.

I like to take the island and burn the boat.

I like to operate without a safety net.

I like intensity.

I like to stomp instead of tip toe.

I like to create storms the weather man couldn't predict.

When the going gets tough, the tough deliver abrasive, devastating effort and work ethic.

Sorry mister mailman...I'll deliver it myself.

Move over Lucifer...I'm more ruthless.

Quitting not an option. Defeat not accepted.

The race isn't won by the swiftest or the fastest...but the one that can endure it to the end.

It's not how you start. It's how you finish.

What happens in between is a direct measure of human will.

Most won't...I will...enthusiastically.

See you at the finish line.

<u>You Must</u>

If you do what you've always done you'll always be where you've always been.

You can't step into your future dragging the mess of your past around.

The possibility of change. The desire to evolve.

The passion to get up off the ground and stop eating dirt.

There are things you must do...

You must be tired of what you used to do.

You must throw it behind you.

You must have faith in those things that are before you and forget those things that are behind.

You must believe the best is yet to come.

You must believe you have the power to make it so.

You must believe you are more than a conqueror.

You must believe in something greater than yourself.

You must believe there's something waiting for you if you just have the courage enough to reach your hand out and grab it.

You must no longer be a liar like the majority of men and women.

You must become something better than you are right now.

Come hell or high water, my God...

You must become better than you are right now.

Some things need to fall apart so better things can come together.

Until you allow that...all your tomorrows will look like today.

Tomorrow is shaped today.

TODAY is the day tomorrow will become different.

Gossip

People that like to gossip are off track with their own life.

The reason they're interested in your life is because they have no life of their own.

See when you get a life you don't have time to think about someone else's business.

It takes all your time and energy to mind your own business.

In fact some people's ability to care about and focus on dumb things as it relates to other people is extraordinarily amazing.

There are some that would be a lot better off if they spent a fraction of the time they do talking about and focusing on other people...talking about and focusing on themselves.

Weak minds discuss people.

I get quiet around gossip because I just couldn't care less about what people are talking about.

Get around people that like to talk about ideas, concepts, opportunities...things of valuable substance.

People who want to gossip with you will gossip about you. If they talk about someone else, rest assured they're talking about you.

Let people talk, it makes them feel better about their own lack of achievement and insecurities.

Winners focus on winning, losers focus on winners.

My level of concern about what another has to say about me or my life is astronomically low.

Whatever you hear about me please believe it. I no longer have time or interest to explain myself...you can even add some to the story if you want.

Have fun...I'm busy.

Weakness In Disguise

There are many strong people in the world, but weak in character.

Those that prey on the weak are despicable...truly the scum of the earth.

People that use their status, position, privilege, and power to be douche bags.

If you want to see a true sign of a person's character give them power and watch what they do with it.

A low life takes a position of power and uses it to take advantage of the weak.

Power without character is a dangerous combination.

How you make other people feel about themselves says a lot about you.

No matter how successful, powerful, talented, rich, and prestigious an individual is, how they treat people ultimately defines them.

Ultimately the ones boasting giant strength externally do so because of weakness internally.

Some "strength" is weakness in disguise.

The truly strong teach the weak strength, not exploit them for what they lack so they can have gain.

Kindness and compassion are true strength.

Have a giant's strength but don't use it like a giant.

The duty of the strong is to protect the weak and always be careful who you mess with...they may be little and weak, but have a giant backing them up.

Entitlement

Entitlement.

The belief that one is inherently deserving of privileges or special treatment.

They want the job promotion but don't want to work.

They want a better life but don't get a better character.

They want to be treated with respect and value but won't drop their ghetto or immature mindset and personality.

They want the finer things in life but forgot about instilling the finer things in themselves.

Here's the truth.

You're eating dirt because you are delusional.

The world owes you nothing. People in general owe you nothing.

You are deserving of nothing you do not work for and earn.

Your gimme mentality will get you no where in life.

Gimme money. Gimme a nice place to live. Gimme a good job. Gimme nice things. Gimme my fair share. Gimme what I want.

Life isn't fair. Favor isn't fair.

You will receive in life a direct reflection of who and what you are.

Your life is garbage because you are garbage.

You want a better life...be better.

Work on yourself. Work harder at the opportunities you've been given.

Until then life will continue to dish out less than your "fair share."

And quite frankly, with that deplorable sense of entitlement, you're getting exactly what you deserve.

"We"

Association brings about simulation.

You act like and become what you are around.

You hang around clowns, your life will begin to look like a circus.

The greatest show on earth.

A sideshow. Come one come all.

Next thing you know you're making balloon animals, and take up juggling.

Be careful of "we".

Many people give up what's the best thing for them to stay committed to the "we" of an organization or relationship.

"We" need to stick together.

"We" need to be committed to the company.

"We" are meant to be together.

"We" are a team.

"We" need to think this way.

"We" are in this together.

People will control you with a "we".

When "we" becomes something that pins you to a place, position, or mindset you don't want or that's not what's necessarily best for you...

Flip that W upside down...screw the "we"...do what's best for "me".

The circus clowns in your life will get over it, besides...genuine concern and tears are all just part of their act.

Focus

Nobody can get what you got until they do what you do.

If you reaped it, you at some point sowed it.

You want to reap different? Sow different.

You've got to define your priorities then put time in.

Where you spend more time sowing you will reap more in that area.

Very straight, very simple....

But, sometimes things are easier to explain than to execute.

People get distracted easily.

Sowing in a million different areas...reaping a little here and there but never a lot in one place.

Wherever you focus it will always be at the expense of lost focus on something else.

Be careful what you focus on.

You are a limited resource.

Sow good seed in the areas that can bear the most fruit. Let the rest die in the ground.

And most importantly, never give up too soon.

There's a tree in that acorn.

Trust Your Hustle

People will try to impose their limits on you.

"That's a rash decision."

"It's a ton of work, I wouldn't want to deal with that."

"How are you going to make that work?"

"You're acting a bit premature don't you think?"

"What are you going to do if this happens?"

"What are you going to do if that happens?"

"You know how many people try and fail at this...you need to be careful."

"You can't do it that way."

"You're crazy!"

"You're thick headed, you should listen to me!"

People always look for logic in everything.

I pride myself on doing illogical things through illogical work ethic.

You'd be surprised how hard you hit it when you have nothing to fall back on.

How hard you'll push...and fight.

What looks insurmountable to an average eye is a sure thing to me.

I can move confidently because I trust my hustle.

I know that I will put in the work. I decide in advance that I'll pay the price, whatever that price may be, to see something through.

See...my hunger is unexplainable.

Anything that steps in my path is feeling it.

You ask why...I ask why not.

You say you wouldn't...I say yes please I will.

Your belief is limited, mine is abundant.

You have a million reasons you can't, I have a million why I can.

You feel uncertainty and fear and remain comfortable, I lean into it, do it anyway, and embrace discomfort.

Take the leap, do it, move in that direction, make the tough decisions, do you, dream, go after it, chase it, seize it.

People don't need to agree or understand.

Eventually they'll see.

Take the advice of very few people. Smile, nod yes like you agree, then do what you were going to do anyway.

That Pain

I'm blessed because I went through so much pain.

That pain pushed me.

That pain provoked me.

That pain started a riot in my soul.

That pain pushed me to work harder.

That pain caused me to try a little bit harder.

That pain made me realize I have nothing to lose.

That pain opened my eyes.

That pain turned a walk into an all out sprint.

That pain pissed me off.

That pain was a gift from God.

That pain was an angel on my shoulder.

That pain was the itch that caused me to scratch.

The song that taught me to dance.

The shock that resuscitated a dead man.

The catalyst to an explosive reaction.

The final second on a ticking time bomb.

The voice only I could hear.

The hand that helped me up.

The stimulant drug that coursed through my veins.

Yeah...yeah, that pain.

I'm blessed because of that pain.

It is good to have been afflicted.

That pain made me...me.

And it's who I always wanted to be.

The Pretentious Ones

Sometimes bitterness doesn't come from what happened to you...but from what is not happening.

There's no bitterness like the bitterness of seeing others step into blessings that you're not.

In fact, when you're a blessed person, you need to be prepared to be disliked by some.

You always know the bitter people by how they act towards you.

The pretentious ones. The ones with the delusional, grandiose sense of self and importance.

They seemingly dislike you for no reason.

Blatantly go out of their way to try and diminish your shine, pick you apart, or in some cases ruin your life.

It's always the people that think they're something that they're not.

People that think they're way more important than they really are.

A false sense of authority, prestige, status, and stature.

Noses up in the air, they truly believe they're better than people.

You see them every day and they don't acknowledge you.

They're always the ones that have the most need to uphold a certain image.

They're pathetic.

You agitate their demons.

Be blessed, stay humble, and never ever dull your shine or limit your potential because some pathetic loser like this is bitter.

Keep winning, keep growing, and keep smiling...they hate that.

Keep giving them something to be bitter about.

Bottom line is that everyone isn't going to like you or be happy for you in life, especially when you win or threaten their delusional grandiosity...and you don't have to care.

After all, the people that aren't happy for you are most definitely not happy for themselves either.

When you're the real deal, you don't have to try very hard, diminish, or hate on other people to prove it.

Revelation

Revelation.

A surprising and previously unknown fact, especially one that is made known in a dramatic way.

It's in our darkest hours we have our greatest revelations.

Things happen to us. Life happens to us.

People spend so much time looking for logic.

How could this happen? How could this be? Why me?

You don't need the reason for it...you need the revelation from it.

You don't need knowledge from it...you need the revelation from it.

You don't need the meaning of it...you need the revelation from it.

Things happen in your life to give you revelation.

The revelation is in the situation.

Revelation defies logic.

Something made apparent in a dramatic way.

Without the drama there is no revelation.

It's not meant to be understood.

It's meant to be revealed to you.

Nothing just happens.

It's all simply preparation for the revelation.

The surprising and previously unknown facts that will guide your life.

You can't see the stars without the darkness.

There's opportunity in your chaos.

But only if you believe.

"Watch Me"

"You'll always be a loser."

"You'll always be a nobody."

"You'll never amount to anything."

And the infamous "you'll be nothing without me."

Sometimes I get tired. Sometimes I want to give up. Sometimes I question whether or not I can do this. Sometimes I doubt myself.

Sometimes I feel inadequate, inferior, and incapable. Then....sometimes I remember what you said...You're going to eat your words. Watch me.........bitch.

Settling

Many stop wondering what's possible for them and start thinking what's probable.

You know what you wanted to be, but settled for what you are.

Making more compromises in life than you would have liked at the expense of your true potential and real desires.

Your "shoot for the stars" hopes turned into modest aspirations.

Placing unproven opinions ahead of the willingness to even try.

Putting all kinds of judgements about what you really can or can't do ahead of a real effort.

Somewhere along the way you bought into the idea that you can't.

That what you're doing now is what you're supposed to be doing.

It's easy to fool people that are fooling themselves.

You have to purify and detach yourself from people...and what they say about your possible outcomes.

Limits that are pressed upon you that you believe and accept as your reality.

You can't set limits on something you haven't even truly given an all out effort to achieve.

Stop selling yourself short.

Forget your preconceived notions about what's realistic and likely based on your history and current capabilities.

And especially based on what other people say.

You can't predict what you can or can't do until you try.

Stop letting blind people proof read your vision.

When you can start imagining better possibilities and a bigger life...

You can have them.

Oh...and it is easier said than done.

There are people taking the same hand you're dealt and winning with it.

The only thing holding you back is the idea that there's something holding you back.

Do it. Right now. Today.

Your tomorrows are running out.

Break The Rules

There are so many rules in life about everything.

Many of the most successful people in history broke the rules.

As children we are taught to color inside the lines...but why should we be confined to the inside of someone else's vision?

Color outside the lines.

Step out of bounds.

If people are going up, I urge you to go down.

If they're going left, I urge you to go right.

Don't follow the crowd, go where it's empty.

Break free from the cage that are your associations.

Get up from the popular table and sit by your damn self.

Be a voice not an echo.

Hand in the uniform for a tailored outfit.

Pave the way don't follow it.

Don't go where they go. Don't do what they do. Don't talk like they talk.

If they're doing this, I urge you to do that.

If they're doing that, I urge you to do this.

If they say you shouldn't do it...do it...aggressively and enthusiastically.

Separate yourself from other people.

Forget them, remember you.

In taking these actions, you may stand alone, but...

One day you'll stand out.

Just Like Them

Much of what we learn about life is from people that don't know what they're doing either.

People with plenty of input, but lack personal output.

Coaching people on life, and can't even handle their own life.

We learn about being a mother or father from people that aren't good parents.

We learn about love by people that never really loved us.

We learn about success from people that haven't accomplished much.

We take swimming lessons by those that are drowning.

Much of what we admire is smoke and mirrors.

We learn how to love who we are by those that can't even look in the mirror.

How to see by those that are blind.

How to cook by those that have no hunger.

How to find ourselves by those that are lost.

How to be genuinely happy by those that live fake.

How to look rich but really be broke.

Most people are unaware of their own shortcomings.

Most people are unaware that they are full of crap.

Double check the advice, stories, and narratives you've been given.

People always give advice and speak from the perspective they have.

Their level. You can't think higher than the level you're exposed to.

Problem with most people is they think their level is something special.

It's up to you to expose yourself to information beyond what you've been fed.

Be careful who you listen to...you might end up being just like them.

In the majority of cases, that's probably not a good thing.

Let God be true and every man a liar.

Silly People

Often times people will always limit you and confine you to the description as they know or once knew you.

The greatest compliment is when a person who knew you when asks "when did you become?"

Silly people.

If you must know...I became when I made a commitment to become.

When I fell out with my old life and decided I wanted way more.

When I refused to submit to that type of limited thinking.

When I pushed forward in spite of fear.

When I resolved to pay the price in advance no matter what it may be and die before I'd ever give up.

When I used all the things people said about me and did to me as power pellets to dominate my life, succeed any, and shove it up their ass.

When I demanded more from myself and my life and rejected the tiny and timid mentality that asks ridiculously stupid questions such as "when did you become?"

Yeah...that's when I became.

Hope that answered the question.

Let Them Walk

You're ultimate destiny isn't tied to the person who left.

People leave you because they're not really for you.

Not really joined to you.

A person that is absolutely, completely, and genuinely joined to you can NEVER walk away from you.

When a person can walk away from you let them walk.

Don't try to talk another person into staying with you.

Into being your friend, being a part of your life, loving you, or caring about you.

Doesn't matter how attractive they are.

Doesn't matter how much money they have.

Doesn't matter how much they've got it going on.

Doesn't matter what they did for you in the past.

Doesn't matter how much history you have with them.

And, most importantly it doesn't matter what comes out of their mouth.

Temporary people teach us permanent lessons.

Many people only come into our lives to teach us who not to be and how not to act.

Know when a person's part in your story is over and burn the book.

Have the gift of goodbye.

Stop begging people to stay, let them go.

You'll be amazed at what you attract once you start believing in what you deserve.

Dead Wood

I'm sorry I spoke and acted that way.

What was I thinking believing something like that?!

I apologize, I should be making better life decisions.

It's too much I know I'm sorry...

Ok ok ok, I'll dumb myself down I promise...now FaceTime me.

I know I'm sorry for trying to be an eagle my fellow chicken.

Look at my new shine! I dulled it down just for you! So where did you want to go for drinks?

Wait! Wait! Let me dilute my character and personality real quick...ok you know there's a really good restaurant I wanted to try.

I'll echo everything you say I promise...call me.

Yes! I'll be your supporting act in the companies puppet show!

Look I'll only use the sad, crying, and angry face emojis...text me.

Alright! I'm limited, insecure, not growing, and want to complain too! Let's take a day trip.

Look! My smile is now upside down. Can we be friends?

I watered down my fire so we can both blow smoke together.

The only thing real here is that I'm fake just like you! Let's go out and wear matching masks.

I will be whatever and whoever you want me to be because I love you.

I don't know what would happen if I lost you...

I mean...besides of course losing some dead wood, thereby freeing up my time, focus, and energy for people and relationships that are more in alignment with who I am, who I really want to be, and want to level up.

Take Control

Your life will expand in direct proportion to your level of courage.

Years go by with very little change because there's no courage.

People are afraid.

It is not human nature to be a champion, exceptional, out of the ordinary, or above average.

It's human nature to be average, blend in, comfortable, stable, and secure.

Look out from where you are...

Look out past the parameters of your present location.

Do you have the courage to think beyond who and what you are?

Do you have the courage to become outwardly what you see inwardly?

What you see is what you'll be.

Do you have the courage to think your own thoughts?

Do you have the courage to give up the "person" you are right now to be who you really want to be?

Do you have the courage to be the Chief Executive Officer of your life and promote or fire people accordingly?

Do you have the courage to stand up for yourself and put people in their place that are using you, manipulating you, and treating you like garbage?

Do you have the courage to give up pride and the job or career that gives the appearance of happiness and success, everyone identifies you by it, but you actually hate?

Do you have the courage to face the resistance, disagreement, and chatter from your parents, spouses, friends, bosses, coworkers, family, or significant others by going against the grain?

It's cute to say you're going to do things, but it's the ugly execution that many fall short and get stopped dead in their tracks.

Everybody wants to be a beast until it's time to do what beasts do.

What do you really expect out of your life?

Expectation shows up in behavior.

I can tell you what you expect by watching what you do.

People with courage look around for the circumstances they want, and if they don't find them, they create them.

I know what you're thinking...it's easier said than done...a statement frequently used by those that lack courage.

There's nothing in this world holding you back from doing what's easier said than done except the story you're telling yourself as to why it's easier said than done.

You're 100% in control of your life.

Stop waiting for your life to get better...life is waiting on you to stop talking and start doing.

I'm Not Supposed To

Struggle is all I know. I come from nothing. No special advantages.

Betrayed, put down, left behind, criticized, talked about, and left for dead.

A fish out water most of my life trying to find my way in a world that was constantly beating me down.

Constantly trying to break me in half.

Given my history...

I'm not supposed to be here. It wasn't in the cards for me.

I'm not supposed to be doing this.

I'm not supposed to think I can be more and have more than what I've been exposed to and experienced my whole life.

I'm not supposed to be moving in this direction. I'm not supposed to be headed down this path.

Always consider what's behind an unusual work ethic.

I've been told I'm crazy for doing certain things, I'm gripping the bat too hard, take it easy, you're going to burn yourself out...

People don't understand what's behind the work ethic.

To know you're on the verge of some of the biggest breakthroughs in your life...

It's the "what if" that drives me.

What if I could pull this off?

What if I could be what no one would ever think I could be?

What if I could pull off a miracle?

What if all this hard work pays off?

What if I can actually make this happen?

What a story that would be.

To me, the work isn't work at all, it's a manifestation of who I'm not supposed to be.

No I'm not crazy, I'm passionate.

Passionate at how proud I will be when I look back on my life knowing I wasn't afraid, wouldn't break, and became what I wasn't supposed to be.

Let's Go

Striking a huge oak tree with an axe is trifling, seems trivial and of no consequence.

But, through childish swipes, consistently, again, and again, and again, and again...eventually the tree will fall.

So it will be with my efforts today.

I understand small attempts repeated will conquer any undertaking.

I know that through consistency I will win.

I will try again and again and again.

One brick at a time, laid daily, will build a massive structure.

I will forget the happenings of the day that is gone and greet the new sun with confidence that this will be the best day of my life.

I will succeed. I will win.

No one can tell me who and what I can be.

I define myself.

I will go beyond the fears and limitations of other people.

I'm determined to see what my life will look like if I don't count the cost.

If I'm willing to go further than I think I can go, all in, unafraid, and committed.

I will be like the rain drop that floods the earth.

The ant that drags a mountain.

There's no plan B only plan A.

I will do today what other people will not do...and I will therefore live the type of life other people will never live.

In taking unreasonable, irrational, and abrasive action to realize an expected end, I often ask myself "who's doing this?!"

Nobody but me. My harvest will be full.

I understand that if I want to be extraordinary I must first become an extraordinary person.

I will look in the mirror and destroy the person I see staring back.

I will give up who I am, COMPLETELY, to become the person I need to be to obtain what I want to obtain.

Sometimes...life is a fight.

Sometimes...it's time to fight.

Struggle has molded my character, adversity has sculpted my will, heartache has shifted my spirit.

So when it is...

Let's go.

Self Doubt

There are times you just get tired. Drained to the point you question your will to keep going.

To keep moving down the path of this journey you started and see it through to the end.

Inevitably along the way, self-doubt, disbelief, and discouragement creep in and start to get in your head.

The voices and opinions of other people convincing you that you can't do something begins to wear on you. You start to believe them.

How much longer can you stand up and stand firm?

Obstacles are put in your way to test whether or not you really want it bad enough.

It's OK to take a break. It's OK to rest. It's OK to stop, be still, clear your head, and re-calibrate.

It's OK to struggle...however quitting is not an option.

You have to remember why you started.

You have to remember what they said about you.

You have to remember where you come from...this wasn't meant for you.

You have to remember that person you aren't now, but are trying to become.

You have to remember, what if you can actually do this, oh how life would be.

You have to remember the self-respect you earn from taking life on and not giving up.

You have to remember that vision no one else can see but you.

You have to remember the outcome you desire.

Rise up inside yourself and remember the people you're proving wrong.

This is a fight. This is a test of your will, your strength, your endurance, your stamina, and your true desire.

If you give up easily then you never really wanted it in the first place.

You need to live for this. Bleed for this. Literally die for this...before you would ever give up.

Get up, stand up, slap yourself out of your stupor, put your big boy and big girl pants on...

Make it happen. Most won't but you will. Remember, something always seems impossible until it's done. DO IT.

Every champion was once a contender that simply refused to give up. Your future self will thank you for staying in the fight.

Don't give up on the person you are becoming.

Interesting Phenomenon

Many of the actions you take are not a result of your thinking.

Those with a PhD in life are not wise due to what they've learned, but because of what they've unlearned.

Growth is really just an unraveling and unlearning of all the garbage that's been fed to you your whole life.

Everything you believe you know to be true about yourself and how your life should be lived was programmed into your mind by somebody else.

Advice you get is always a reflection of the advice giver's perception and values. Their perceptions and values aren't always necessarily good for you.

Some of the most miserable periods of my life were a direct result of following someone else's advice and skewed perception for my own life.

Interestingly enough, after following their advice for a while, my life started to take shape and become a mirror image of theirs, which wasn't anywhere near what I really wanted for my own life.

Follow your parent's advice, your father or mother in-law's advice, your blind friend's advice, your teacher's or professor's advice, or even your spouse or significant other's advice, and miraculously your life begins to look eerily similar to theirs.

Don't allow yourself to be programmed. Question everything. Go against the grain.

It's YOUR life. Time is limited.

Follow that inner whisper, your heart and intuition. They know where you really want to go.

And most importantly...you don't owe anyone an explanation.

Defiance

When your mind tells you you can't, what if you didn't believe it?

When it gets tough and your mind is saying just stop, what if you thought you're unstoppable?

When discomfort starts to set in and your mind is screaming slow down, what if you pick up the pace?

When you're afraid and your mind is convincing you to shy away, what if you leaned in anyway?

When you're doubting yourself and your mind whispers it's probably not possible, what if you try anyway?

Where the mind goes the body will follow.

Where the mind goes your life will follow.

Imagine what your life might look like if you controlled your thinking and didn't let your thinking control you.

If you moved forward without limiting beliefs.

The external world doesn't matter when your inner world is relentless.

Your world is an outer expansion of what's going on inside your head.

Show me your life I can tell you your thoughts.

Reject and discard every thought that insults your spirit.

Fully embrace the fact and realize that your thoughts control your life.

Become careful what you think about.

<u>5 Years Ago</u>

People would have laughed at me had I said in five years I would acquire $4 million worth of real estate.

They would have laughed if I said I was going to be doing large renovation projects.

Five years ago I knew hardly anything about real estate.

Five years ago I had to google how to swing a hammer.

All I knew was how to slave for a commission check and pucker my way up a corporate ladder in a cushy job that was considered normal by most people's standards.

I had no special training. No special licenses. No special degrees. No special certificates.

No special nothing.

People would have looked at what was realistic. What was likely. The evidence that was right in front of them.

I don't write this to impress you, but to impress upon you that the person with big dreams is more powerful than the person with all the facts.

When you're hungry you don't care about the facts.

Logical practical thinking says you can't do it today.

You want to produce unreasonable results in your life, you've got to be an unreasonable person.

You've got to be an uncommon person.

I intentionally stepped into one uncomfortable situation after another.

I didn't wait for the perfect moment.

I wasn't "ready."

I didn't have the perfect plan.

I didn't have all the answers.

I had a made up mind and a determined heart.

See, people don't lack the perfect moment, the readiness, the perfect plan, or all the answers.

They lack the true burning desire to obtain what they say they want.

They lack the action that matches the words fluttering out of their mouth.

You don't transition to another level when you're comfortable with the level you're on.

Comfort makes you weak. Comfort is where dreams go to die. Comfort is where you go to die.

If you're going to change your life and go where you've never gone before you need to have courage.

You will not find toughness in a comfortable environment.

Something has to give. Has to break.

That something is you.

I suggest you live in fear everyday of your life...

The fear of missing out on all you could be, because you're wrapped up in what you are.

Advices

Take the advice of very few people.

Sadly many people are misled and fail because they are listening to the advice of their parents, in-laws, siblings, friends, teachers, coaches, bosses, coworkers, etc.

Pay closer attention to the advice giver than the advice itself. Most people are full of it. It's not that they don't mean well, it's just that they have never actually done what you are wanting or trying to do and therefore can't advise you on how to proceed.

Knowing something isn't enough. What have they actually done? The proof is in the pudding.

We're afraid to go against the grain, upset someone, or be disrespectful to someone we love.

Advice always stems from the givers perspective. It's always a reflection of their perceived limitations based on what they've experienced, have done, or have failed to do.

In some cases it's a pure manipulation that's in the advice givers best interest not yours. Just because they can't do something people want to convince you that you can't do something.

Never let anyone push their limitations on to you. Take a closer look at the advice givers in your life. Although they may mean well, they may be destroying your life and holding you back tremendously.

No Love

Where were you when I fell and needed help up?

You get no love.

When I cried myself to sleep?

When they were stitching me up?

When I was hopeless and afraid?

You get no love.

When I was sleeping on the floor in a strange place?

When I needed guidance?

You get no love.

When I was crying for help?

When I needed a place to stay?

You get no love.

When I needed someone to give a shit?

When my life was falling apart?

You get no love.

When I was strung out?

Where were you?

Nowhere to be found.

I couldn't find you...

But I found me. I found pride. I found purpose. I found my true abilities. I found my way.

I found a life that will be well lived.

I found love for myself...and I am enough.

I don't need ya.

Although you get a middle finger and a have a nice day....

You get no love.

Trapped

You can't drive forward looking in the rear view mirror.

You will never move forward if you're wasting all your energy on what did happen.

You're fueling your history at the expense of your destiny.

Here's the truth...

The person you're mad at is out having a good time and done moved on with their life.

They're not thinking about you and they don't care you're mad.

You've got to have enough respect for yourself and your life to stop allowing someone to control you.

You're not free.

You're trapped in a state of mind and being controlled by someone else.

They own you.

You're limited and they could care less.

Aren't you smarter than that?

You're not hurting them with your anger.

You're hurting yourself.

Focus on where you're going not where you've been.

Let it go move on because I assure you that there's much better quality out there.

You'll never know what could be until you let go of what was.

I'm sorry to say that being mad at them isn't going to change them or the situation.

I mean mad or not...

They're still going to be the same piece of shit.

You're better than that.

Mental Diet

Make no mistake about it. Highly successful people think differently.

Very differently.

Success is a mindset. You must learn it by consuming material and content that will cultivate it.

You upgraded your phone, your membership to the jelly of the month club, and your subscription to People magazine...

But what about upgrading your thinking?

Candy Crush Saga, please no.

Reruns of Seinfeld, just stop.

Celebrity gossip, oh my, no.

Howard Stern on your morning drive, come on now.

Don't keep up with the Kardashians.

ALWAYS sharing pointless memes and posts, what's going on here?

Religiously following the latest shenanigans of your friend Claire or Cousin Jimmy on Facebook, OK, enough is enough.

You get the point. Ditch the distractions. Ditch the crap.

Just like you are what you eat, you are what you mentally consume.

There's such a thing as junk food for the mind, and you can always tell when someone has a shitty diet.

Hallucination

Loosen the tie around your neck, take off the uniform, throw the name tag or name plate in the garbage...

They just may be causing you to hallucinate.

I know you're popular, have a reputation, and are known for what you do...but you may be majoring in a minor thing.

Double check the narrative you're being fed.

Many miss out on the narrative they really want or is best for them because they're believing someone else's narrative hook line and sinker.

Believing another idea of what success looks like or should be.

Cross reference what you're being told.

Many can't think for themselves so they submit and fall into a group think strategy.

Hypnotized, bamboozled, influenced by your social and work environment.

If I think like everyone else I'll be accepted.

I'll fit in.

Life can be a lot broader. You can be a lot broader.

But, you can't think higher than the level that you're exposed to.

Think bigger thoughts.

See yourself beyond where you are.

Don't cheat yourself following the herd off the cliff of life.

Don't be a prisoner to someone else's imagination, agenda, or plan.

Be careful of the influences you allow into your life.

If you can give up the title, the ridiculous ego, and the reputation that comes along with it...you can become what you know deep down you can really be and most importantly...want to be.

You're not fooling anyone but yourself.

And when you're receiving "advice" always remember it's easy to fool people that are fooling themselves.

<u>Know It Alls</u>

Some people have an answer for everything.

A snappy comeback.

I mean they just know EVERYTHING. They've experienced it ALL. Done it ALL. Made EVERY mistake imaginable.

A living breathing instruction manual for life.

You need to listen to them.

They can tell you how to do everything.

They know exactly what everyone else needs to do to live better, be better, and improve their life.

But...when you look at what they've actually produced in their own life....it is very confusing.

So if I do what you say, believe what you believe, and go through the motions you go through I'll have a life that looks just like yours?

I can be living far below my potential?

I can be unhealthy or overweight?

I could be a yes man?

I can live a life of excuses for my incapacities?

I could settle for FAR less in my life?

I could live in denial?

I could be average in every aspect of my life but fool myself into thinking I've done more or are doing more?

I could grow up and be just like you?

So do as you say but not as you do?

Excellent.

When you have all the answers, you've lost.

Reality Check

Why so mad bro?

I see you're big in stature....oooh baby boy, but you're weak where it counts.

Sweety, why so hateful?

I see you're a celebrity in your own movie, oooh but sweety you're nothing more than a stand in extra.

Insecurity is loud. Confidence is so quiet you can hear a pin drop.

Insecurity is verbal. Confidence is action.

Insecurity is stuck. Confidence is free.

Insecurity is surface level. Confidence runs deep.

Insecurity is dumb. Confidence is intelligent.

Insecurity knows not that it knows not. Confidence knows that it knows.

Read that one again bro...sweety. Slow...make sure you get it.

"Knows what?", you ask? Exactly..........

Insecurity puts others down. Confidence lifts others up.

Don't be mad bro. Don't be hateful sweety.

Someday you'll wake up and understand how ridiculously immature and pathetic you are.

And maybe...just maybe you'll develop strength where it counts.

And when that day comes...

The day you give up your weak ego that really doesn't impress anyone that can see straight...

You'll begin to walk without a delusional self-image of grandiosity that is a figment of your imagination. And on that day, the world will greet you with loving open arms and a warm soothing hug, and say...."welcome to reality."

<u>The Truth</u>

Adversity introduces a man or woman to themselves.

Your life...whatever it looks like right now...is a reflection of you.

The choices you've made, the things you believe are possible or not possible, and disciplines or the lack thereof you worship.

If you're looking at your life right now and don't like many things about it, it should be a no brainer that things need to change.

Unfortunately for many that's not always the case.

You can't change what you are not willing to confront. What you're not willing to face.

A rejection of truth, is a deadly disease.

A virus that eats you alive from the inside out.

True bondage has nothing to do with physicality.

You just have to be tied up in your head.

Hard headed people that are set in their ways and beliefs cut off any possibility of an interjection of truth.

The truth pisses them off.

Many only want to accept words that are a confirmation of what they already believe.

People don't like their beliefs to be challenged.

Not a condemnation of their perspectives, but a confirmation and validation of them.

It's hard facing the truth about different aspects of your life.

It's much easier to believe your opinion without fact.

Set in their ways, they'll believe what they want to believe and think what they want to think no matter how you beg, how you plead, how you explain, or how you hit them over the head with obvious truth.

Don't waste your breath wrestling with people that are committed to misunderstanding you.

Become more proficient in your silence than you are in your speech.

It's easier to stay in a known hell than to venture out into an unknown heaven.

Changing your life is hard. People are afraid.

If only they realized the only thing they should be afraid of is the regrets they'll have because they didn't have the courage to change.

They didn't have the courage to take control of their one life.

Unfortunately everyone can't be saved.

The truth hurts, but it's THE ONLY thing that will set you free.

I'm Busy

I'd love to talk and listen to your excuses as to why you can't live a better life but I'm sorry I can't...

I have things to do.

It's not that I don't care...well maybe it is a little bit...

But see I'm busy...

I'm busy actually doing all the things with my life you swear up and down that you can't do.

I'm busy throwing my whole self at a commitment of change.

I'm busy reevaluating my priorities.

I'm busy doing whatever it takes.

I'm busy creating a higher better expression of myself.

I'm busy being relentless.

I'm busy doing what's easier said than done.

I'm busy going beast mode on my life.

I'm busy getting after it.

I'm busy evolving.

I'm busy developing myself.

I'm busy doing instead of talking.

I'm busy finding solutions instead of problems.

I'm busy taking control of my mind, my excuses, and my life.

I'm busy living, not dying.

I'm busy doing EVERYTHING IN MY POWER to be a victor not a victim.

Hopefully that explains it.

Let's catch up next week...you can fill me in on the latest developments that aren't happening with your life then.

Enemy Within

If there's no enemy within, the enemy outside will do you no harm.

No one will do it for you but you.

A made up mind.

A decision that you are moving in a new direction.

And although you can't see what's around that corner as you move further away from the dead zone that is your life, you know it will be no match for a determined heart.

You can only see so far ahead. Your visibility only goes so far.

It's only as you continue to move and get closer does your visibility stretch further.

If you are not severely conflicted within, there's no need for worry.

You will not move, you will not change, you will not shift, you will not explore, you will not turn the corner.

You will be safe. You will be secure.

The enemy outside will not hurt you because it's got you right where it wants you.

Comfortable, convenient, unchallenged, and limited.

Submissive to the comings and goings of the world...

Dead but still alive.

Pick a fight within.

__Becoming__

It shall come to pass.

Your ability to believe that determines your ability to receive that.

Your ability to believe begins to shift only when certain things become another.

When I should becomes I must.

I want to becomes I will.

Maybe becomes hell yes.

Probably becomes certainty.

I think becomes I'm firmly convinced.

I want it becomes I HAVE TO HAVE it.

Fear becomes nothing.

Self-doubt becomes self-confidence.

Passively looking becomes diligently seeking.

Stagnation becomes movement.

Faith becomes works.

They love me becomes I love me.

Immaturity becomes mature.

Distraction becomes focus.

Pettiness becomes foolish.

Perfection becomes imperfect.

Popularity becomes isolation.

Comfort becomes uncomfortable.

Talking becomes doing.

Well organized becomes a hot mess of massive action.

Ultimately what becomes is a new belief, which becomes a new attitude...

New attitude becomes new altitude...and it shall come to pass.

POOF!

The blocking feature on social media is a beautiful thing.

One tap of a button and an annoying, ignorant, crude, or rude person disappears.

Just like that...poof! They're gone.

In an instant you don't have to see them or hear from them again.

I love it. It's wonderful.

There are some people who exist that need to be blocked who are unfortunately not on social media but living and breathing in real life.

If only there was a block button for real life.

There are some people that when they just go away it seems like life is so much better.

They're like a thorn in your ass or torrential down pour on your parade.

Or like an annoying fly that keeps landing on your food when you're trying to eat.

You try to shoo them away they just don't take a hint.

They bless us with their absence not their presence.

You know those types of people.

Any interaction with them is about as enjoyable as sticking your hand in a boiling pot of water or jabbing yourself in the eye with a pointy object.

When they disappear its like weights have been lifted off, dark clouds have dissipated, or that migraine headache finally went away.

Things flow smoother, the air seems lighter, and the sun shines brighter.

I've come to be a black belt ninja at blocking people.

I have an allergic reaction to ignorance...

So if you fit the description I know it's 100% guaranteed you're not aware you do...but please entertain me with a magic act.

POOF!

Disappear.

I Told You So

I told you so. What people say when they get some level of satisfaction out of seeing you fail.

Satisfaction that justifies their lack of courage and inaction.

It's real easy for a coward to criticize a risk taker.

I told you it wouldn't work!

Translation...I feel better about being a coward.

I told you you should have stayed there! You had a good job!

Translation...puppet master, I'm validated, I'd like to move my arms now.

I told you you shouldn't have moved there!

Translation...I feel better about the fact I'm afraid to move further than 5 minutes away from my parents.

I told you, you should have listened to me!

Translation...I feel better and more validated about what I think I know that I really don't.

I told you, you shouldn't have caused any waves!

Translation...I feel much better about the fact I conform, allow people to control me, and live a lame life.

Look...

It's not the critic that counts.

Don't let the chatter stop you.

Cowards will always chatter about how the strong and the brave stumbled.

What they don't realize is it's supposed to be hard.

It's not always going to go as planned.

It's not always going to be seamless.

No one ever accomplished anything extraordinary without conflict, strain, and struggle.

If it was easy everyone would do it.

But that's why everyone doesn't do it...they stay weak, afraid, and safe.

Why in the world would you ever allow an opinion from someone like that to make you question yourself?

Keep pushing, truth is, those people wish they had a fraction of the guts you have to live on their terms.

You're doing the things they would do if they had the guts.

Drown out the noice. Keep going.

Posers

The life of a poser is exhausting.

Those that give the impression they're something they're not.

A shirt and tie doesn't mean you're important, successful, or professional.

Being popular doesn't mean you're worth knowing.

A Mercedes Benz doesn't mean you're rich.

A college degree doesn't mean you're educated.

Serving people doesn't mean you're moral, ethical, or a nice person.

A relationship status and profile picture doesn't mean you're faithful.

A title doesn't mean you're fulfilled.

Having kids doesn't mean you're mom or dad.

Being religious doesn't mean you're perfect.

A ring doesn't mean you're a husband or wife.

A smile doesn't mean you're happy.

Just because you sit in a garage that doesn't make you a car.

Get the point?

Posing is hard work.

I'm exhausted just thinking about it.

Be who and what you appear to be...or don't appear to be it.

Life gets much easier that way.

Outgrown

Through your journey of growth you'll eventually come to realize just how much you've outgrown certain people.

Those whose voices, comments, and opinions all of a sudden look very sad, petty, and ridiculous.

You've become so far beyond them that it's hard for you to even believe you were once at their level.

They cannot make this connection, but you can.

They do not and will not ever have this revelation, but you have.

They do not understand you any further than their extremely limited perception and perspective of human nature.

Every time they speak you're reminded of just how much you've grown as an individual.

You feel sorry for people more than anger.

When you open your mouth to speak you tell the world who you are.

We're all self-made, only the successful will admit it.

It is ok to drastically outgrow people.

It is ok to leave some people behind.

There are many people that do not understand the concept of growth, of change.

There are some that do not understand or actively engage in the evolvement of their heart, mind, and spirit.

They stay EXACTLY the same FOREVER.

I've come to see that these types of individuals do hold some value in our lives.

They show us and help us measure just how much we in fact have altered.

They are our measuring stick by which we know we're in the right track.

You don't need people to understand you. Many won't.

Separate yourself, detach, leave them behind, or love them from a distance...

It is not mean or cold hearted. It is a necessary requirement if you want to evolve.

Associations matter. Environment matters. Influences matter.

Protect who you've become and are becoming.

What seeps into your heart and your mind changes who you are. Changes your spirit.

Delete negativity ruthlessly.

NEVER stop evolving. See, I heard what you said, I'm not angry or bitter, I'm just up here now.

Keep It Moving

Becoming more in life is determined by your ability to keep it moving.

You can't be sure how everything is going to turn out, I know you're afraid.

Keep it moving.

They'll try to bring you down, you'll have all kinds of things said about you.

Keep it moving.

It's got you up tossing and turning until 2 in the morning, worry, anxiety.

Keep it moving.

Crying often, I know it's hard.

Keep it moving.

Frustrated, fed up to the max.

Keep it moving.

You can't see any way in the world you're going to be able to get over this or get through this.

Keep it moving.

Seems nothing is going your way, I know there's little faith.

Keep it moving.

I know you're thinking you can't take any more of this, and you're going to give in to the urge to quit...but you're failing to realize the secret that's going to get you right where you want to be.

See, in order to keep growing...

You have to keep going.

Keep it moving.

Go Out and Get It

You opened up two gifts this morning...

Your eyes.

Progress is happiness. Progress is fulfillment.

Assess your true intentions.

Are you really not in need of certain things or don't want certain things or...

Are you just lazy, uninspired, afraid, and most importantly...

Stuck in a life you absolutely believe you cannot get out of, take control of, or change?

You don't have what you want in your life not because you really don't think you need it or want it, but because you don't really believe you can have it.

You do not think it is really practical or possible.

It's much easier to live in an abyss of nothingness, expecting and wanting nothing more out of life.

You won't be disappointed if you just say you don't want it or need it. It helps you rationalize how what you do have "is all you really want or need".

A life of average mediocrity and small easily attainable goals.

But I promise you there's danger in low exceptions.

You generally get what you expect.

Money, promotion, great relationships, love, wealth, and happiness.

There's nothing evil about it.

What's evil is squandering a beautiful life away and not doing everything within your power regardless of what other human beings think about it.

Abundance in every aspect of your life is always there, always available.

It's all around us.

It's YOUR MIND that creates limitations.

Stop selling yourself short.

God created you in his image.

What are you going to do about it?

You Chose

So your life sucks.

Yes you could be clinically depressed...

But before you believe that diagnosis and buy what the doctor is selling, make sure you're just not in fact simply suffering the consequences of your own lifestyle choices.

You may in fact just be surrounded by assholes.

You're choosing to work there.

You chose that man or woman.

You chose to eat the pancakes.

You're choosing to live there.

You chose to get hammered last weekend.

You chose to spend your money on that.

You're choosing that habit.

You chose to sit there all day watching re runs of Seinfeld instead of working out.

You chose to cut off your nose despite your face.

You are choosing not to see things for the way they really are and dealing with them.

You may be depressed, or you may need to just slap yourself in the face and wake up.

Perseverance

Perseverance.

Steadfastness in doing something despite difficulty or delay in achieving success.

The race isn't won by the strongest or the fastest but by the one that can endure it until the end.

The one with the ability to stay on track.

Many start off strong, but end up in a much different place than they intended.

When it got hard they stopped. They submitted to the pain in the process.

Consistency and patience are two superpowers many don't possess.

Fast "success" isn't what you want.

Speed for a moment doesn't mean progress. A lot of people are going nowhere fast.

It's a long way between where you start and where you finish and a lot can happen along the way.

ONE DROP of water will eventually cave in ceilings...because it's diligent.

It drips again, and again, and again, and again, and again.......

Just do not stop.

Be like a drop of water, do a little thing a long time until it becomes a big thing.

<u>Underprivileged</u>

Some are blessed being born into privilege.

Entitled, they have advantages many don't have right out of the gate.

A head start in life. It's a beautiful thing.

The best education, a father, married parents in a loving home, inheritance, the family business, never worrying where they're going to live, what they're going to eat, or how they're going to get by.

They have more opportunities and the ability to do things and get further much easier and much faster than those that are starting the race from a much different place.

A lead in the race of life through nothing they've done.

The privileged have a clearer path to run while the underprivileged path is full of hurdles.

The underprivileged path starts from a place much further behind.

Privileged or underprivileged EVERYONE still has to run their race.

Fact is many underprivileged people that grew up in ghettos, broken homes, no parents, in abuse, poor, etc...

In a fair race from the same starting line...

Would SMOKE the privileged in this race we call life.

I know personally many people that if I had what they had I would blow them away so unbelievably, incredibly, and unapologetically to the point of complete utter annihilation.

I assure you they would be ashamed of themselves.

I said it and I'm here to represent it.

Always count your blessings, lend a hand to those less fortunate, and keep your head out of your ass.

Underprivileged people that create privileged lives out of nothing are the biggest badasses there are.

The circumstances you're born with aren't your choice or your fault.

The circumstances you die with are.

Rude Commentator

Don't ever be upset by a person's rude and ignorant comments and remarks.

See they're just responding based on their capacity to think and understand.

The level that they're on.

Whenever exceptional thinking people get around ordinary thinking people there's going to be conflict.

The best response is always no response, not because they're right and you're lost for words, but because...

When you're an ocean person you don't fool with a water drop person.

When you're a mountain person you stop messing with mole hill people.

A whale will never jump out of the ocean to dive in a fish bowl with the goldfish.

Sunflower people don't come down to the level of dandelion people.

See, when you're an eagle soaring way up here, how would you look pecking around on the ground like a chicken?

When you're a 20 foot deep pool of water...pouring into a cereal bowl person might overwhelm their capacity to fully hold and contain what you're saying.

Remember people communicate based on their capacity to think and understand.

When you think and understand little...you act, speak, and communicate little.

Pray for them though...I mean it's hard to go big when little has a grip on you.

I'd love to respond to your ignorance but I don't stress about a can of sardines...

I'm too busy exploring the world of deep sea fishing.

Cast Me Out

Not everyone's acceptance is a blessing.

In fact there are some you should consider it a blessing they cast you out.

You don't owe anyone an apology for your life, who you are, or who you're trying to become.

You're going to do great things and you don't owe anyone an apology.

You're becoming a better version of yourself. You don't owe anyone an apology.

You've changed. Same DNA but a different presentation. You don't owe anyone an apology.

You changed your mind. You think differently about it now. You don't believe that anymore. You don't owe anyone an apology.

You're focusing on you now. You don't owe anyone an apology.

You said it and you meant it. You don't owe anyone an apology.

You're going to be an exception to the rule. You don't owe anyone an apology.

You're cutting negative people off. You don't owe anyone an apology.

You're choosing to get up out of the same sewer others live in. Sorry they'll have to find someone else to keep them company. You don't owe anyone an apology.

You've decided enough is enough, no more, you've had enough, it ends today, you'll suffer no more, the rest of your life is going to be the best of your life.

Growing is about saying no to more and more things.

Stop apologizing.

You don't owe anyone an apology.

Shine Through

Life breaks everyone.

But there are some that find strength in the broken places.

Everyone has cracks and breaks that go unnoticed from a distance.

But...if you get close enough, somewhere, in some way, everyone has blemishes.

Broken pieces can never be put back together the same way again...but it's in the breaks and the brokenness that the real beauty lies.

When you've been brutally broken to pieces and are trying to rebuild yourself, don't waste the scraps.

I assure my friend...there's some treasure in that trash.

You might take a different shape than you had before using pieces that seemingly don't fit the way they once did...it's the perfectly imperfect fit that creates the real masterpiece.

Through the seams of shattered pieces that have been mended back together, room has been created in the cracks to allow what's inside to be revealed.

Only with fractured scars of brokenness can your light start shine through.

It's when you discover your light, your true depth, the whole game will change.

What breaks isn't in fact broken at all.

First it hurts then it changes you. What hurts you today makes you stronger tomorrow.

Strength is made perfect in your weaknesses.

There's nothing on earth stronger than a broken man or woman that has been put back together again.

My Side

It's said there's two sides to every story.

I used to feel like my side of the story needed to be told to keep the facts straight.

Now I've come to a point in my life I don't care what story anyone chooses to believe.

I can care less about explaining my side.

I'm ok with your side.

Sounds good to me.

Explaining myself to insignificant people whose thoughts and opinions have no direct bearing on my life seems like a waste of precious energy.

Energy I reserve for important matters that actually move the needle in my life.

So I'll leave it to you to fill them in.

After all I'm happy to help you look good at my expense.

Each and every one of us is the villain in someone's story.

We all have enemies we've never even met who don't even know us personally.

People that accept a story they're told.

So whatever you hear about me please believe it.

Matter of fact you can add some to the story if you want.

I don't have interest, the energy, or most importantly the obligation to explain myself to anyone.

Let whoever say and think whatever, just keep getting better.

Call Me Crazy

I'm dancing...but you can't hear the music.

I'm singing...but you don't know the song.

I'm speaking...but you don't know the language.

I feel the rain...you're just getting wet.

I see...but you're only looking.

I'm laughing...but you didn't get the joke.

I'm enlightened...but you're stuck on stupid.

I'm free...but you decorated your jail cell.

I'm truthful...but you live a lie.

I'm present...you're stuck in the past.

I'm imagining...but your stuck on knowledge.

I'm hopeful...but you're realistic.

I'm awakened...but you rolled over and hit the snooze button.

I'm misunderstood...oh but I understand.

I'm crazy...but only to someone like you.

I've Been

It's not that easy they said. Just not that simple. Doesn't always work that way. Easier said than done.

I'm strong because I've been weak.

I'm wise because I've been stupid.

I'm hopeful because I've been hopeless.

I stand firm because I've been brought to my knees.

I'm fearless because I've been afraid.

I'm bold because I've been spineless.

I shine because I've been dark.

I smile because I've frowned.

I'm fixed because I've been broken.

I'm whole because I've been pulled apart.

I'm healthy because I've been sick.

I love because I've been unloved.

I appreciate because I've been unappreciated.

I'm free because I've been stuck.

My entire life wasn't that easy. My entire life wasn't that simple. My entire life was easier said than done.

Prove them wrong. Prove yourself right.

EVERY. SINGLE. DAY.

Karma

Life has a way of coming around full circle. Put out good and you get what you deserve. Put out bad and you get what you deserve.

Most times you'll get what you deserve in such a way no one else can even see it.

It's delivered privately in your own heart, head, and conscious.

So don't worry about someone that did you dirty. They will eventually face the wretched dirty old man staring back at them in the mirror.

Envy

Don't live miserable to impress other insignificant people. If you're a prisoner in your own life for an image you have a serious problem.

You don't have to have the same size house as your friend.

You don't have to have a car just as expensive as your sibling.

You don't have to over budget your wedding so everyone is impressed.

You don't have to take your girlfriend on an extravagant vacation you can't afford.

You don't need to wear expensive name brands to prove you're the man.

You don't have to slave at a miserable soul sucking job that you have no emotional connection to all because you have a fancy title and need to assure you can pay for an image that has no real substance behind it.

Imagine the day you just give it all up without any care in the world about someone else's perception about it?

Collect assets not liabilities.

I used to envy and think someone with a lot of things was a success, now I envy those with inner peace.

Life Lessons

I didn't always have my head on straight. I didn't always know how to deal with life.

I've learned many things about life the hard way.

I've learned that life doesn't play games with anyone. No one is exempt.

It doesn't care who you are, where you're from, how much money you have, how much people like you, how beautiful or muscular you are, or how big your heart is.

Life is rough and tough. It is no match for the man or woman that is not equipped to deal with or handle it.

It will inevitably deliver tragedies, hardships, tough lessons, losses, heartbreaks, and traumas. Life doesn't wait for anyone to grow up, become mature, more level headed, more conscious, more capable, or more equipped.

Life happens how and when it wants to happen. It's unapologetic. It doesn't feel sorry for anyone.

Life will teach you that there's only so much you can do to control it or dictate it.

Life demands your full respect and attention. It doesn't sit and wait for anyone to finally figure it out.

Disrespect life and it will disrespect you. It will spiral out of control, beat you down, and punish you on its own terms.

Life isn't always logical. Life doesn't always make sense.

When you approach life haphazardly and without direction, it will use you. It will spin you around in circles.

Life has its own agenda. It will screw up your plans, and force you to your knees.

It'll force you to tap out into submission.

Abuse life and it'll abuse you.

You can make life your worst enemy or your best friend.

Life will treat you exactly how you treat it. It can work for you or against you. It will humble you and force you to shut your mouth.

Life doesn't give you what you want. It gives you what you are.

Life is a great teacher. It will force you to open your eyes and learn its lessons. Heed the lessons.

Some only love you when they have something to gain from it.

You learn a lot about people when they don't get what they want from you.

When you no longer serve any purpose in their overall personal agenda or immediate personal needs.

People love you when you're up and flying high.

You find your true friends when you fall down, regress, and are eating dirt.

The harsh truth is that when it REALLY comes down to it...the vast majority of your "friends" don't give a shit about you.

When all hell is breaking loose and the fire is raging, there really aren't many that would even piss on you to put it out.

Hey, rightfully so, people have their own life, agenda, and problems. You really only ever have a few real ride or dies in your entire life...

If you're lucky.

Keep those people close, appreciate their presence in your life, and put your total investment in on them because they're hard to find.

Feed what feeds you. Starve the rest.

Know the difference between an acquaintance and a true committed friend that is really FOR YOU no matter the circumstances or what other people think about it.

If someone can walk away from you let them walk.

NEVER travel a million miles for anyone that wouldn't cross the street for you.

Givers have to set limits because physical and emotional takers have none.

Get Distant

I don't mind hanging around people that don't have anything, but I'm absolutely afraid of hanging around people that don't want anything.

See, I'm afraid it's contagious.

You have to be positioned to flourish.

There are narrow limited places that never let you stretch or reach your full capacity or potential.

Communities that limit you.

Jobs that don't advance you turning your sky into a ceiling.

Mindsets that contaminate and infect you.

Families that don't support you.

Friends that are going nowhere, serve no purpose, and add no value.

Relationships that put a ball and chain around your ankle.

Like trying to take a bath in a cereal bowl or leap off a diving board into a glass of water.

A seed can't grow planted in a teaspoon of dirt. A seed will only root when planted in a environment bigger than itself.

You've got to put yourself in an environment that is beyond you. That is bigger than you. That forces you to step up your game and pick up the pace.

You've got to get out of the place that you're secure and sure.

Where you're not the smartest, best, brightest, or most successful one in the room.

There's no misery and frustration bigger than the misery and frustration of being confined to an environment that is too small to contain your vision.

See you come to realize how big the world is when you get out of someone else's.

Distance yourself for a bit, you'll realize a lot.

Weary Spirit

It doesn't matter how focused, how disciplined, how consistent, or how dedicated you are...sometimes you get tired.

EVERYONE gets tired.

But I don't mean the kind of tired you get from not getting enough sleep.

I mean the tired that wears your spirit.

Hope deferred makes the heart sick.

I've learned you have to be tough to wait.

You have to be tough to grind it out every day with no immediate show of accomplishment.

No immediate gratification.

To wait upon something that requires faith to ultimately receive because today's logic and reasoning are telling you a different story.

Until you change the voice inside of your head in times of need you will never become what you're trying to be.

How you respond to challenges will ultimately tell whether you are wise or foolish.

Challenges show up to test your faith and beliefs.

In times of need...I've learned strength and might only get you so far.

I've learned to crave and develop endurance and stamina within my spirit to keep going.

Hear Me

It's hard to really hear in a listening world.

Many listen but don't really hear.

Well what's the difference?

When you listen things fly by, go right over your head, and flutter away in the wind.

You are left the same.

But when you hear...listening sticks to you.

It bonds itself like glue.

Finds a place to stay.

Gets down in your gut and gets on your nerves.

You can tell when a person hears by their actions.

By the way they start acting out of character.

See, hearing confirms something you already knew but didn't know.

It reveals teachers that have been there all along...ready to teach...waiting for you to be ready to learn.

Hearing causes irrational decision making, defiant behavior, and abnormal speech.

In a world where there's a lot of noise...we listen to a lot of things...

But I suggest you develop selective hearing.

Begs the question..."What am I trying to hear exactly?"

You'll find out once you stop listening.

Mirror Mirror

Someone's opinion of you does not have to become your reality.

I know many, if asked, would have a clear and precise opinion about who they believe me to be or what I'm about.

If you asked those same people what their opinion of themselves is...

Looking in their magic mirror..."Mirror mirror on the wall who's the fairest of them all?"

You'd be indulged with a colorful answer. A delusional description.

When a person's opinion of themselves is anything but reality, their opinion of you is laughable and certainly not anymore real.

How can someone see you clearly if they are blind to themselves?

People don't even know who they really are, let alone know you.

Most would be better off getting real about who they believe themselves to be first...then their opinions might have more bearing and hold more weight.

Someone who's kidding themselves has to be kidding me.

My level of concern about another's opinion is nonexistent.

I see, accept, and own my imperfections, no matter how ugly or messy they might be...and I know you're ugly just like me.

Keep gazing into your magic mirror...after all...

Beauty is in the eye of the beholder.

Winning

The bullies are getting bullied.

Those that don't have enough elasticity in their character to experience success and not become arrogant.

Becoming condescending and self-consumed.

Elitism and superiority.

Strong enough to win but not humble enough to receive the reward without becoming a stuck up pompous prick.

To be winning in life and still remain humble...

Not placing yourself on a pedestal.

That's where the real power is.

Pride comes before a fall.

Never say something wouldn't happen to you.

Success has a way of seducing many into thinking they can't lose.

You're not done living yet.

At the end of the day our graves will be the same size.

How people handle winning in life says a lot about them.

It Is What It Is

Sometimes we get stuck in what people expect.

Sometimes we get so wrapped up in a persona we forget to be a person.

Sometimes the way people describe you can become a prison.

Living up to someone else's description, boxed in.

When you're authentic to your core you're not incarcerated by a title... by a description, by a way of life.

You're free to be what you are not what they call you.

There's a freedom in not fitting in. There's a freedom in not belonging.

Sometimes being cast out by certain people and places is a blessing.

Growth occurs when you realize you don't have to experience life the way you have been told to.

Yeah there's going to be many that will not agree with you. Many that might not talk to you anymore. Many that say stuff about you.

Once you develop that "it is what it is" mentality a lot of things stop bothering you.

Screw them.

You never know who would love the person you hide.

Intentionality

Live intentional.

Most flap in the wind and just get blown around trying to hold on for dear life.

Reacting not acting.

I don't know about and I'm not really concerned with anyone else...but I want increase.

In EVERY area of my life I want increase.

I want my cake and I want to eat it too.

Not in one area at the expense of another because society says one should deem it more important or more valuable.

EVERY area is important. EVERY area is valuable. Family, spiritual life, finances (aka MONEY), legacy, health and fitness, environment, intellect, relationships, love, skills, business, you name it, I want increase.

And I want increase BY ANY MEANS necessary...

Now before you demonize me, drop the lazy, excuse making, determined to justify your inaction on the things you want in life mentality...

Whatever it takes is the means by which I will operate.

Like shedding blood if I have to, working myself to death if I have to...

Not by breaking the law but by severely breaking some rules.

Not by stepping on people but by leaping over them if they're in the way.

Like facing whatever I have to face no matter how uncomfortable, how difficult, how insurmountable, no matter what.

Regardless of the resistance. Regardless of the obstacles.

I'll never submit to the idea of using "being grateful" as an excuse to lie dead and dormant and never strive for more.

As an excuse to die before I'm dead.

I'm grateful, I'm blessed indeed, now give me increase.

A tree tries to grow as big and tall as it possibly can.

Where I end up 12 months from now...I intended to end up there.

Set a goal, a vision. Designed a strategy, a blueprint, a course of action that will put me there on purpose.

The way I intended...because I execute and take action.

There isn't any what if or maybe about it.

See you can count every chicken before they hatch.

Cause and effect.

I'm the devastating cause and what I intended to have happen is the submissive effect.

I don't sit around and hope or wish for it. I forget those things that are behind and STRAIN to reach those things which are ahead.

Intentionality.

Life doesn't happen to you, it happens because of you.

I suggest the realization that often occurs later in life for many people of the things they claim they really don't need is in reality an excuse.

Truth is they just don't have the balls to go out and get them.

You will always generally get what you expect. If you don't expect much you'll never receive much.

<u>Get Worse</u>

You walked through the fire but don't have to come out smelling like smoke.

Everything you go through can be used for your good if you let it.

You can choose to use it to your advantage or disadvantage. To become better or worse.

It's not about finding the light but learning how to see in the dark...because darkness is inevitable.

Sometimes bad has to get worse before it gets better.

Storms make rainbows.

Pressing grapes makes wine.

Pressure creates diamonds.

Stars become visible only in darkness.

Strength is made perfect in weakness.

In times of confusion, sadness, and struggle, not certainty, happiness, or ease.

Not when you're winning, but when you're losing.

I'm strong because I've been weak.

I'm hopeful because I've been hopeless.

I stand firm because I've been brought to my knees.

I shine because I've been dark.

I smile because I've frowned.

I'm fixed because I've been broken.

I thrive because I've suffered.

I'm whole because I've been pulled apart.

I'm healthy because I've been sick.

Had I not been made weak, I would have not been made humble.

Weakened humbleness is the seed that great strength grows.

Embrace the struggle.

Best Position

When you're at the mercy of someone else to give you things you can't give yourself you're not free.

When they don't come through you have pain.

There's a position in life that I believe is the ultimate wealth. The ultimate place to be. The ultimate achievement.

The "fuck you" position.

Living a life totally free to be who you want to be and what you want to be.

Where you don't have to conform or kiss anyone's ass to make sure the hand that feeds you doesn't punch you in the face.

You just can't put a dollar amount on it.

Freedom is priceless.

You're in control of your own life, your own outcomes, your own time, your own paycheck, your own place to live, your own growth, your own everything.

You don't need anyone for anything, just in my fortress of solitude and independence minding my own business.

A position of complete independence. Complete liberation.

This position is hard to achieve.

Freedom comes at a massive price. Your time, your energy, your sacrifice, and even at times your sanity.

A price way too expensive for most to pay so many are bought at a price to give it up.

To give up their freedom, their dreams, and their own best interest at the expense of being liked, being accepted, and fitting in...

And most importantly to pay for a life full of a bunch of stuff with money they don't have to impress people they don't even like.

I'll give it all up any day of the week...Hey I just got to be me. I just have to be free.

Perhaps

If truth sets you free why then would it ever be rejected?

Why would it be rejected even in the face of confirmed concrete evidence?

Perhaps there are many reasons.

Perhaps it's because in truth, normal blindness is disrupted with a sudden glimpse of light.

Like suddenly turning the light on early in the morning. Forced to squint. Forced to feel discomfort and unease. Forced to bear the sting of the light.

Perhaps it's because truth cuts like a knife that slices through even the toughest skin. The toughest people.

Exposing vulnerabilities and weaknesses through the cuts and incisions.

Perhaps it's because people don't really want to be free.

Why be starving and homeless in truth, when you can seek refuge in a place you can be fed and have a place to stay.

Perhaps it's because many run, but in truth there's nowhere to hide...

From themselves.

Perhaps it's because truth takes the loaded gun many point at other people and forces them to turn it on themselves.

Hard to pull when their truth is in the trigger.

Perhaps it could be a lot of things...who knows, perhaps.

Blind Leading the Blind

The world is full of blind hypocritical idiots leading the blind.

Do as I say but not as I do.

Well done is better than well said.

Many proclaim to be certain things, know certain things, or to have done certain things.

When you look beyond their mouth you find little to no evidence of an actual produced result.

Words are easy. Actual production around what those words represent is hard.

Embody what you proclaim you are and what others should be.

Don't inform others on information you don't even use and put into practice yourself.

Develop eyesight before you instruct others on how to see.

Take the plank out of your own eye before you inform others on how to remove the splinter out of theirs.

Bear fruit before you tell me how to plant seeds.

Judge a tree by the fruit it actually bears.

By the fruit it actually produces.

Not the fruit it claims. Not the fruit it talks about.

If you're going to preach it, practice it.

Otherwise do yourself a favor and shut your mouth...less talking, more producing. Results speak for themselves.

Talk is cheap, prove it...then people might care what you say.

<u>You're Better</u>

You know why you think some people's lives are better than yours?

Because you see the part that they show you.

Better is a perspective. Better is subjective. Better compared to what?

So you thought you'd be better by now. You're better than you think.

Sometimes you have to stop and look over your shoulder at where you started.

You're not where you want to be but you're further than you were.

You're better.

You've got much further to go but look how far you've come.

You're better.

I know you thought you should have been there by now but you needed to learn some things along the way.

You're better.

You think you should have more to show by now but we all know not to judge progress by the harvest reaped but by the seeds you planted.

See, you just have to give the cake time to bake.

You're better.

Stay focused. Stay consistent. Keep going.

It's only a matter of time...but don't stop at your best...because when you keep bettering your best your best keeps getting better and better...

Look forward, head down, work.

Soon enough you'll look over your shoulder once again and see...

You're right where you wanted to be.

And...Isn't that better?

Participation

Unfortunately in life everybody doesn't win.

Life doesn't give out participant trophies.

Life doesn't reward people that simply show up and tried.

Unlike friends and family...

Life doesn't feed into, coddle, or pander insecurities and weaknesses...telling people what they want to hear.

Life doesn't give a damn.

Life will chew you up and spit you out.

It'll kick you while you're down. It'll glorify its unfairness and laugh in your face while it's doing it.

It doesn't care how upset or sad you are about it.

Life happens whether you're ready or not, or understand it or not.

It doesn't care you're afraid, timid, or uncertain.

It will strip you of your confidence, your will, your dignity, and your belief...and it'll smack you in the face while it's doing it.

Life demands you toughen up. It demands you figure it out.

It demands more out of you if it's going to pour more into you.

You have to be tougher than your life.

Don't show up in life to participate...show up in life to take over.

Show up in life to win, or don't show up at all.

Slow Cooking

People don't like building and creating too much.

Most like the quick fix, the straightest path to what they want which involves the least amount of work.

Shake and bake, microwaveable success. Easy.

But see, anything that's worthwhile and extraordinary is going to require a little elbow grease.

You're gonna have to withstand some heat, spend some time in the kitchen.

See you can't just toss this thing in a bowl, pop it in the microwave...done in five minutes.

You're gonna have to put in some work to make it.

Things always taste better made from scratch, slow cooked with patience.

You're gonna have to plan this thing out.

You're gonna have to bust out some serious ingredients to make this thing happen.

If you want the sweet taste of real success, you better forget that shitty method of preparation.

See, you gotta get this recipe just right.

And when you do, the smell of success is so good you can almost taste it.

If you're hungry and never satisfied it's hard to wait, but have patience...

Because after you've given that cake time to bake...

I assure you my friend you're gonna have it...and you're gonna eat it too.

Say Goodbye

Stop being so forgiving, people know exactly what they're doing.

"But baby she didn't mean anything to me."

"I slept at my friend Kate's house last night why don't you believe me!?"

"We've been married 30 years she's used to it, she knows I don't mean it."

"I'm sorry for calling you a bitch and a horror, I love you."

"I would never intentionally try to hurt you, I don't know what came over me."

"I was drunk, it just sort of happened, I'm sorry it will never happen again."

"They're just a friend, nothing more."

"I lied to protect you. I didn't want to hurt you."

When you use red flags as blindfolds...

Sooner or later...

Time will bring to reality of what lies underneath the surface.

You know what you're worth...enforcing it is the problem.

You know what you want and deserve but take what you get.

You devalue yourself and compromise your life and dignity for a person that doesn't really care about you.

Doesn't matter what they said...their actions confirmed it.

You'll be amazed at what you attract after you start believing in what you deserve.

Someone you never dreamed of losing can be replaced by someone you never dreamed of having.

You are responsible for your own happiness, not someone one else's.

Don't be afraid of the solitude that comes from raising your standards.

It's your obligation to you to love and respect yourself.

Sometimes you have to gift the gift of absence to those that don't appreciate your presence.

You can cut someone off and still wish them the best in life. You can genuinely love someone and never want to see them again.

Stop holding on to people just because you have history together.

Some people only enter our lives as an example of what to avoid.

Sometimes solutions aren't so simple.

Sometimes goodbye is the only way.

<u>Triggers</u>

Some people are so amazing.

They appear to just have it so together all the time.

One couldn't help to beat themselves up in comparison.

They never seem to struggle.

They always seem to be perfectly perfect.

Everything they touch turns to gold.

They have such a beautiful and supportive family.

They're so happily married. Look at that ring.................wow.

Their significant other is the bomb. So attractive, treats them so good.

They never seem to feel pain or turmoil.

They're always smiling. Amazing smile.

I mean their life is like a fairy tale.

Their children seem so perfect with their elaborate and sophisticated names.

Their career is so wonderful. They look so important.

They're always having fun. YOLO.

Their life is just absolutely amazing.

I wish I could just be them. Oh how great my life would be.

Bummer I'll just have to settle for the reality of me and the reality of my life.

Here's the truth, no one knows what they're doing.

No one has it all together all the time. No one's life is picture perfect all the time. No one feels like smiling all the time. No one is happy all the time.

In a world full of highlight reels, don't be hard on yourself.

When you're real about your struggles and shortcomings you are given the power to change them.

You are enough, you're doing just fine.

If this post offended your perfect life and existence, be grateful for triggers...they point you where you're not free.

What You Need

Sorry to break it to you.

Unfortunately sometimes you can't have fun accomplishing your goals.

Sometimes it sucks.

You need to embrace the suck.

People on top of their game in anything in life do what they hate...and do it like they love it.

They sacrifice what most won't, have tunnel vision, and a ferocious work ethic.

And most importantly they don't go with the flow, they create the flow.

It is a very simple equation.

You don't need a masters degree to understand this.

You don't need to take a class.

You don't need a certificate or license.

You don't need to drive a BMW with $20 in your bank account.

You don't need a $200 pair of shoes.

You don't need to smooch your bosses ass cheek.

A dry cleaned suit isn't going to get the job done unfortunately.

You don't need a desk or a name plate.

Titles don't mean shit unfortunately.

Don't worry about updating your resume.

When it REALLY comes down to it many of the things people worship have nothing to do with getting the success they're after.

See you're going to make it a lot further in life trading all of these things in for the most important things of all...

A nice big set of cojones.

Hand Picked

Hand pick your associations.

Your crew, your team, your peeps.

Your homies, girlfriends, squad, or click.

Run with people that want more out of life...you might get some new desires.

Those that are actively engaging in the process...you may stop talking and start executing.

People that are hungry...you may feel your stomach start to growl.

Those that are unstoppable...you may become a force to be reckoned with.

Those that are unreasonable...you might start pushing back.

Be down with people that don't take no for an answer...you might keep asking for it.

People that mean what they say and do what they say...you might stop bullshitting.

People with fire in their eyes...you might start seeing flames.

People that are evolving...you might start a metamorphosis.

Those that are looking up and leveling up...you may get a better view.

See when everyone else around you is running you tend to pick up the pace.

There's simulation in association.

You're not asking for too much, you're just asking the wrong people.

And if necessary, don't be afraid to be a one man army.

My Way

What you allow will continue.

Every day of your life you teach the world how you should be treated.

See sometimes there are people that treat you like a door mat, a piece of meat, or a worthless piece of shit...

The way they look down on you, laugh at you, demean you, belittle you, or walk around on you...

See there are some times, some things, turn into dumb things...and it's time to put your foot down.

There needs to come a day you decide that you've had enough of this.

A day you decide you're pissed.

Everyone look out when ONEday becomes TOday.

Today it's gonna go your way.

Today it's your way or the highway.

Today there will be no doubt.

Today you're gonna let it all come out.

Today you're gonna stand up and shout.

Today they're gonna see a side of you that they'll never forget.

Today they're gonna have some serious regret.

Today you will be respected.

Today you understand and demand what you deserve.

Today they can take that shit somewhere else...

Today you're adopting a higher better expression of yourself.

Today, you love you enough.

Today they're gonna see things your way...or today they become a part of your history.

Just Do It

When I started in real estate I had zero experience.

I didn't have a real estate license or a college degree.

Never took a single real estate class.

There wasn't some magical real estate success fairy that tapped me on the head with a magical answer to the perfect question granting me guaranteed success.

Sure I read books, listened to podcasts, asked questions...but it was with a serious intention to take action.

I learned by DOING.

Could I have made better decisions along the way? Sure, but $4 million worth of real estate later who gives a shit. It's just the cost of the tuition I had to pay for the things I didn't know.

No different than wasting money on learning a bunch of useless shit in college.

I would have accomplished far less if I sat analyzing the shit out of everything, afraid to actually do anything.

Paralysis by analysis...overthinking the end of something before it ever had a chance to start.

You and the people around you will always find a reason not to do something.

What are the reasons why you can?

Calculate the risk then just fucking do it.

Sloppy action trumps perfectly neat inaction any day of the week.

I'd rather be a hot mess of decisive action than a well-organized coward.

Truth is you can tell the majority of people the exact way to the holy grail of guaranteed success and they still wouldn't do anything about it.

Stop being afraid. Stop doubting yourself. Stop playing it safe.

If you're waiting for all the right answers, the perfect plan, the right time, to be ready, to have it all figured out...you're going to be waiting forever because none of that exists.

Everybody has big ideas...people romanticize their plans.

The magic you're looking for is in the work you're avoiding.

THE EXECUTION!

Some spend their whole lives "getting ready".

Getting ready to do nothing.

Fortune favors the bold.

Those that actually go out and do shit.

Just do it already.

Cut It Off

Sometimes the person you want most is the person you're best without.

Some people can stay in your heart but not in your life.

Sometimes your significant other needs to become your insignificant other.

"The one" might be better off being "the ex".

It's absolutely amazing how many people go back to relationships that have definitively proven to be toxic, not good for them, not what they want, or extremely dysfunctional.

Low self-esteem, poor self-image, and lack of self-love and respect are ALWAYS the reason why.

You have to lose the expectation around things that don't work.

I'd be ready and willing to cut off ANY relationship before I allow anyone to suck the life out of me, disturb my peace, dilute my spirit, and infect my mental health.

All relationships are either adding to you or subtracting from you.

Lifting you up or holding you down.

Helping you or hurting you.

When ANYONE is attempting to take withdrawals without making any deposits you need to let them know there's insufficient funds...and if they keep overdrawing...

Close the damn account.

Delete anyone that is toxic to your environment, not because you're petty or childish, but because you have decided to prioritize peace and optimism...

You will be amazed at how quickly and profoundly your life, your mentality, your progress, your outlook, and your outcomes will improve when you just cut certain people off.

Lose anyone or anything before you lose your mind.

Before you diagnose yourself with depression...first make sure you're just not in fact dating or married to an asshole.

Come on...you've got to see you're better than that.

Get It Back

I know you think you're special.

I can tell by the way you looked down on me, talked about me, and treated me.

Bringing me to my knees doesn't make you stand.

Sometimes your history determines the fierceness with which you fight what is front of you.

See I got some resolve.

You may see me crying. You may see me down here, can't hardly lift myself up..

Best believe when these tears dry up I'm gonna be swinging on you.

See regardless of what you say, I got some good stuff down in me...

I will not be defeated by what you say about me, I will only be defeated by what I say about me.

I got some resolve down in me.

I got some fire down in me.

I got some press down in me.

I got some fight down in me.

I may be down but I'm sure as hell not out.

Yeah...yeah...yeah I've got some good stuff down in me.

Resolve...I can feel it rising up in me.

Yeah...push is about to come to shove.

Bend is about to come to break.

My God, I got a spark down in me that's about to explode.

I got a chip placed firmly on my shoulder now.

I got my fight back. I got my groove back.

I got my stance back.

Yeah I got some resolve.

Sometimes things happen in life that force you to pick up the pace.

This ain't no time to cry...I'm gettin ready to run.

I'm gettin ready to be the person I was before you did all that stuff that dimmed my fucking shine.

34 Things

34 Things I would have told my younger self...

1. The wisest most enlightened people aren't found in crowds.

2. You're looking up to the wrong people.

3. Don't buy a house. If it has one door rent it. If it has multiple doors own it.

4. The high on life is so much better than cocaine.

5. Popularity is overrated. They're popular because they're fake. If everybody likes you, you're doing it wrong.

6. The answers you need are found looking inside, not outside of yourself.

7. Take the advice of very, very few people.

8. Fuck what they think.

9. It's ok to live a life and think in ways others don't understand.

10. College is overrated. A degree is just a piece of paper, your education is seen in your behavior.

11. Be an investor not an employee.

12. Don't cry over what you didn't cause or can't control.

13. Don't believe everything you hear. Formulate your own opinions.

14. Trust but verify.

15. How a person treats you is often just merely a reflection of the personal stuff they're dealing with at that moment, don't take it personal.

16. The less you need and want, the more you'll have.

17. Opinion isn't always fact and perspective isn't always truth.

18. Poverty, middle class, or being rich is a mindset. It's not what you are, it's what you believe you aren't that'll determine where you end up.

19. One day you'll look back and understand and see why they're so screwed up...it's got nothing to do with you.

20. That broken heart is fixing your vision.

21. People have their own shit to worry about, don't take it personal. Do you.

22. Distance yourself you'll realize a lot.

23. It's ok to be anti-social, it's a sign of intelligence.

24. There isn't a person on earth that will make you happy.

25. Your thoughts are destroying your life. The key is in the thoughts you think.

26. People come and go, here today gone tomorrow...love yourself first.

27. It's not other people's job to love you...it's yours.

28. She's not as pretty on the inside as she is on the outside. Run.

29. Be the opposite extreme of everyone else around you.

30. Nobody knows what they're doing.

31. Don't be mad at your parents, they're just extremely weak, blind, and ignorant...they did the best they could considering.

32. Fret not, nothing you're going through will be wasted. The steps of a good man are ordered by the lord.

33. Don't sweat it, very little matters, we're all just passing through in a moment of time.

34. Someday you'll have a great story to tell, but no one cares about your story until you win...so win.

Are You Ready?

Opportunity and abundance is all around us for the taking. It's our mind that creates limitations.

We build up evidence to talk us out of dreams.

Evidence to dissuade us from going forward.

A way to cope with our limitations.

Blaming everyone and everything else for the reason you can't become.

Rationalizing why it makes sense to not expect much from yourself or your life.

Developing all the reasons why you can't, while dismissing all the reasons why you can.

Don't expect much from me...

I'm a minority.

I come from the neighborhood.

I grew up without a mother or father.

I was abused or taken advantage of.

I was adopted, abandoned, or left behind.

I couldn't go to college. I didn't get the education.

I'm a recovering addict.

I'm too old now.

That's not in the cards for people like us.

I'm stuck.

I don't have the support.

I got the diagnosis.

I'm not as smart or talented.

I don't have any special advantages.

Tear down the story that supports who you believe yourself to be...and build up the story of who you could be.

See, you fail in something you can see because you lacked in something you can't see.

Attitude, faith, and belief.

When you make excuses for your limitations you get to keep them.

Wipe the slate clean today. Pick a new direction and just start going that way.

I promise you there are people with your same circumstances...and they're winning with them.

Find them...model their mindset and your behavior will follow.

You'll be amazed at what you can do when you move forward without limiting beliefs.

Truly I tell you...you're a testimony waiting to be delivered.

But, no one can do it for you but you.

Don't wait on the world, the universe, or God.

See...the world, the universe, and God are waiting on you.

Waiting for you to adopt an insufferable belief that you're greater than your circumstances.

Question is, are you ready?

People might try to remind you of who you were...

Make sure they get the new definition.

Killer Instinct

An instinct to increase. To pounce. To take action.

Some have it, some don't.

To get after it. To grab it. To hold it in the palm of their hand.

To wrap their hands around the neck of life, and snap it.

Demand it.

They don't knock politely. They find ripping the door off its hinges to be a bit more effective.

They KNOW they can have it, because they KNOW themselves.

They trust their hustle.

Not much for gambling, but bet on themselves regularly. It's an addiction.

Fishing for sharks, reeling that sucker in.

Some just play this game of life better than others.

Mind over matter.

The further OVER one gets...the further along one will go.

They look around for the circumstances that they want and if they don't find them...they create them.

They do more with less.

Pull rabbits out of hats. Abracadabra. Magical, like a fucking magician.

Kick them while they're down, you just may break your leg.

Instinctive to defeat, not be defeated.

Victimizing the victimizer. Sending them running with their tail between their legs.

They aren't subject to life, life is subject to them.

When its do or die, has to work, and failure just isn't an option...

No plan B, safety net, nothing to fall back on, the one chance you've got.

When mommy and daddy can't help...

Survival of the fittest.

It's that killer instinct to stand up and fight, go all out, not take no for an answer, and make it happen that separates the men from the boys.

Let's see what ya got.

Against The Grain

My whole life I've seemed to just go against the grain.

In high school I quit the football team, walked off, and started sitting by myself.

Got into bodybuilding, everyone thought I was weird. All I wanted to do was work out and stick to my diet.

Then I won Teen Mr. Connecticut and Teen Mr. America.

I never fit in any company I worked for. Company "leaders" were always trying to push me out.

God bless them. Pushed me in the right direction.

I administer and control myself now.

I used to be concerned about keeping certain people, relationships, etc.

Said fuck it, just started being the real me unapologetically, let it all go, not much stayed.

Realized everyone you lose isn't a loss, oh well. It's a freedom that's priceless.

I used to think I was the man because by most people's standards I looked "successful".

The fully loaded brand new vehicle, the clothes, the career, the paycheck, the title, the condo, the "friends".

Traded in the car for a beat up pickup truck, started wearing plain cheap clothing from Walmart, walked out on my career, took a massive pay cut, accepted the title of crazy asshole by most, moved into a mobile home that cost next to nothing to live in, and started spending most of my time by my damn self.

Now I have assets that pay me and I'm utterly free indeed.

I just love going against the grain.

It has always made all the difference.

Patient Gangster

Has anyone ever had a complete disregard for you or your life?

Treating you like nothing more than a worthless piece of dog shit stuck to the bottom of their shoe...and act like it wasn't nothing at all.

To add insult to injury, they're not even purely, genuinely, or sincerely sorry in their heart.

You see them experiencing "success" and "happiness" while you're sitting, staring, and sure as hell not having a similar experience.

Seemingly there are no consequences to their actions.

Why does it seem good things happen to bad people, while bad things happen to good people?

Watching their prosperity becomes the source of your agony. The type of agony that's enough to make you question life as you know it and the point of continuing on.

Agony that causes so much frustration you sabotage your own life and progress because you don't see a point in trying.

The agony of watching these people prosper can cause you to draw a premature conclusion about life.

Don't make a permanent decision about the possibilities in your own life because you must realize that they will soon be cut off.

Sooner or later the evil deeds of those that do them will come around full circle in one form or another.

Maybe not in a day, a year, or even a decade or longer.

But, we all create our own destiny.

It's not where you start, it's where you finish.

Destiny ALWAYS speaks to THE END of a thing, not the beginning.

A lot happens along the way.

Eventually those that did you dirty will lie in the bed they made, alongside those they made it with.

Even though today they lack a real understanding of self-awareness and think they're many things they are not...

Behind their fake smile, life, and personality...

They will eventually understand what a pathetic human being they really are.

Then maybe, just maybe, they might actually be sorry.

Karma is a patient gangster.

For those that ever walked all over me and didn't give a fuck...if you're wondering if this is directed towards you, I'll make it easy on you so you don't have to wonder.

It is.

Disillusionment

When you distance yourself...unplug from people, society, and life as you know it, it does something to you.

Isolation, solitude, being alone.

You realize a lot. It's where revelation, disillusionment, enlightenment, and strength of mind are fed.

It's extremely hard at first. Like ripping off a band aide.

But once you get used to it, it becomes addicting. Intoxicating.

You crave it. Need it. You can't wait to have it.

Not because you necessarily like being a loner or always being by yourself...

But because you've tried blending into the world before and people continuously disappoint you, are exhausting, draining, complex, and complicated.

Once you get a taste of how peaceful being alone is and start enjoying your own company you don't want to deal with people anymore.

We spend a lot of time making friends and focusing on external relationships, but oddly still feel alone.

If you make friends with yourself, you'll never be alone a day in your life.

Being alone doesn't necessarily mean you're lonely.

Far from it.

It means you don't need other people to fill space because none is empty.

To win me over your presence needs to feel better than my solitude.

You can't play games with a person that isn't afraid to be alone...

Come correct or you'll get cut off real quick.

Good Focus

It is easier said than done but I can and will do it. It is that simple.

I can make it happen. It will work.

I can and will do it. Nothing will stop me.

I believe this can happen...this will happen.

There's a way, I just need to find it.

Impossible is nothing. Nothing can hold me back.

I am better than this. This isn't it for my life.

I can decide my own fate. I can do anything I set my mind to.

I will realize my dreams. Good things are supposed to happen to me.

I refuse to feel sorry for myself. I will not be defeated.

I refuse to be denied. No one can tell me who and what I can be.

I define myself. I'm going to get it, period.

I can and will overcome this. I'm in control of my life.

Imagine what your life might look like if you dismissed and replaced your negative attitude and limiting beliefs with what you just said to yourself above...and really meant it and believed it.

If negative words have power to bring you down...positive words have power to lift you up.

Where focus goes, energy flows.

When you focus on good, the good gets better.

A negative mind will never give you a positive life.

Focus on positivity my friend...and watch your life begin to change.

Rob Them

Imagine if you had the power to rob other people of their power by being able to see into the depths of their character.

Always being able to understand the roots driving behavior...why they do what they do.

There's a reason everyone does everything they do.

There's a reason why that person has a delusional sense of superiority.

There's a reason they're lashing out at you.

There's a reason that person is talking badly about others.

There's a reason those parents don't give a shit about their kids.

There's a reason that person is a sloppy drunk.

There's a reason she's a slut or he's a player.

There's a reason they always need to be the center of attention.

There's a reason they treat you like shit.

There's a reason they're so insecure.

There's a reason behind every personality, every behavior, and every characteristic in every person.

Most people are a pawn to their subconscious state of mind.

People have issues. Issues that have nothing to do with you but are all rooted out of some personal battle they're fighting within.

It's then put on display through the things they say, actions they take, and how they treat other people...

Many aren't even conscious of the fact that they have the issues they have.

Distance yourself, disconnect, disassociate from whoever you're plugged into that has irrational and toxic behavior...you'll realize a lot.

Don't be a passive slave or victim to human nature...

Decode it. Actively transform it.

Eventually when you master this....

You understand the reasons behind why people are who they are and do what they do... nothing ever upsets you anymore.

It's human nature...don't sweat it.

Leave people to do the dumb shit they do, it's got nothing to do with you.

Checkmate

You become your mental and social environment over time.

Your brain absorbs it, mentally rehearses it, and manifests it automatically.

Drink enough Kool-Aid and you become like the Kool-Aid man busting through walls saying OH YEAH!

It's really amazing how many of the thoughts you think are a reflection of those around you.

The words you speak are an echo, and the character you portray, a mimicking act of those around you.

You don't even know it's happening until your behavior isn't producing the kind of life you want.

Until your dissatisfaction and lack of fulfillment cause you to start Googling your own existence to try and understand how the hell your life ended up where it is.

There are many times in my life, I all of a sudden stopped, looked around, said "fuck this", and never looked back.

I've never regretted it one single time.

I didn't know exactly where I was going or what I was doing, but I sure as hell knew I didn't want to be where I was at the time.

You may be a big fish in a small pond, everyone respects you, you're the shit...but there are oceans out there.

Unfortunately most don't have the guts or self-esteem to leap out of their fish bowl and swim with the sharks.

But see when you consciously swim around sharks you become one.

Don't miss out on becoming all you could be because you're hypnotized and brainwashed into being who and what you are.

Is your nature authentic to you or are you a pawn in someone else's game of chess?

As for me, I think I'll be the pawn that dictates my own moves...

Checkmate bitch.

Choose Your Battles

I've learned to pick and choose my battles wisely.

Especially with irrational people.

Irrationality makes people look for evidence that confirms what they already want to believe.

Even when that evidence is blatantly stupid and far from the truth.

Only arguing a point that supports what they need to believe to provide them comfort in an area they lack.

No matter what you say, how truthful you are, or how valid your point is, some people will only ever see things from their desired perspective.

It's not that these people are ignorant...they just know SO much that isn't so.

The sky is blue, but they need it to be green.

No matter how blue the blue of the blue sky is...they will find a way to make it green because that's what's going to support the story they're telling themselves.

I have absolutely no interest in arguing with a color blind person.

Once I come to the understanding that a person is irrational, lying to them self, and just won't budge, I get real quiet.

My responses become very short, reduced to single word answers.

Only talking to agree, concede, tap out, and surrender to their desired perspective.

Ultimately, if it's a battle that has no direct bearing on my life or my outcomes...I can care less.

I will reserve my two cents for a better investment that will pay much better dividends.

A Bulldog can whip a skunk any day of the week, but it just isn't worth the fight.

Eventually I get to the point where even if they tell me 1+1=5........yes, yes indeed it does....congratulations.

<u>Take The Steps</u>

Everything and everybody has to start somewhere.

Truly I tell you, one step at a time is not too difficult.

But, so many want to go from the basement to the penthouse suite in one step...I assure you that's not what you want.

They try to run up the steps fast and that's great...until you trip on the steps and they teach you to respect them.

They send you back and force you to retake the steps you skipped.

You want the money, the notoriety, the success, and everything that comes along with those things, but you won't be able to handle it.

Those that stand the test of time and last long term in anything understand that life takes you along in steps and stages.

It's only through steps and stages that you become who you need to become to handle what you have to handle at a higher level.

Get to one level, master it, become comfortable with life on that level...

Then take another step.

Getting to the penthouse suite is one thing. Staying there is another.

You can't thrive in a penthouse situation with a basement mentality, understanding, or work ethic.

It's through the steps and stages a basement person becomes a penthouse person.

You can't think higher than the level you're exposed to.

When you see up you can go up.

But that's going to require you to look beyond where you are...as well as become someone else.

To he or she much is given, much is required.

Despise not the day of small beginnings.

I promise you my friend there's a tree in that acorn...

Don't be afraid. Don't be intimidated.

Go ahead...take the steps.

See you at the top.

Advice

Oh I'm sorry when was the last time you did or accomplished anything in what I'm trying to do?

Oh never in your life?

When you plan to set your life on fire, some are going to fan your flames and some are going to try to put the fire out.

Truth is many fail in life because they're listening to and taking advice from their friends and family who have no business even giving the advice they give.

It's amazing how much some people know about something they've never experienced or done first hand.

Many know exactly what you should do but barely know what to do in their own life.

Once you learn how to hear nothing...life gets real good.

Drown out every voice but your own.

You know, background noise.

Chitter chatter from the peanut gallery.

You need selective hearing.

Ear plugs are a good investment.

That's how you get quiet in your head so you can hear your own voice.

When you listen to everyone around you, you become trapped in a life based on someone else's thinking.

Always listen to your heart and own intuition.

Only seek advice from people that have experience and have excelled in the EXACT thing you're trying to do.

Someone you would gladly trade places with.

Take the advice of very, very few people...

Everyone doesn't need to agree with or understand what you're going to do.

Eventually they'll see and will probably start asking you for the advice.

But you know you don't need to be rude.

Have some decency why don't ya...

Shake your head like you agree so they change the subject, then do what you were going to do anyway.

I Told You So

I told you so. What people say when they get some level of satisfaction out of seeing you fail.

Satisfaction that justifies their lack of courage and inaction.

It's real easy for a coward to criticize a risk taker.

I told you it wouldn't work!

Translation...I feel better about being a coward.

I told you you should have stayed there! You had a good job!

Translation...puppet master, I'm validated, I'd like to move my arms now.

I told you you shouldn't have moved there!

Translation...I feel better about the fact I'm afraid to move further than 5 minutes away from my parents.

I told you, you should have listened to me!

Translation...I feel better and more validated about what I think I know that I really don't.

I told you, you shouldn't have caused any waves!

Translation...I feel much better about the fact I conform, allow people to control me, and live a lame life.

Look...

It's not the critic that counts.

Don't let the chatter stop you.

Cowards will always chatter about how the strong and the brave stumbled.

What they don't realize is it's supposed to be hard.

It's not always going to go as planned.

It's not always going to be seamless.

No one ever accomplished anything extraordinary without conflict, strain, and struggle.

If it was easy everyone would do it.

But that's why everyone doesn't do it...they stay weak, afraid, and safe.

Why in the world would you ever allow an opinion from someone like that to make you question yourself?

Keep pushing, truth is, those people wish they had a fraction of the guts you have to live on their terms.

You're doing the things they would do if they had the guts.

Drown out the noise. Keep going.

Nothing To Lose

This is not your practice life.

There's no "let me try this again." No reset button. You don't get a do over.

This isn't a dress rehearsal. Life is happening now.

People think they have time. A lifetime is shorter than you realize.

People get hung up on dumb shit while life is passing them by.

Held in one place by people and places, not physically chained, but mentally chained.

Fail often and course correct as you go along.

Don't like your job? No worries! Quit, get a new one. It's not your boss's life it's yours.

Can't stand your boyfriend or girlfriend anymore? It's all good! Cut them off. There's plenty of fish in the sea.

Don't like where you live? No biggie! Move.

Everyone says not to do it? Well you know what you have to do then! Do it.

Loser friends holding you down? No problem! Become better, attract better. Get some new friends.

No hope for your marriage? No worries! Face it, it's unfixable or should have never happened. Get a divorce.

Yes it's just that simple.

Life is way too short to live in ANY way that doesn't serve your true happiness and desires.

The #1 regret amongst old people living out the last days of their life is regret in not living the life they really wanted to live.

Even if you're 99% happy....

Let that 1% that you're not be the reason you flip the whole thing upside down.

Ultimately, what in the hell do you really have to lose?

Eventually we are all going to go far away from here.

What is REALLY going to matter when you're facing death?

I promise you very little of the dumb shit that's got you all choked up now that's for sure.

Think deeper thoughts, take more chances, live intentionally for yourself first.

Make sure you can smirk on your death bed knowing you left nothing on the table.

Small Beginnings

Everything and everybody has to start somewhere.

Truly I tell you, one step at a time is not too difficult.

But, so many want to go from the basement to the penthouse suite in one step...I assure you that's not what you want.

They try to run up the steps fast and that's great...until you trip on the steps and they teach you to respect them.

They send you back and force you to retake the steps you skipped.

You want the money, the notoriety, the success, and everything that comes along with those things, but you won't be able to handle it.

Those that stand the test of time and last long term in anything understand that life takes you along in steps and stages.

It's only through steps and stages that you become who you need to become to handle what you have to handle at a higher level.

Get to one level, master it, become comfortable with life on that level...

Then take another step.

Getting to the penthouse suite is one thing. Staying there is another.

You can't thrive in a penthouse situation with a basement mentality, understanding, or work ethic.

It's through the steps and stages a basement person becomes a penthouse person.

You can't think higher than the level you're exposed to.

When you see up you can go up.

But that's going to require you to look beyond where you are...as well as become someone else.

To he or she much is given, much is required.

Despise not the day of small beginnings.

I promise you my friend there's a tree in that acorn...

Don't be afraid. Don't be intimidated.

Go ahead...take the steps.

See you at the top.

Images

A lot of people like to show their stars but not their scars.

When you work more on your image than you do your reality...you become an imposter in your own life.

Living the image but resting your head at night with the reality.

I know many people that live it...but would never admit it.

You'd be shocked at the people you think you know...but really only know their image.

You see a picture, portrait, snapshot, image of them living the dream, never knowing the special effects are fake props used to create an Emmy award winning performance.

Quiet desperation. Screaming but no one can hear.

That's a stressful life to live.

An unsustainable life to live because you have to fake it every day.

No one ever knowing that behind that smile and that "hello how are you?"...

You're suffocating from the choke hold of life and the top of your head is about to blow straight off.

Sooner or later the unsustainable becomes too much to bear.

Things begin to break.

Time always reveals the reality of what lies underneath.

Underneath an inauthentic reflection of an image that is not at all in fact real.

Anything built on inauthenticity will collapse...and if it doesn't collapse...

It will just remain barely standing, propped up with bitterness, resentment, unfulfillment, and misery...

All because there's too much fear, pride, and ego to bring in the bulldozer and wrecking ball to tear down and reveal a closely guarded secret...

An image that is far from reality.

<u>Crying</u>

You DESERVE to cry your eyes out.

That's right...I hope you ball your eyes out on a regular basis.

From the outside looking in, one would think you were upset or extremely saddened.

But you should cry because you are eternally grateful for what you've been given.

Even if it's a little bit.

Grateful for occurrences along the way that keep you moving in the right direction.

I believe genuine tears of this type keep you grounded.

It's through those tears you praise not how you got it, but who gave it to you.

Whether it's more or less than others is beside the point.

It's about gratitude for what YOU have been given and what you're doing with what YOU have been given.

I don't even understand myself sometimes how or why I got what I got.

It was and has been more than I ever expected, and it wasn't supposed to be...but it is.

I've broken down in tears more times than I can count.

You've got a lot more than you realize.

Be grateful over a little, no matter how insignificant or minor you think it is or other people are telling you it is...and you'll be given a lot.

Despise not the day of small beginnings.

Don't sleep on a little bit.

How you handle a little bit determines how much more you will be given.

There are some tears that bless you as they run down your face.

Tears of joy.

Cry me a river my friend.

Chapters

Don't judge me by the chapter of my life you walked in on.

The book of my life is just beginning. I'm only on chapter one, but don't count me out.

See chapter one lays the foundation. The premise to which the rest of the book is written.

Chapter one is the beginning of a beautiful story that gets better and better as you read on.

Every word is carefully chosen. Every sentence carefully written. Every paragraph carefully crafted.

I know you might judge me by what you're reading now.

Keep reading.

This is a book that gets better and more interesting.

My chapter one contains a strong foundation of positioning. A position of which I will surely prosper.

So, when chapter 20 is written, don't be surprised by what you read.

I wasn't surprised when I was writing it.

In Conclusion

I sincerely hope this book has introduced some fresh perspectives, impacting you heart, your mind, and most importantly, your outlook and beliefs as to what is possible for you in your life.

Remember, everyone's journey through life is different, but no matter where life takes you...

Play the hell out of the cards you're dealt, delete all negativity from your life, self-improve on a daily basis, aim high, and don't stop until you get there.

And most importantly have an insufferable, radical belief that you are greater than your circumstances.

Never let anyone turn your sky into a ceiling.

Made in the USA
Middletown, DE
28 June 2022